WEST EUROPEAN PACIFISM AND THE STRATEGY FOR PEACE

Edited by

Peter van den Dungen

St. Martin's Press   New York

© Professors World Peace Academy in Europe 1985

All rights reserved. For information, write:
St. Martin's Press, Inc., 175 Fifth Avenue, New York, NY 10010
Printed in Hong Kong
Published in the United Kingdom by The Macmillan Press Ltd.
First published in the United States of America in 1985

ISBN 0–312–86284–9

Library of Congress Cataloging in Publication Data
Main entry under title:
West European pacifism & the strategy for peace.
Papers from a colloquium held in Paris, Sept. 1982
under the auspices of the Professors' World Peace Academy
in Europe.
Includes index.
1. Peace–Congresses. 2. Europe–Defenses–Congresses.
I. Van den Dungen, Peter. II. Professors World Peace
Academy in Europe. III. Title: West European pacifism and
the strategy for peace.
JX1952.W463 1985   327.1'72   84–11585
ISBN 0–312–86284–9

Contents

Contents

Preface

In September 1982, a 2-day colloquium was held under the auspices of the Professors World Peace Academy (PWPA) on the phenomenon of the European peace movements. The PWPA is an association of scholars from a diversity of backgrounds, disciplines and political persuasions, working cooperatively for the peace and prosperity of the world. It grew out of a series of friendship meetings of scholars from Korea and Japan, initiated in 1972, to promote peaceful interaction between these two previously hostile nations. In pursuit of its goals, the Academy, which is now active in over 70 countries throughout the world, sponsors a wide range of study groups, seminars and publications.

The meeting, organised by the French section of the PWPA, took place in the *Maison des Polytechniciens* in Paris and brought together some twenty, mainly European, specialists on questions of peace and security, defence and disarmament, and Communist thought and practice regarding peace. This volume is a selection of the papers presented on that occasion. They have been brought up to date where necessary, although most papers deal with questions of fundamental and lasting importance, which surpass the specific issues that are central in the current debate on European peace and security. For this reason it was felt that the publication of these papers was justified as a worthwhile contribution to the already voluminous literature on the subject.

I am grateful to Patrick Litherland, Penny Lord, Sarah Martin and Kathryn Pritchard, all graduates of the School of Modern Languages of the University of Bradford, for their help with the translation of some of the papers; to Angela Hicks for improving the readability of the text, and to Françoise Demunck for typing it. I would also like to thank Don Trubshaw, secretary of the British branch of the PWPA, for his help.

Peter van den Dungen
School of Peace Studies
University of Bradford

Notes on the Contributors

Professor Stanislav Andreski is Head of the Department of Sociology at the University of Reading.

Dr Armand Clesse is an independent researcher into problems of nuclear strategy from Luxembourg.

General Pierre M. Gallois is a Former Head of the French Air Force.

Claude Harmel is General Secretary of the Institute of Social History in Paris and a former editior of *East and West*.

Professor Morton A. Kaplan is Director of the Centre for Strategic and Foreign Policy Studies at the University of Chicago.

Dr Jean Klein is Senior Research Fellow at the French Institute of International Relations in Paris.

Professor Gerard Radnitzky holds the Chair in the Philosophy of Science at the University of Trier.

Dr Alexander Shtromas is Reader in Politics at the University of Salford.

Professor Hylke Tromp is Director of the Polemological Institute at the University of Gronigen, Netherlands.

Dr Peter van den Dungen is Lecturer in Peace Studies at the University of Bradford.

Professor Wolf Graf von Baudissin is Director of the Institute of Peace Research and Security Policy at the University of Hamburg.

Part I
The Idea of Pacifism and Peace

1 Pacifism and Human Nature

STANISLAV ANDRESKI

1 THE NOVELTY OF PACIFISM

Any rational justification of the hope for permanent peace must depend on our view of the causes of wars. It is equally obvious that no action for the promotion of peace (that is the prevention of wars) can be effective unless it is based on a correct understanding of the causation, just as you cannot cure anyone without a proper diagnosis.

An adequate explanation must refer to factors of the same order of generality as the phenomenon to be explained; in the present context it must account for the fundamental fact that the practice of war is old and general while the idea that permanent peace might be possible — let alone that it ought to be maintained — is very new in relation to the total history of mankind. All the thinkers of Antiquity and the Renaissance as well as of the Oriental civilisations regarded war as part of the eternal order of things, just as inalterable as births and deaths.

The 17th century Dutch jurist Hugo Grotius was the first writer to envisage the possibility that one day mankind might live without war. Only during the second half of the 18th century did the view begin to spread among philosophers (in the old and broad sense of this word) that war was something barbaric that ought to be superseded. This idea did not begin to gain adherents outside the narrow circles of intellectuals until the second half of the 19th century. As a massive current of opinion, pacifism emerged only after the World War I. However, it was weak enough to be almost completely stifled in some countries on the eve of the World War II. It was not until after its end that pacifism began to strike roots in the masses.

The last 38 years constitute a new era in the history of mankind: for the first time nobody praises war and everybody professes to love peace,

3

while even aggressors disguise their attacks as defence. Ministries of War have everywhere been replaced by Ministries of Defence. True, the latter change may have less to do with altered attitudes than with the general craze for euphemisms which has prompted innumerable renamings: 'sick rooms' have become 'health centres', 'prisons' — 'rehabilitation or resocialisation centres', while instead of 'the poor' we have 'underprivileged' (the most idiotic euphemism of all since not even in paradise could everybody be privileged). There are no longer any old people but only 'middle-aged', no 'mental defectives' but only 'retarded' (although they will never catch up), while the backward countries have become 'developing' and so on. Nevertheless, whatever might be the case in other aspects of life, in the matters of war and peace the advance of euphemisms appears to reflect a real change in attitudes. Oscar Wilde's saying that 'hypocrisy is the homage which vice pays to virtue' seems to apply here.

To ensure their posthumous glory, the Assyrian kings had inscriptions on their tombs which listed how many enemies they had mutilated, blinded, skinned or impaled. In contrast, in our times even Hitler did not advertise his mass murders while Stalin made not unsuccessful efforts to conceal them. Nor did Harry Truman boast about the fact that on his orders more people died in a second than ever before. It is even more remarkable that nowadays nobody maintains that war is a good thing whereas before and during the World War I in all countries there was a flood of books and articles praising war as the supreme test of nations and men which brings out the best in them. Between the two world wars the fascists took up these themes and went on proclaiming the glories of war. Nowadays such attitudes are never openly expressed and, presumably, rarely held. Nobody openly takes pride in conquest which in the past was regarded as the greatest title to glory.

Is this change likely to be permanent or is it just lip-service which merely camouflages the old warlike propensities? How can we reconcile the hope of avoiding war with the knowledge of its ubiquity in the past? Perhaps we can but we should not do it by denying this fact, as some optimists try to do.

2   THE UBIQUITY OF WAR

As far as recorded history is concerned there is little doubt for argument on this score: all the states of which there are records waged wars — most of them virtually non-stop. The Old Kingdom of Ancient Egypt appears as the most pacific state that ever existed, although this might be because of the paucity of records. It is likely, however, that this impression is not false because, as the first large state, it had no rivals for a long time. Skirmishes with surrounding tribes might have been regarded by the scribes as too trivial to be worth recording. On the other hand, there is good evidence of protracted warfare during the process of the unification of Egypt. In any case, during the second millennium B.C. Egypt was conquered by the Hyksos, and the New Kingdom, which arose after their expulsion, was much more warlike than the Old. Even if the Old Kingdom was less warlike than other states, it constitutes no exception to the rule that all states waged wars. There is no lack of records of wars waged by other states. Indeed, very often this is the only activity which was recorded – which is not surprising since history began as tales of martial exploits written down by court chroniclers to immortalise the glory of their masters.

Although history is unambiguous on this score, some thinkers sought consolation and hope in the idea that war is a relatively recent invention – not older than written history – and that prehistoric man was peaceful. Generally speaking, the image of the savage oscillated between Hobbes' notion of primaeval ferocity and Rousseau's of gentleness. The picture presented by the recent generation of anthropologists gave a boost to the belief in the peacefulness of primitive man, not so much by arguments to this point as by omission of the subject of war. The standard textbooks and treatises on general anthropology have no chapters on war.[1] In the dozen *Source-Books in Anthropology*,[2] only a quarter of one volume is given to war, incongruously tacked on to the discussion of law. The *Notes and Queries on Anthropology*,[3] for the guidance of field researchers, has no section with questions about war, which gives the impression that the authors do not want to know about it. There is some justification for this omission because recent generations of anthropologists have studied tribes which for many decades (in some cases more than a century) had lived under colonial governments which permitted most customs to continue but put a stop to tribal wars as soon as they were established. Taking as their task the description of what they had seen, most anthropologists had little to say about war. In consequence, books of synthesis based on recent field studies throw no light on the problem which interests us here because the picture they paint does not correspond to the situation when the tribes were independent and able to fight one another.

A more adequate picture of primitive warfare can be obtained from Davie's *Evolution of War*[4], which is based on older field studies, made when the experience of war was still within living memory of some tribesmen. The most thorough inquiry into warfare among the simplest known peoples is *Ontstaan en Eerste Ontwikkeling van den Oorlog*[5] (Emergence and Early Development of War) by T.S. van der Bij (Groningen, 1929) where the scattered information about the times of the first contacts with the Europeans is collated. Writing about 60 years ago, the author already came to the conclusion 'that no new source-material can come to light on the problem of primitive warfare'. He was right as far as reports of observations were concerned. The only new factual information has come from the study of oral history and literature such as tales transmitted by bards. A more famous Dutch scholar, Rudolf S. Steinmetz, wrote a long review[6] of van der Bij's book – *De Vredelievendheid der Laagste Volksstammen* (The Pacifism of the Most Primitive Tribes), where he disagrees with the conclusion that the most primitive peoples were less aggressive than the more developed. The dispute hinges largely on what we mean by 'peaceful' and 'aggressive', and therefore is partly, but not entirely, verbal. On balance, it seems that van der Bij is right in maintaining that the simplest known peoples – those who lived in very small bands and had the most rudimentary tools and weapons – were less inclined to start wars and to wage them energetically than peoples with a more complex culture. This conclusion also agrees with the statistical survey of ethnographic data by L.T. Hobhouse *et al.*[7] Two reservations, however, must be made before we draw any inferences about our prehistoric ancestors. The first is that the most primitive peoples on record were living at the time they were observed in inhospitable areas, surrounded by more powerful neighbours. It is not surprising that they were not keen to attack them, but this tells us little about their propensities. Second, these peoples had been pushed into undesirable environments by others who must have been better warriors. It is very likely, therefore, that the ancestors of more advanced peoples were more warlike – or at least better at fighting – than peoples who were on the same level of culture much later. In any case, none of the aforementioned authors maintains that the most primitive peoples fought no wars but only that their wars were milder and rarer than those of big tribes.

It is indeed likely that warfare intensified as the weapons and organisation became more efficient, at the same time as the pressure of the population on resources increased and the amount of wealth which could be carried away grew. Such wealth was particularly important among pastoral nomads in the shape of herds.

A glance at ethnography exposes the vacuity of the recipes for peace, propounded by anarchists and people who call themselves 'ecologists' (and make ridiculous a very worthy cause), which assume that decentralisation and smallness entail peacefulness. Unfortunately, there is no guarantee that the opposite remedy — a world government — would ensure peace either, because history has recorded many civil wars often more murderous than many international conflicts. Even atomic weapons might be used in a civil war if it were to be as bitter as some of the past have been. More people died in the American Civil War than in any other war between Napoleon and the World War I. More Americans died in the Civil War than either in World War I or II. More Spaniards died in the Spanish Civil War than Britons in the World War II. Perhaps a certain kind of world government might be able to ensure peace throughout the world but there is no reason to suppose that any kind would do so.

3   IS THERE AN INSTINCT FOR WAR?

The ubiquity of war has led many thinkers (including the famous psychologists Pierre Bovet and William MacDougall) to postulate an instinct for it. There is a long tradition of regarding man as inherently violent and vicious, although few writers went so far as Leonardo da Vinci who said that 'the beasts kill to live but men live to kill'. However, although it is obvious that men have no genetically transmitted constraints on killing their fellows — of the kind which prevents wolves and lions from killing one another, there are good reasons for doubting the existence of an instinct — similar to those of thirst, hunger, sociability and concupiscence — which would evoke the desire to kill other men. The first argument against postulating such an instinct is that, despite their ubiquity, wars do not occur with the regularity which might be expected if an instinct were at work. Often a country remains at peace for a generation, and it is not very likely that there is an instinct — that is a genetically transmitted, practically universal propensity — which may skip an entire generation. Secondly, wars between states were mostly waged by specialised, often very small, sectors of the population. It follows that if the willingness to fight in a war were due to a genetically transmitted propensity — an instinct of pugnacity, as MacDougall calls it, or of combativity, as Bovet calls it — the genes for it could have been present only in the small minority of men who were doing the fighting. This is not impossible, since there are inclinations (such as the love of music or mathematics) which seem to have a genetic component, but appear only in a minority. But it would be confusing to apply the same term to a propensity which is rare (even if genetically transmitted) as to propensities which are so nearly universal that a departure from them is regarded as abnormal.

If it were true that wars resulted from genetically transmitted propensities of a minority of men, important theoretical and practical conclusions would follow. They would be very different from what would follow from the conclusion that all men are endowed with such propensities. The first view derives some support from the common knowledge that there are big differences in aggressiveness between men. These differences, however, may be due at least as much to the influence of the environment as to heredity. Furthermore, the link between personal aggressiveness and the readiness to take part in a war is far from direct.

Even a restricted explanation in terms of an instinct founders on the fact that in all armies punishments and rewards are used to induce men to fight. This would be superfluous if they had an inherent desire to do so. No society has found it necessary to have inducements to make people want to eat or seek company and sexual gratification. Shootings, whippings, keel-haulings and all kinds of other cruel punishments were meted out to those who tried to avoid fighting, whereas valour was rewarded by prestige, decorations, admiration and often wealth. The prospects of sexual gratification were often used as an incentive. Among the Galla of the Horn of Africa, a man could not marry until he brought genitals cut from an enemy. The Zulu king, Chaka, used to apportion wives to his warriors in accordance with their performance on the battlefield: the heroes got many while the laggards got none. In many Amerindian tribes, men who did not want to be warriors were debarred from access to women, obliged to dress like them and to live in the section of the village reserved for the homosexuals. The low status of women in most societies can be seen as an arrangement which helped to instil into men the will to fight, by making them afraid to be regarded as effeminate.

On the other hand, there could be no wars if men were endowed with an innate inhibition against killing their fellows, of the kind that many animals have; but the lack of such a genetically-determined restraint does not imply the existence of a generalised desire to kill. All that is needed to make warfare possible is a certain plasticity of behaviour which permits men to perform murderous acts. Furthermore, even if it is true that men are innately aggressive, they may well be able to assuage this propensity by non-lethal fights. Indeed there are very good reasons against postulating any kind of instinctual determinant (a sufficient as distinct from a necessary condition) of war.

The first argument is deductive: namely, that an innate propensity to kill its own kind would make any species unviable. Every adult has had many opportunities to murder someone with impunity; and if a sizeable fraction of the population were inclined to avail themselves of such possibilities, the murder rate would soar to such heights that the population would become extinct in a few generations. It might be objected that this argument applies only to individual behaviour but not to collective conflicts where people aim at killing enemies only, while aiding and protecting members of their own group. This is true, but if the warriors — especially the victors — always killed everybody they were able to kill, mankind would have become extinct soon after such a habit became general. In reality, very few (if any) wars have led to a total extermination of the vanquished; and although there are examples of defeated populations and races dwindling and eventually dying out, such processes have been much slower and rarer than would have been the case had most acts of collective aggression been prompted by a desire to kill rather than to rob, enslave or merely humiliate and subdue. I conclude therefore that the survival of mankind despite countless wars proves that men (though perfectly able to kill as a means to other ends) are not normally prompted by a desire to kill for its own sake.

Apart from the foregoing abstract argument, the latter view is supported by the evidence about soldiers' feelings on a battlefield which clearly shows that by far the most common emotion is not any kind of blood-lust but fear. Swayed by the sentiments of honour or duty a soldier may overcome his fear, but seldom (if ever) is it some simple aggressive impulse that motivates his bravery; on the contrary, much docility is needed to make a good soldier.

Organisation enables the individuals who decide on aggression to avoid physical involvement, while those who have to commit violence may experience no feelings of aggression. With a hierarchy the direction and form of collective action will depend on how the occupants of the top positions are selected. Consequently, populations which do not differ in the average level of combative propensities may display striking contrasts in collective bellicosity according to whether more or less aggressive individuals obtained power.

There are many examples of leaders being more peacefully disposed than their followers, but, on the whole, power tends to fall into the hands of those who thirst for it and these people are likely to be more aggressive than the average. The incidence of war strengthens this tendency as its conduct requires combative leaders who are likely to embark upon more warlike adventures. Such rulers, moreover, tend to carry over their militancy into internal affairs and to abuse their power, thus exacerbating internal conflicts. These tend to tilt the selection for leadership in each faction in favour of more aggressive individuals who are likely to initiate bellicose external policies.

Whereas the art of organisation has introduced the possibility of dissociation between the decision and the physical deed of violence, the general development of mental powers has called forth a whole gamut of motives for aggression which have little to do with any instinctual aggressive drive; for instance a decision to attack in order to forestall being attacked under more adverse circumstances. Even a purely offensive war is usually waged not for the sheer pleasure of fighting but as a means towards other ends such as greater power and glory, increased security or opulence at other people's expense.

The realisation that life can be made easier by exploiting others, and the invention of various ways of doing this, constituted a very significant step in cultural evolution and it has brought into action powerful motives for aggression which have nothing to do with a spontaneous and unforeseeing animal impulse. Furthermore, the invention of personal names and of the concept of glory has enabled men to experience insatiable cravings for limitless aggrandisement, thus also creating new specifically human motives for aggression.

Of equal importance was the invention of weapons, which has altered the nature of fighting not only by making a killing likely even when it was not specifically intended, but also by creating a prudential reason for killing. If no weapons exist and you have thrashed your enemy once, you should be able to do it again any time, as an unarmed man has little chance of disabling a stronger opponent by surprise. But if he has a lethal weapon, then the only way to make your victory safe may be to kill him.

The use of weapons both determined and required other decisive turns in human evolution. Once the predatory animals were eliminated as the main obstacle to human proliferation, the numerical expansion of a horde came to be limited chiefly by the appropriation of the living space by other hordes. True, had men been as incapable of killing their own species as many animals are, they would have starved rather than embarked upon fighting and killing one another; but, given the adaptability of human nature, war must have imposed itself as soon as it became clear to our pack-hunting ancestors that they could nourish themselves and their children only if they pushed away the strangers from the hunting grounds or water sources. In other words, given the adaptability of our species, the tendency for births to exceed deaths (due to causes other than mutual killing) constituted a sufficient as well as a necessary condition for war to become a constant feature of social life.

We can explain a phenomenon only by a factor which is neither less nor more prevalent: for this reason we cannot explain war by the existence of sovereign states because civil wars amply demonstrate that a common government is not enough to prevent fighting. On the other hand, the pressure of population on resources has been just as prevalent in human history as all forms of organised lethal fighting and has been absent in all cases of a combination of internal with external peace. The proposition that, given the propensities of human nature, the tendency of the population to grow beyond the resources has ensured the ubiquity of wars, does not imply that every single instance of war must have had this factor as an immediate cause.

An analogy might make this point clearer: the fact that everybody who survives to a certain age enters a phase of senile decay ensures that everybody eventually dies. The statement that senescence is the cause of men being mortal remains true even though only a minority (perhaps very small) die simply of old age. In the same way, the statement that the tendency of the population to grow faster than the resources makes wars inevitable is in no way invalidated by finding that many wars have occurred without this factor being in operation. Most of the criticisms of the demographic theory of conflict are based on the elementary logical error of imagining that a proposition '*A* implies *B*' is invalidated if we find that *B* has occurred without *A*. It seems, therefore, that wars might not cease to be a permanent feature of social life until after the restoration of the demographic balance whose disappearance at an early stage of cultural development made them inevitable. This condition would make peace possible, though not guaranteed.

4   THE GROWING UNATTRACTIVENESS OF WAR

The military hierarchy is usually so arranged that power and exposure to dangers and privations are inversely related, so that the commanders are able to push the underlings into the battle while remaining safely behind. This gradient varies according to time and place. In tribal and feudal warfare, the leaders led literally in the forefront, whereas the World War I was perhaps the safest ever for the generals. The World War II was slightly less safe for them because of aerial bombardment.

An interesting feature of human nature is that real heroes are often less revered than the bosses who have exposed themselves to little danger or privation while sending vast numbers of others to their death. Napoleon deserted his army twice — in Egypt and in Russia — and twice surrendered rather than fight himself. Despite the defeat (after causing the pointless death of more than a million Frenchmen), he continued to be adored in France and his cult persists to this day. Bismarck was adored as 'the

Iron Chancellor' although he never went anywhere near where iron might be flying about. In order to feel safe in the republic established after the World War I, the Germans chose as their president general von Hindenburg — one of the chiefs who led them to defeat. Although his main contribution to victory consisted of signing death warrants on deserters and mutineers, Pétain was known as 'the hero of Verdun' and was chosen to rule France at the hour of its defeat. Similar examples can be found everywhere. Although it was often otherwise in more primitive forms of warfare, a more descriptive term for 'war leaders' of recent times would be 'pushers' because they pushed others from behind instead of leading them in front.

The material rewards of war were perhaps greatest for nomads who were able to conquer a much greater sedentary population and set themselves up as its rulers. When a Roman soldier brought home a gang of slaves he could put them to work on his farm and lead a life of relative leisure. Feudal warfare had many attractions: the battles never lasted more than a day and campaigns were usually short, seldom lasting more than three months. In exchange for incurring a momentary danger, the warriors were exempt from constant heavy toil. The economic rewards were considerable as the victors usually acquired land with bondsmen to till it, in addition to movable booty. The most eager volunteers for wars were the younger sons of the nobility for whom this was the only way of acquiring estates of their own. The danger to an iron-clad knight was smaller than in most forms of warfare because he could be knocked off the horse and immobilised without a very serious injury, while the prisoners were normally released for ransom. Only the Swiss regularly cut the throats of dismounted knights, for which reason they were greatly feared.

Even when knights were replaced by mercenaries, the profession of arms remained fairly attractive to those who would otherwise be obliged to lead a life of back-breaking toil and poverty. The battles were still one-day affairs and, although the campaigns now lasted much longer, often several years, the soldiers spent most of the time in camps or in winter billets, gambling, drinking and wenching. As the armies were still small the pay was good in comparison with what could be earned in humdrum civilian jobs. The booty was often large, especially in Italy where some of the condottieri amassed sizeable fortunes.

For the common soldier all these advantages disappeared when organisation was improved, which enabled the armies to grow large and entailed a lowering of the pay. This occurred first in France. An even more drastic deterioration of the condition of common soldiers occurred when the lure of pay was replaced by the press-gang and selective long-term conscription. In modern Europe, the latter method was introduced first in Prussia, whose impecunious monarchs built by this method an army which was extraordinarily large in relation to their resources. By following their example, Peter the Great built the largest army in Europe. Even larger armies were put into the field by Sadi Carnot, the organiser of the armies of the French Republic who invented the general call-up. Owing to the revolutionary enthusiasm, he needed less compulsion than the monarchs. Napoleon inherited this system, and his victories were due as much to the numerical superiority of his troops as to his skillful generalship.

A cheapening of the weapons and the invention of drill made this evolution possible. A rifle was much cheaper than the armament of a knight not only in relation to the improved capacity of production but even absolutely, as measured by the amount of the steel it contained or the labour used to make it. Larger armies could, therefore, be maintained. They were useless, however, without more order on the battlefield which, in turn, required training in groups — that is drill.

Having fallen into disuse since the fall of the Roman Empire, drill was introduced by the Dutch for their mercenaries during the war of independence against the Spaniards. It was perfected by the monarchs of Prussia for whom it was the method for making good soldiers out of conscripts and press-ganged vagabonds. Peter the Great applied it on a vaster scale to the Russian serfs. As the fear of punishment replaced the lure of pay and booty, military service in the lower ranks became very unattractive; and the nobility avoided it except in the higher ranks. Having little to offer, the soldiers were no longer accompanied by crowds of camp-followers, as was the case during the Thirty Years War and before. Being closely supervised (to prevent desertion) they had fewer opportunities for looting and raping. Napoleon's soldiers had ampler opportunities of this kind because he dispensed with the practice of trailing waggons and made his troops live off the country, which enabled them to move much faster than their enemies burdened by supplies. This method outraged the conquered populations and among other things stimulated the growth of German nationalism. Nevertheless, Napoleon's soldiers were too many to profit from booty or to live off the country as successfully as Wallenstein's mercenaries did during the wars of religion.

Conditions reached their nadir for the common soldiers during the First World War which was the first to have a permanent front on which the battle never ceased. The pay was miserly and the reward for victory was nil or rather negative because the ex-soldiers often found it difficult to find jobs. Objectively, the consequences of defeat were not (or would not have been) important to common people because under a liberal economic system even an annexation did not make much difference, while the colonial empires brought profit only to the upper classes. The war was caused by petty squabbles about prestige. The economic interests of the masses were almost as little involved as in the recent war in the Falklands. To compensate for the lack of material incentives, governments prepared the cannon fodder by systematic indoctrination with nationalism and then sponsored a barrage of insidious propaganda mendaciously vilifying the enemy nations. Owing to the gullibility of the masses, it was very effective.

The economic gains from a victory to the victorious nation as a whole had become by then even more negative than hitherto. Indeed a war between agricultural peoples could benefit a substantial part of the victorious population only if it resulted in an acquisition of a territory on which the surplus population could be settled, thus relieving the pressure of population on resources and raising the standard of living. This however, could only happen if the indigenous population was driven out or exterminated. In modern times this happened only in North America, Australia and Tasmania. In feudal wars, as we saw, the noblemen could gain a great deal while the commoners could only lose by suffering devastations, but at least they did not have to do the fighting, apart from a small number of henchmen. Under dynastic absolutism, wars were waged at the behest of the monarchs (though with some regard for the desires of the nobility), by mercenaries and later by conscripts — both drawn from the destitute sector of the population. There was no question of these wars being fought for the sake of the interests of the common people. There was no hypocrisy: it never occurred to the rulers that they ought to be acting for the benefit of their subjects.

It is a myth that businessmen were usually the chief warmongers or imperialists, or that wars served the interests of their class, although it is true that restricted business circles profited by and instigated some pushover affairs like the Opium Wars, or the Boer War or the sending of a few gunboats to force the Cubans or Venezuelans to pay their debts. A big and costly war was never good for business and there is no evidence that any such war was instigated by commercial or industrial interests. At the onset of the World War I, the City of London Banks asked the Governor of the Bank of England to convey to Lloyd George (then the Chancellor of the Exchequer) their unanimous opposition to Britain's entry into the war. Under liberalism, business could operate everywhere and did not need an extension of political dominion to make profits. The only class which always gained something from territorial expansion — even of such minor kinds as the transfers of Alsace and Lorraine – was the officialdom because this was the only class which was replaced in the wake of a conquest even in liberal states.

World War I was perhaps the most irrational ever fought because it was very costly and yet served nobody's interests as even the victors were worse off in the end. This was inevitable because the complexity and interdependence of the national economies increased enormously the costs of dislocation (which were probably greater than the costs of physical destruction), while their liberal institutions made it impossible for the victors to squeeze much wealth out of the vanquished without further dislocating their own economies. Given this irrationality, it is not surprising that once the wave of nationalist intoxication had passed, a strong current of pacifism swept the victorious as well as the defeated countries. What is surprising, however, is that 15 years later Hitler was able to whip up so much enthusiasm for his programme of conquests. It remains true nonetheless that, despite all the efforts of his propaganda machine, the outbreak of the war did not evoke such a wave of pugnacious euphoria as had accompanied the declarations of war in Germany, France and Britain on the previous occasion.

With some initial success, the Nazis attempted to make it possible for the entire nation to profit from a victory by jettisoning the corner-stones of modern European civilisation: the respect for the rights of property and residence, and the freedom of movement and work. They expelled entire populations from their homes, confiscated property and revived serfdom and slavery. In Poland, they attempted to exterminate the entire educated class. Whereas the extermination of the Jews was prompted by the obsession of Hitler and his cronies and served no further goal, the treatment of the Slavs was a part of the plan to create in Eastern Europe an empire where a German aristocracy would be served by Slavonic serfs and slaves. Thus every German would have become an aristocrat like every white man in South Africa. Although many people derive a satisfaction from bossing others, the progress of technology – especially since the advent of automation – has made bondage unprofitable. Unfortunately, however, technology has created a new source of conflict which in the future may become extremely important: namely, pollution. Once it becomes unbearable, people may be ready to go to war in order to prevent others from polluting their environment. And, as everybody knows, an all-out war may end with an extinction of mankind or even all life on earth.

5   THE PROSPECTS

So long as there was no technical progress and the fertility of populations remained near its biologically determined maximum, there were always people who could obtain the means of existence only by grabbing them from others. For this reason it is no accident that the idea of putting an end to wars began to be entertained only when technical and economic progress was a perceptible fact and when the belief that it would continue came to be widely held. Nor is it an accident that a disinclination to kill is prevalent only in societies where the pressure of population on resources is not extreme, owing to the combination of sufficient wealth with a check on the growth of the population through birth control. Although, unfortunately, there is no reason to assume that absence of poverty is a sufficient condition for a spread of humane and pacific attitudes, there is good evidence that it is a necessary condition. Technology has eliminated, as well as the struggle for survival, another great incentive to war and conquest: when productivity was low nobody could attain comfort and leisure without harshly exploiting others. Machines made it possible for people to live well without pushing others to the subsistence minimum or below. Unfortunately, the scarcity of space, the exhaustion of the natural resources and accumulating pollution threaten to put an end to the happy and unprecedented situation reached by the fortunate countries, and to keep the unfortunate in the abject condition in which they are now. This means that the prospects of peace will be very dim unless some means are found to arrest the four processes which threaten to make the struggle for resources more brutal than it has ever been: the population explosion, soil erosion, pollution and the exhaustion of natural resources.

The prospect of general suicide provides a strong disincentive, particularly as the rulers can no longer ensconce themselves safely behind protective barriers. Nevertheless a grave ecological crisis might produce ever larger waves of fanaticism and irrationality which will make the balance of mutual deterrence increasingly vulnerable, not to speak of the ever-present danger of a holocaust triggered off by a technical error.

NOTES

1. This is true, for instance, of R.H. Lowie's *Primitive Society*, London, 1921; A. Goldenweiser's *Anthropology*, New York, 1937; Raymond Firth's *Elements of Social Organisation*, London, 1951; Ralph Piddington's *Introduction to Social Anthropology*, London, 1950, and Alfred Kroeber's *Anthropology*, New York, 1950.

2. *Source Books in Anthropology*, American Museum of Natural History, 1959–68.

3. *Notes and Queries on Anthropology*, Royal Anthropological Institute, 1951.

4. Maurice R. Davie, *Evolution of War*, Yale University Press, 1929.

5. T.S. van der Bij, *Ontstaan en Eerste Ontwikkeling van den Oorlog* (Emergence and Early Development of War), Groningen, 1929.

6. Rudolf S. Steinmetz's review of T.S. van der Bij's *De Vredelievendheid der Laagste Volksstammen* is reprinted in volume III of his *Gesammelte Kleinere Schriften zur Ethnologie und Soziologie*, Groningen, 1935.

7. L.T. Hobhouse, M. Ginsberg and C. Wheeler, *Material Culture and Social Institutions of Simpler Peoples*, London, 1911.

2 Pacifism: Sources of Inspiration and Motivation

PETER VAN DEN DUNGEN

From those who belong to or participate in the peace movement as well as from those who comment on it, one sometimes gains the impression that this movement is a phenomenon of the contemporary world, unheard of until comparatively recent times. The great number of peace organisations and movements currently existing and the substantial following some of them attract, coupled with the unprecedented attention they receive in the various media help to reinforce this impression and to provide material evidence for the assertion. Within the peace movement itself there exists, however, a section which knows better — consisting as it does of those whose involvement in campaigns for peace goes back as far as the days of the World War I. Next to the many newcomers there are thus the stalwarts of the peace movement, who 'have been here before', and who, for a variety of reasons and irrespective of the outcome of their previous involvement, are taking part again in current activities. But the most conclusive evidence for the fact that peace movements have existed before is to be found, of course, in the records of history. Man's longing for peace and his incessant strivings to bring it about before the present time is documented in the rich legacy which these movements have left behind, and which is preserved in a number of famous libraries throughout the world. We wish to refer here only to the collections of books, pamphlets, journals and archival and other material in the libraries of the Peace Palace in the Hague, the Nobel Institute in Oslo, and the United Nations in Geneva. The recently published catalogue of another celebrated peace collection in Swarthmore College (Pennsylvania) provides further vivid testimony of the universality and permanence of the peace impulse. The Swarthmore College Peace Collection is the repository of the papers and documents of many organisations and individuals active in the field of peace. Amongst its holdings is material from almost one thousand different peace groups which were active during a period of over 150 years (1820–1980) in the USA alone! A cursory glance at the catalogue reveals not only the great number of peace movements which have existed in the past, but also the variety of their aim, outlook and inspiration.[1]

Despite this variety, it is customary to group all peace movements together and to refer to their underlying philosophy or ideology as being that of 'pacifism'. An observation which virtually every student of pacifism makes, however, is the inadmissibility of dealing with the peace movement (or pacifism) as an undifferentiated whole. A few examples may suffice. A prominent American writer who is also a leading member of the Peace Section of the Mennonite Central Committee, John H. Yoder, writes: ' "pacifism" is not just one specific position . . . but rather a wide gamut of varying, sometimes even contradictory, views. . . . There is no such thing as a single position called "pacifism" '.[2] In his book Yoder attempts to devise a typology of pacifism, by asking how many different types of pacifism exist and indicating their differences and similarities. Although he confines his study to religious pacifism only, he nevertheless identifies some eighteen different positions! If one's survey is not confined to the religiously inspired variant of pacifism, it is inevitable that several more 'pacifisms' will be identified. A wider survey was undertaken by the German philosopher Max Scheler in the 1920s as part of his study of the idea of peace and pacifism. He writes: 'Ideas and movements of what is called *pacifism* are by no means uniform. There exists not only one form of pacifism: there are many of them. Although I shall attempt to present only a rough division of pacifism in general, I think that there are at least eight typical forms. These pacifisms are different in essence with regard to their respective origins in the human history of ideas and real history, with regard to the types of ideas of pacifism and their ethoses, and with regard to the means and ways in which they propose to realise eternal peace.'[3] We will return to Scheler's typology and to his masterly little work shortly, but first we want to draw attention, if ever so briefly, to another point of interest concerning the definition of the word 'pacifism'.

One author, in his attempt to define the word 'pacifism', discovered that the word itself is of much more recent origin than the phenomenon which it refers to: 'it must be stressed that (the phenomenon of) pacifism . . . did not at all come into existence only yesterday and that it is indeed much older than the word itself which was created fairly recently'.[4] He goes on to say that according to the *Encyclopaedia Britannica*, the word dates from the turn of the century only, which is implicitly confirmed by the absence of the terms 'pacifism' and 'pacifist' from the French equivalent of that period, the *Nouveau Larousse Illustré* (published about 1900). To be more precise, the word 'pacifist' was coined at the International Peace Congress held in Glasgow in 1901 by the Frenchman Emile Arnaud. It seems that the British tried, unsuccessfully, to insist on the adoption of the word 'pacificist'. It was agreed that a pacifist was anyone who, in a general sense, was working to create or perpetuate peace.[5] Apparently the word 'pacifism' first appeared a few years later in the writings of another Frenchman, Emile Faguet, whose book, *Le Pacifisme*, was published in 1908. Although the words 'pacifism' and 'pacifist' were absent from the *Larousse*, mention is made, however, of '*le pacifique*', and this is defined as: 'He who loves peace, he who searches for peace (*qui recherche la paix*)'. It is, by the way, interesting to note the second part of this definition. The academic discipline called 'peace research' only established itself, and then very gradually and in the face of much opposition from several quarters, after the World War II. In France, Gaston Bouthoul coined the term 'polémologie' (and established his institute bearing the same name) to denote the scientific study of war as a sociological phenomenon – an approach which was neglected in the traditional study of war in military academies and 'Ecoles de Guerre'. To find a reference to 'peace research' in a volume published as early as the beginning of the century is remarkable – it indicates an awareness on the part of the author that, at the time when he was writing, there were the first beginnings of an attempt to make the peace movement more effective (and respectable) by adopting an objective and scientific approach, so that the traditional means employed to advance the cause of peace, namely, appeals to morality and sentimentality, were, if not supplanted, at least reinforced by rationality.

According to J.-B. Barbier, the 1935 edition of the *Dictionnaire de l'Académie Française* offers the best definition of 'pacifism': 'The doctrine of those who believe in the possibility of establishing universal and perpetual peace and who endeavour to prepare its realisation.' The author does not consider himself to be an adherent of pacifism so defined. Yet, he argues, love of peace is not incompatible with a critical assessment of pacifism: 'There is no contradiction between, on the one hand, desiring peace and, on the other, denouncing the repeated and obstinate errors of pacifists, which are tragic in themselves and for our country.' He points out that it is most unfortunate that, as regards the French language at least, the poverty of terminology is apt to lead to a confusion which allows of no position in between that of pacifism on the one hand and militarism or bellicism on the other. How can one denote that tendency which, while being expressive of a strong desire for peace, nevertheless does not subscribe to the essential features of pacifism? In Barbier's words: 'If, as is indeed the case, we have today the word "pacifism" to indicate the doctrine of those who are called *pacifists*, we have, unfortunately, no noun which could be applied to the propensity, so different, of the *"pacifique"*, i.e. the propensity of the person who loves peace and searches for it without, however, maintaining in principle that the means exist to safeguard peace totally and indefinitely.' The absence of the term described has resulted in adding yet another interpretation to the word 'pacifism' and thus in further confusion about what it stands for. The following exchange (in the 1930s) between Wickham Steed, editor of *The Times*, and Lord Ponsonby, chairman of the War Resisters International and advisor on foreign policy to the Labour Party, is typical: Wickham Steed: 'I hate war and want to put an end to it. To this extent, you may call me a pacifist.' Lord Ponsonby: 'I beg your pardon. But *you* a pacifist!'[6] Not only does the French language appear to be suffering from this defect. In fact, the very differentiation which Barbier makes between *'le pacifiste'* and *'le pacifique'* (and which may well be his own, far too subtle distinction which is perhaps not generally adhered to in the French language) is one which appears not to have an equivalent in most other languages. In English, a distinction is sometimes made between *pacifism* and *pacificism*, whereby the first is 'the belief that all war is *always wrong* and should never be resorted to, whatever the consequences of abstaining from fighting' and the second assumes that war 'though *sometimes necessary*, is always an irrational and inhumane way to solve disputes, and that its prevention should always be an overriding political priority'.[7]

Returning to the substance of the matter, Barbier maintains that the difference between the two 'pacifist' positions resides in a fundamentally different interpretation of history and human reality — or, rather, the 'pacifist' ignores the lessons of history and fails to grasp the shortcomings inherent in the human condition: '[*Le pacifique*] has some reservations regarding the possibility of a general and eternal peace. For he believes that peace will never assume the character of a static reality for the simple reason that, as the wisdom of ancient Greece has already taught us, *"panta rei"*. Indeed, everything perpetually changes. In other words, *"le pacifique"*, unlike the pacifist, takes full account of this precariousness and imperfection which are inherent in the human condition.'[8]

The achievement of perpetual and universal peace — which is tantamount to the abolition of all war — is generally taken to be the aim of the peace movement. But if this definition is rigidly used, many groups and movements which are active in the peace field would not be included in one's survey or account. The English historian A.J.P. Taylor has distinguished two types of peace movements, namely, those which aim to eliminate all war, and those which try to end particular wars or to prevent certain wars from taking place. Bob Overy, in his useful descriptive classification[9] of contemporary peace movements, has further refined this typology by calling to mind those movements which aim to eliminate particular aspects of war. With the help of these three categories it will be possible to include virtually all the movements, campaigns, groups and organisations which are currently active in most countries of the Western world. The validity of this scheme can be readily demonstrated by applying it to the variety of peace movements currently existing in, for instance, Britain. The first category – *movements to eliminate war* – comprises some of the long-standing, traditional peace organisations, several of which are rooted in or closely linked to religious denominations. Examples are the Quakers, Pax Christi, the Fellowship of Reconciliation (FOR), the Peace Pledge Union (PPU).

An organisation which has been inspired by Gandhian and Tolstoyan ideas and practices is the War Resisters International (WRI). Whilst opposing all war, these organisations have in practice translated their activities in specific concerns such as the right to conscientious objection to war-service or the elaboration of alternative, non-violent means of defence and struggle. Movements in this category are, on the whole, not mass movements, but they constitute rather a 'permanent minority', upholding in their best form the highest moral principles. More popular in terms of gaining wide support are *movements to stop particular wars* or *movements to prevent certain conflicts from developing into war*. The prime example of the first is the anti-Vietnam war movement in the USA and in various European countries in the 1960s. Another example is the emergence, in the second half of the 1970s, of the Northern Ireland Peace People, and the formation of affiliated or supporting groups in Britain and abroad. Virtually every war is likely to call into existence a movement to stop it; its success, not so much in achieving its aims as in gathering public support and attention, is dependent on a number of factors, including the proximity and 'visibility' of the conflict, the level of 'exposure' to it (media-attention), the nature of the conflict and the parties involved. In Britain, the war in El Salvador (in which Britain was not a participant) and the war with Argentina over the Falklands (in which the country was directly involved) led to the emergence of movements opposing those conflicts; the Russian war in Afghanistan has not – or at least has not resulted in an organisation which has attracted national publicity.

Peace groups which aim to prevent certain wars from breaking out are, at the present time, numerous. The war they have in mind, of course, is the one between East and West. Virtually all the big peace movements which have sprung up in Europe in the last few years find their *raison d'être* in this concern. The main groups in Britain in this field are the Campaign for Nuclear Disarmament (CND), whose foundation goes back to the late 1950s (when there was a similar anxiety), and the European Nuclear Disarmament campaign (END), which aims to embrace all of Europe. These groups, which have caught the public's imagination, partly also belong to the third category of peace groups we have identified, viz. those which want to *stop particular aspects of war*.[10] As their names imply, both CND and END have as their first priority the abolition not of war but of nuclear weapons. The present popularity of both movements, and of their counterparts in other West-European countries, can be attributed to several factors. Prominent among these is the decision or intention to introduce new nuclear weapons (Cruise and Pershing II missiles, replacement of Polaris submarine fleet with Trident missiles, the neutron bomb). Just as virtually every war seems to bring forth a reaction from the peace movement, so does every new weapon. It is, again, recognised that it is only the West's own new weapons (sometimes deployed in a defensive reaction) and not those of the other side which seem to have this consequence. Suffice it here to say that whereas it would be unwise to discount the influence of the Soviet Union in all this, it would be equally unwise and inappropriate to let everything hinge on this single factor. I agree with Bidwell when he writes: 'It is both insensitive and politically naive to write off the peace movements in the Western world as Lenin's "useful fools", or to suggest that they are simply tools manipulated by Soviet agents disposing of "a billion dollars in hard currency". To acknowledge their sincerity and their strength is not necessarily to agree with them.'[11] One could, for the sake of completeness and, above all, clarity, expand the typology used by a fourth category, which would encompass all those movements which are sponsored by the Soviet Union and in which the directing hand is clear to see. This group would thus consist of peace movements and groups which would not be regarded as bona fide, unlike those which belong to the other categories. That many of the latter do contain communists is wellknown and not surprising; it becomes a different matter, however, if communists are the sole or dominating influence in such a movement. This is, for instance, the case in the World Peace Council (WPC). The blatant one-sidedness of this and similar organisations often gives the game away at an early stage. The fact that a peace group is bona fide does not, of course, necessarily mean that its analysis is sound, its programme commendable, and the attainment of its immediate objectives a guarantee for peace.

However, one should not lightly brush aside people's feelings of anxiety and worry of which peace movements are a sincere expression, nor reject their arguments without a full and objective examination. One of the main tasks of peace research, in my opinion, is the sympathetic yet critical assessment of the analyses, proposals and strategies emanating from the peace movement. I have the strong impression, however, that this is far from being the case today. Many of the speculative (and sometimes naive and dangerous) assumptions of the peace movement and much of the wishful thinking which pervades it have also become characteristic of much peace research – explaining both its lack of success (in terms of growth, respectability and credibility) and its controversial standing. A 'Science of survival' is badly needed; but whether, after some 25 years, peace research can justifiably claim to be this 'science' is doubtful. The mere fact that there is no consensus (to put it mildly) on a great many issues touching upon the subject of war and peace between scholars in such traditional disciplines as history and politics on the one hand and those engaged in peace research on the other, can be regarded as a clear manifestation of this failure. Whereas in the past peace movements have been blamed all too readily (and often falsely) for inviting aggression and war,[12] the same accusation, which is being levelled against it again today, is not entirely without ground.

In this connection, it is worth pointing out that one has to be equally careful in evaluating criticisms which emphasise the 'peace at any price' attitude of peace movements. Since their beginning, at the end of the Napoleonic Wars, peace movements have been part of a much broader re-form movement which included such causes as temperance, anti-slavery, penal reform, women's rights, free trade. The same is true today: although there are groups which limit their activities to the narrow field of peace and disarmament, many others are also involved in such issues as colonial liberation and world poverty, racial and sexual discrimination, human rights and civil liberties, and – particularly with the growth of the nuclear energy industry – ecology. The main achievements of Mahatma Gandhi and Martin Luther King – two of the best-known and much-admired peace leaders of our century – were the peaceful liberation of a country and race respectively. Whether one refers to Carl von Ossietzky or Andrei Sakharov, to Albert Schweitzer or Dominique Pire, amongst the Nobel Peace prize laureates there are few, if any, whose concern for peace did not also embrace freedom, liberty, justice – without which true peace is inconceivable. Particularly since the 1960s, many peace movements have again become part of a wider movement for changing society; the 'alternative society' envisaged is one which wants to remove the threat of nuclear holocaust, but also the many other blemishes which make our societies less than peaceful. As Bob Overy has rightly argued: 'Peace movements . . . have not succeeded in defining themselves in more than a narrow and oppositional way which is perhaps negative. But the concerns of peace movements of whatever type are almost always broader and more positive than opposition to war and stretch right across the spectrum of political and social activity.'[13]

This concern for a truly comprehensive peace has, even among principled or total pacifists, led to agonising decisions, occasionally resulting in the abandonment of the pacifist stance. This was, for instance, the case with Quakers during the American War of Independence and, almost a hundred years later, the Civil War, when they were torn between remaining loyal to their peace testimony and their commitment, no less deeply rooted, to the cause of human dignity and freedom.[14] In our century, the Spanish Civil War and the rise of fascism witnessed similar discussions in the pacifist movement about priorities and the precise meanings of the pacifist creed in the particular circumstances of the time. In the 1920s, many rallied to the pacifist movement without having fully considered the implications of their stand. The appearance of totalitarian states was to change this. As a leading peace historian has written, Einstein's pacifism is typical of much of the anti-war sentiment of the post-World War I era: 'In the first place it was largely an emotional response, a repulsion against the horrors of modern war and an expression of the disenchantment that had followed World War I. Einstein did not hide this fact. "My pacifism is an instinctive feeling", he wrote in 1929. "My attitude is not the result of an intellectual theory". . . . Einstein and many others found that the same emotional impulse that had made them espouse war resistance now propelled them into the camp of those who urged armed resistance. For Einstein, the path that conducted him away from pacifism led him (to his shocked horror, let it be added), toward the creation of the atom bomb.'[15] The conclusion Peter Brock draws from the travails of the peace movement of the inter-war period is one which has not diminished in validity and which can, to a lesser extent, be applied to the contemporary peace movements: 'The mistake made by the pacifist movement in the half-decade before World War II was in trying to sell pacifism as an immediately viable political programme without imparting sufficient insight into what its adoption would require or attempting to develop in any detail the positive aspects of non-violent action as an alternative to military power.'[16]

Before returning to the forms of pacifism distinguished by Scheler, it is useful to refer to Peter Brock's analysis of the 'Varieties of pacifism at the outset of the twentieth century'.[17] He identifies four sources of 20th-century pacifism:

(a) The doctrine of non-resistance as developed by the Anabaptists and the Mennonites of the Reformation era.
(b) The peace testimony of the Quakers, dating back to Cromwell's England. They were to contribute substantially to the creation of an organised Anglo-American peace movement in the 19th century.
(c) The institutional approach to the problem of war evolved by these 19th-century peace societies.
(d) The socialist anti-militarism which emerged, along with the organised labour movement, in the half century before 1914.

A crucial difference between the first two mentioned groups is that whereas the Mennonites not only separated from the established church but also attempted to live in isolation from the state (believing that nothing good could be achieved by political action), Quakers sought to transform the world, not withdraw from it. Their aim was to christianise, not repudiate, politics. In contrast to the inward-looking Mennonite tradition of non-resistance, Quaker pacifism became an outreaching creed, seeking to find expression in both domestic and international political activities. This development explains the heavy Quaker presence in many social reform movements, first and foremost amongst them those concerning peace. They were a major influence on the creation of the first organised peace societies which started in the USA and England at the beginning of the last century. (Contemporary peace research is equally unthinkable without the impetus provided by Quakers from the same two countries.) In addition to the support derived from Quakers and other religious groups, the first peace societies also drew support from the Enlightenment period: whereas Christian pacifists condemned war as sin, the men of the Enlightenment condemned war as both inhumane and irrational. In the peace societies, the religious and secular case against war thus came together. Their fundamental aims were the promotion of (a) arbitration and arbitration treaties, (b) an international authority or tribunal, (c) the codification of international law, and (d) simultaneous and proportional disarmament. These objectives were regarded as being interdependent. Although the impact of the peace societies was small in terms of their political effect, they were nevertheless successful in several ways: they countered the age-old glorification of war, pressed the material and moral case against war, and made proposals for international organisation to replace international anarchy. The fact that these notions and insights are widely accepted now and taken for granted does not detract from the real merits and achievements of the peace societies in this respect.

With the growth of the labour movement, a distinct socialist anti-militarism began to appear towards the end of the last century. Although no socialist party adopted a completely pacifist stand, Marxist parties indeed rejected pacifism categorically and many socialists favoured the class war, socialism, with its ideal of human brotherhood, somewhat bordered on pacifism. In its attempt to prevent war in 1914 — by organising a general strike — the international socialist movement failed, thereby demonstrating that its prescriptions were no more able than those of others to bring about international peace. In a more general sense, however, the socialist movement brought about a greater awareness of the connections between the evils of war and the shortcomings of the economic system, stressing the need for social change to eliminate war and violence. It thus added a new dimension to pacifism. Each of the four varieties mentioned by Peter Brock which, having progressively emerged in the course of the last 400 years or so, together provide the main source of contemporary pacifism, thus has unmistakenly contributed a distinct element to the pacifist doctrine, accounting for the rich variety of the phenomenon.

We devote our last few pages to Scheler's reflections on peace and pacifism — they deal with the essential issues, and make his essay, much as it appears to be a child of its time, 'a major contribution to the cause of peace'.[18] Scheler's work is an attempt to answer the following four questions:

(a) 'Is the idea of eternal peace a *positive value* and a polar star guiding all political actions for any statesman? Put negatively: is war a part of human nature or is it not? Is 'eternal peace' at all possible with human beings?

(b) Can an *evolutionary* direction towards a gradual realisation of the idea of 'eternal peace' be traced within *history known to us*?

(c) Does the *present* situation and phase of human history point to a somehow *foreseeable* realisation of this idea — that is to say 'foreseeable' in a practical sense, not in the sense of a specific date?

(d) Are there systematic and practical methods of will, techniques, and institutions already at hand which would *today* allow us to set out to bring about some kind of 'eternal peace' — for example through legal institutions (League of Nations), through the moral axiom: 'Do not resist evil' (passive politics), through refusing conscription in times of war; or through a dictatorship of the proletariat and communism;

through formations of group interests in Western and American capitalism; or through a Europeanism (United States of Europe) and a struggle against nationalism; through a church or the arbitrator-ship of a Pope?'[19]

Scheler calls 'general pacifism' that way of thinking which answers affirmatively all four questions, especially the last two, and defines 'militarism' as that which provides negative replies to the same questions, and specifically the first one. These two positions, pacifism and militarism, define the extreme ends of a spectrum[20] of possible points of view and convictions which can be found in between ('Instrumental militarism' is the somewhat unfortunate term which Scheler uses to designate collectively these non-extreme views).

To the first two questions Scheler replies positively, to the last two his answers are, however, negative. His fairly extensive discussion of the first point is, as he makes clear, meant to be a rebuttal of the erroneous and dangerous views which, through such figures as Hegel, Nietzsche and von Treitschke, had become the dominant views on the subject in 19th-century Germany. 'Perpetual peace *is* an "ideal" ', he concludes in the first section of his analysis. 'It is not a dream as Immanuel Kant had already seen – and it is a beautiful and good ideal' (p. 161). Although the problems raised by the second question are 'very difficult', Scheler believes that a positive answer is likely. From his interesting and penetrating discussion the follow-ing observation is worth quoting: 'If there is at all the possibility of a history of humanity as a whole, it has begun only in our own day, perhaps in 1914. It is humanity, i.e. humanity not as a name for a species but understood as a historically-real specific subject – which is history's *task*, and perhaps its result. Humanity (as a whole) is *not* history's point of departure' (p. 161). Looking at the multitude of conflicts and tensions around him, the author has no option but to reply negatively to his third question; a similar answer is given to the final one. Scheler's typology of pacifism, briefly mentioned earlier, is developed in the corresponding chapter, by far the largest, of the book.[21] We will do no more than enumerate the eight types of pacifism which he mentions, and say a few words on each.

Heroic pacifism is the only one which is 'pure' and not the (conscious or unconscious) expression of some ideological interest. Its real home is not so much the Christian as the Buddhist world. Because of the spiritual values which underlie it, this pacifism merits the highest moral considera-tions. It has proved inefficient, however, in attaining its goal. *Christian pacifism* is very relative: the Church's doctrine of the fall and original sin, as well as that of the Just War, excludes the possibility of total pacifism, whereas in the period when the power and influence of the Church and the Pope were at their height, peace was hard to find. *Economic-liberal pacifism* (closely identified with the Manchester School) totally ignores the role played by the will to power and to dominate, which has a wider ambit than merely serving the instincts of self-preservation and the desire for gain. To expect perpetual peace from free trade is to put the cart before the horse: 'Should world peace come about by way of moral, political and legal developments, then a free trade will come about automatically. Economic pacifism mistakenly takes the effects for the causes' (p. 41).[22] *Juridical pacifism or pacifism by law* errs in over-estimating the power of law; the highest achievement of this pacifism is to be found in the creation of the League of Nations, the efficacy of which is very limited. *Marxist, socialist and communist pacifism* sees in the final victory of the working class also the triumph of perpetual peace. It is a pacifism of a completely different kind from the other forms of pacifism which are being considered here − yet, because of its belief in the ultimate extinction of war, it is a pacifism all the same. Scheler quotes from Lenin and Zinoviev's *Socialism and War*, in which they write: 'Marxism is no pacifism. . . . Our cause is not to be seen in a general disarmament, but in the disarmament of the bourgeoisie and the armament of the proletariat' (p. 47). Scheler's conclusion on this particular variant of pacifism is worth quoting: 'An eternal peace to be erected upon the blood of a world revolution is probably the most questionable form that this most changing idea of peace has ever assumed. For we are concerned here not only with bloodshed but also with the destruction of the entire history of Western culture! A war of world revolution represents a great danger for peace' (p. 47). Faced with this prospect of world-wide revolutionary wars, as preached by the Bolsheviks, Western circles of high finance and great industry began countering this threat with an ideology of their own; in this Scheler detects the beginnings of a *Conservative pacifism of the greater bourgeoisie*. Despite some of its positive aspects, it lacks a moral basis and to expect universal peace from it would be naive. This form is somewhat related to another type of pacifism, *Imperialist Empire pacifism*. It refers to the tendency, which can be seen in history every so often, to bring about universal peace through the hegemony of a single state − so powerful and extensive that no other can threaten it. This kind of pacifism is the exact opposite of the first kind, i.e. instead of a 'pacifism of non-violence' we are confronted here with a 'pacifism of total violence'. The author finally identifies a *Cultural pacifism* − a conglomeration of ideas and attitudes which find expression in such manifestations as a new cosmopolitanism of cultural milieux, the internationalism of the sciences and technology, a new European spirit, in educational endeavours to revise school text-books, etc. Laudable though these initiatives and developments are, by themselves they will not be able to bring about perpetual peace. Thus, none of the forms of pacifism discussed by Scheler ('instrumental pacifism') is able to bring about, in the foreseeable future, perpetual peace.

Scheler concludes his concise but convincing analysis thus: 'From the above it follows that we must reject all old forms of militarism much as we must reject all forms of instrumental pacifism proper. We must demand a character-pacifism that grows out of the moral tenor of the person, and an instrumental militarism; we must enhance all endeavours directed to-wards an eternal peace' (p. 50). The 'call of the hour' is a notion dear to Scheler; the first requirement of his day is also that of ours, namely, 'to save Europe from another war which would amount to total destruction, i.e. a "Twilight of the Gods" for European culture and for everything that our ancestors have loved and honoured since Homer' (p. 50). In his passion-ate but serene appeal to the new generation of his country — divided between those who want a war of revenge and who believe in a romantic militarism, and those who, disillusioned as a result of the war, have aban-doned themselves to utopian pacifist theories which do not stand up to the critique of reason — Scheler, on the contrary, stresses the need for a sane intelligence which has not lost touch with reality and for a firm spirit which together will provide the best guarantee for the maintenance and consolidation of peace. His directions to this cherished goal of mankind, so tragically ignored by his own generation, are as valid today as when he first suggested them, over 50 years ago.

NOTES

1. *Guide to the Swarthmore College Peace Collection*, 2nd edn, Swarthmore College, Swarthmore, Pennsylvania, 1981, 158pp.
2. John H. Yoder, *Nevertheless: A Meditation on the Varieties and Shortcomings of Religious Pacifism*, Scottdale, Pennsylvania, Herald Press, 1971, pp. 5–6.
3. Max Scheler, 'The Idea of Peace and Pacifism', translated by Manfred S. Frings, *Journal of the British Society for Phenomenology*, vol. 7 no. 3, Oct. 1976, pp. 154–66 and vol. 8 no. 1, Jan. 1977, pp. 36–50. The quotation is on pp. 165–6. This is the only English translation available. In one or two places I have departed from Frings's translation. Scheler's book is based on a series of lectures held in Berlin in 1927 (the year before his death), and was first published in 1931. A French edition was published in 1953 (Paris, Aubier/ Editions Montaigne).

4. J.-B. Barbier, *Le Pacifisme dans l'Histoire de France*, Paris, La Librairie Française, 1966, pp. 7–11.

5. Keith Robbins, *The Abolition of War: the 'Peace Movement' in Britain, 1914–1919*, Cardiff, University of Wales Press, 1976, p. 10.

6. 'The Way of Peace: a discussion' in *The Listener* (London), 16 Feb. 1938.

7. See Martin Ceadel, *Pacifism in Britain 1914–1945: The defining of a faith*, Oxford, Clarendon Press, 1980, p. 3. The first chapter of this book traces the development of the meaning of both concepts. In the second chapter a new typology is suggested, in which six types of pacifism are identified in order to make distinctions on the one hand, about the inspiration of the pacifist, and, on the other hand, about the attitude he adopts towards the society he lives in.

8. Barbier, op. cit., p. 13. In the first chapter of his book (pp. 9–21) which is devoted largely to matters of definition, the author, as we have indicated, makes some interesting and valid points. Despite appearances to the contrary, his work is, however, polemical and it betrays, at times, a very superficial and overtly hostile view of the peace movement. In this respect, the treatment by Scheler is much more objective, fair-minded and far more penetrating. Scheler's work, it must be remembered, is philosophical whereas Barbier's is historical in approach. The latter's work, moreover, is not at all a history of pacifism or of peace movements in France (as one might suspect from the title) but, more in accordance with the author's career as plenipotentiary minister, an interpretation of French foreign policy from a particular (partisan) point of view.

9. Bob Overy, *How effective are peace movements?*, London, Housmans & Bradford University, School of Peace Studies, 1980, pp. 3–4.

10. One of the most prominent organisations whose aim is to eliminate particular aspects of war is the International Committee of the Red Cross (ICRC), and the affiliated Red Cross societies in many countries. The work of the Red Cross concerns the interdiction of certain weapons and categories of weapons in war, the treatment of the wounded and prisoners of war, etc. Its humanitarian concerns have, from its inception, been regarded by some (extreme pacifists) as making the Red Cross an upholder of the 'war system', by trying to legislate and humanise the inhumane. The World Disarmament Campaign (WDC), the Campaign against the Arms Trade (CAAT), the various campaigns to bring about nuclear-free zones — these are all instances of movements which, by addressing themselves to a specific issue, aim to reduce the likelihood of wars taking place.

11. Brigadier Shelford Bidwell, 'Fighting Talk' (A review of General Sir John Hackett's *The Third World War*), p. 948 in *The Times Literary Supplement* (London), 3 Sept. 1982. The attempt to counter the peace movement by alleging that it is financially backed by a country's opponent is an old and largely discredited one. In the First World War, for instance, Scotland Yard seized the accounts of the leading British anti-war organisations and scrutinised them for evidence of German money or influence, but nothing was found. Cf. Robbins, op. cit., p. 147. This is not to deny that Nazi Germany and Soviet Russia have pioneered methods which may lend substance to the allegation.

12. For a brief but convincing study see, e.g., D.V. Glass, *The Role of the Peace*

Movements in the 1930s, London, University Group on Defence Policy, 1959, 16 pp. 'That the peace-movements of the 1930s were in any significant sense preparers of, and contributors to, "appeasement",' Glass concludes, 'is a myth.' For the same period and country see also: ' "King and Country": did that 1933 Oxford Union debate really sway the Führer?', pp. 196–8 in *The Listener*, vol. 99 no. 2547, 16 Feb. 1978. (The episode referred to in note (6) is also taken from this issue.) For a dissenting view, see e.g. Kaplan (infra).

13. Bob Overy, op. cit., p. 5.

14. For an excellent discussion of this dilemma see D. Elton Trueblood, *The people called Quakers*, Richmond, Ind., Friends United Press, 1980, esp. ch. 10, 'The Struggle for Peace'.

15. Peter Brock, *Twentieth-Century Pacifism*, New York, Van Nostrand Reinhold, 1970, p. 132 (section: 'Pacifism and the Growth of Totalitarianism').

16. Ibid., p. 136.

17. The title of his first chapter (pp. 1–13); what follows is directly based on it.

18. Thus Manfred S. Frings & Kenneth W. Stikkers in 'Introduction to Max Scheler's "The Idea of Peace and Pacifism" ', pp. 151–3 in *Journal of the British Society for Phenomenology*, op. cit.

19. Scheler, op. cit., pp. 155–6.

20. The German–American historian Alfred Vagts has argued that the true counterpart of militarism is not pacifism but civilianism. See Volker R. Berghahn, *Militarism. The History of an International Debate, 1861–1979*, Leamington Spa, Berg Publ., 1981. What Berghahn writes about militarism is to some extent also true of pacifism: '... there is no general agreement on its meaning. Worse, like imperialism, militarism is and always has been a word of political propaganda and polemic' (p. 2).

21. Op. cit., pp. 165–6 and 36–50.

22. That the growing interdependence of economic and other interests of states is making war increasingly impossible – a contemporary variation of economic-liberal pacifism – is one of the two pillars supporting Werner Levi's thesis concerning *The Coming End of War*, Beverly Hills & London, Sage Publications, 1981. The other factor which is bringing this about is the system of nuclear deterrence; Levi entitles this part of his book 'Weapons Wipe Out war.'

3 Pacifism and the Contemporary International Situation

ALEXANDER SHTROMAS

1

Whatever the objections to pacifism – the view that peace is the highest value of all and that no goal, however lofty, is worth fighting a war for – one has to admit that in the nuclear era it makes at least some sense, which even the fiercest opponents of pacifism cannot entirely deny. For the highest value of all, indeed a value without which all other human values lose their very meaning, is life. A nuclear war, insofar as it puts at high risk the continuation of all life on Earth, seems therefore not to be worth fighting, even if the defence of such precious values as national independence – let alone territorial integrity – or any lesser ideological or political values, is at stake. The provocative catchphrase 'better red than dead' expresses this attitude in a nutshell and was formulated on the basis of such reasoning. Indeed, it is hard to disagree with the elementary truth that it is better to be anything but dead, because as long as there is life there is also hope. After all, as long as people stay alive, humanity, as an inherent and irrepressible part of any individual, will – under any external circumstances, however adverse – remain alive too, and there are strong reasons to believe that, in the end, it will have to assert itself, against all the odds, over all forces trying to suppress it. And if this is so, why not agree, in order to survive, to become 'red' for a certain limited period of time?

2

Not many Western pacifists preaching unilateral disarmament are, however, willing to admit that their logic is based on the above arguments and that what they advocate amounts to unconditional surrender to the Soviet Union. Instead, they try to attribute to the Soviet Union entirely defensive and even benevolent intentions and thus do everything they can to deny that the Soviet threat is real. According to them the only reason why the Soviet Union is so militantly militaristic is the hostile attitude and threatening posture of the West towards it. In other words, many pacifists are keen to explain anything the Soviet Union does on the world scene, even its most brutal acts of aggression and expansion, as something that is essentially determined by a justified feeling of insecurity and by a real need for making itself less vulnerable to an external attack from the overwhelming hostile forces encircling the USSR. The conclusion that logically follows from this reasoning is that if the West were seriously and credibly to the 'beleaguered Soviet leaders', to change its anti-Soviet stance, for example by disarming or taking other similar unilateral steps, not only would the imminent threat to world peace entirely disappear, but genuine trust and friendship among the nations of East and West could firmly and swiftly be established. By assuming that the USSR is a benign and besieged power, the pacifists lay the whole onus for keeping the world on the brink of a nuclear war, on the 'cruel, militaristic West', which is thus supposed to be the world's only authoritative force on whose will and decision the fate of peace depends fully and exclusively.

This one-sided, West-centred (and therefore, provincial) stance is clearly assumptious and self-deceptive. It deliberately ignores any of the existing, contradictory interpretations based on expertise and analysis (including the official Soviet one) of the same phenomenon, together with the facts on which these other interpretations are based. For the proponents of this stance the urge to obtain a simple answer to an extremely complex problem — an answer that would give them comfort and make their wishful views appear uncontroversial — is so compulsive that everything that complicates the issue is treated as pure anathema, which must be rejected out of hand, however true in factual or persuasive in logical (but not emotional) terms it might be. No one can claim infallibility in his interpretation of a complex political reality, neither the pacifists nor even their more sensible and analytically minded opponents; but those who assume that they are infallible and therefore reject in advance everything that challenges this assumption are by definition bound to be wrong.

In this context, however, the whole argument of who is right or wrong — indeed the very discussion about the essence and goals of Soviet foreign policy — as well as of the nature of the East—West relationship in general, should be deemed to be entirely beside the point. A pacifist stance that is honest, realistic and adequate to the essence of pacifism must be able to meet the requirements of any of the possible interpretations of these problems, including the one that posits that the only realistic alternatives are either unconditional surrender to the USSR or nuclear war if it becomes necessary to deter Soviet aggression. Those pacifists who place the emphasis not on the straightforward choice between these two extreme alternatives but instead on a wishful interpretation of Soviet intentions and plans, are trying to avoid tackling the real issue — the issue of principle — and thus miss the point entirely. Any pacifist worthy of that name should dismiss as irrelevant all political interpretations of the behaviour of the sides involved in the conflict and boldly state that, if it were the only choice given, he would above all prefer surrender to an outright war.

As should be clear from the opening paragraph, there is nothing objectionable, in my view, in choosing surrender rather than a nuclear holocaust, provided that one is absolutely honest about this and, more importantly, has reasonable grounds based on analysis for believing that such a choice is viable; in other words, provided that by choosing to be 'red' (or to surrender) one can really put an end to the threat of a nuclear holocaust and thus save human life from extinction. But can one? This is the question that must be posited and answered in the first place, before one goes any further; however, since so far no Western pacifist has ever attempted to do so, I will try.

3

The peoples of Communist countries (and especially the Russians themselves) undoubtedly had such a real alternative. Their, on the whole quite submissive, existence under the oppressive Communist rule shows that, after repeated but unsuccessful and desperate attempts at resistance, they reluctantly preferred turning red (though only outwardly, not in terms of their real inner selves) to being extinct. Indeed, history has proved that, under the conditions of 'capitalist encirclement', individual nations under Communist rule were on the whole physically able to survive in spite of the heavy losses in human life that were inflicted upon them by the Communist regimes.

However, under today's conditions of the continuing East—West confrontation, the choice between 'red' and 'dead' has to be made no longer only by individual nations but by the entire world. For the East—West confrontation is now nothing else than a struggle for the establishment of a *universal* world order. The issue at stake here is the system, either democratic or totalitarian — and these systems are incompatible — on which this universal world order is going to be based. Hence, by choosing to be 'red' (or, which is the same, surrendering to the Soviet Union), one chooses to submit the entire world to a Communist totalitarian system with no 'hostile environment' left in sight at all to keep the Communist powers in check.

This is what entirely changes the whole situation of mankind's ability to survive under Communist rule. First of all, the Communist power will impose on all genuine conflicts and differences of interests its own preconceived solutions, as it always has done, but this time on a global scale. These solutions, being unsatisfactory to any of the parties involved, will have to be ruthlessly enforced by the powers that be, and instead of removing the genuine issues which cause conflicts, will (as even the present experience of the countries under Communist control shows clearly enough) only artificially suppress them. The effect will be to create an even more potentially aggravated and explosive situation which sooner or later will erupt, causing extensive bloodshed and, in the absence of outside (i.e. non-Communist) regulative forces, produce a protracted and utterly uncontrollable overt confrontation of 'all against all'. A nuclear holocaust is the very likely result.

Secondly, for the above as well as many other reasons, a totalitarian universal world order can hardly be stable and lasting. After a certain time it will inevitably collapse, and a polycentric totalitarian world — (in a totalitarian environment any newly established entity, in order to survive, will have no choice but to be totalitarian, too) — in which the constituent parts will be constantly fighting one another, will emerge in its place. Incidentally, this was prophesied by George Orwell in *Nineteen Eighty-Four*, and is already corroborated by the actual cases of splits and conflicts between the USSR and Yugoslavia, China and the USSR, Vietnam and Kampuchea, China and Vietnam, and Albania and the rest of the Communist world. One should remember that were it not for the restricting influence of the Western world on Communist powers, a Soviet–Yugoslav war would certainly have erupted in 1948, and a Soviet–Chinese war in 1969–70. The latter, as we know, was prevented exclusively by the drastic intervention of Nixon and Kissinger and by a radical change in the USA's China policy, which was first expressed at the time in the rudimentary form of the so-called 'ping-pong diplomacy' and later acquired the character of a regular 'Soviet-sustaining' relationship between the two countries brought about by Nixon's historic visit to China in 1972. It goes without saying that Communist totalitarian powers, free of any checks and balances, and able to ignore or suppress public opinion, if left on their own, i.e. without the 'restraining' influence of the presence of external 'hostile' forces, will find it so easy to engage in wars against one another that these wars will become the inevitable reality of their co-existence. What this means for mankind in the nuclear age does not need much elaboration — the human race will hardly be able to survive its totalitarian experience.

The Western world's surrender to the Soviet Union (or, in other words, its becoming 'red') is thus undesirable, not simply because a bad and inhuman system of the world order would be established; if only this were the case, it could be accepted as a relatively small price to pay for mankind's security of existence, especially because, as has been said, totalitarian Communism is unviable as a long-term system of rule and, sooner or later, is bound to collapse in any case. Surrender is, however, entirely unacceptable since it is by no means certain that the human race will not be extinct even before the signs of the collapse of Communist totalitarianism are in evidence. This is why 'becoming red' almost certainly means becoming dead too, whereas staying 'not red' and resisting the 'red menace' by all means in one's power is the only way of enhancing the chances for remaining alive and well.

Hence, the whole dilemma of being either 'red or dead' is entirely illusory and the very formula 'better red than dead' — fatuous. For, if we accept it, we will most certainly be both red *and* dead in no time at all. This makes the present pacifist stance not only assumptuous but obsolete; moreover, it makes it a stance contrary to everything the pacifists are supposed to stand for. I am afraid that the pacifists have to go over this ground and then change their message, so that it could counter the above challenge and become consistent with the facts behind it. If, however, they refuse to do so, their pacifism should be put to serious doubt.

4

As has already been mentioned above, whatever the appearances, claims and interpretations, the East and the West confront one another about nothing less than the underlying principles on which the universal world order should evolve. Their antagonism is therefore basically ideological: two incompatible world views are opposed — totalitarian and liberal—democratic (not Communist and Capitalist as many people tend to believe) — and thus also two world futures. For reasons explained in the previous paragraph, the genuine pacifist undoubtedly should be on the liberal—democratic side of that confrontation. And he probably also would be, if only he were able to recognise clearly enough that the West really is such a side, defending not so much its egoistic power-based interests as the democratic and peaceful future of the world.

Of course, it is plainly inconceivable for some people in the pacifist camp to recognise this because of their ideological 'anti-capitalist' or 'anti-imperialist' bias. The problem, however, is that it is difficult, even for those who do not share this bias. The West so conspicuously lacks ideological self-consciousness and so stubbornly refuses to treat its confrontation with the East as being about anything other than conflicting national interests between 'normal' states rather than about the future, indeed about the survival, of the human race, that general confusion about the functions and goals of the West in this confrontation is bound to arise and persist. For by mistaking the Soviet Union for an ordinary imperial power, whose pursuit of its national interests differs only from that of other such powers, e.g. those of the West, not so much in content as in its inordinate manner and excessive scope, the West shows itself to be confronting the East for the mere sake of preserving (and, in favourable conditions, also expanding) its own position of power and privilege in the world. But if this is really so, and if the only thing at stake in a confrontation fraught with the danger of a nuclear holocaust is the share of influence, natural resources and prestige enjoyed by the parties involved, is the West really more worthy of support than the Soviet Union, whatever its goals are or could be? This, to a large extent self-depicted, image of the West conceals the whole liberal–democratic, peace-assuring side, within the context of the East–West confrontation, so well that for many people, especially the pacifists, it seems to be totally non-existent. Hence, people who would enthusiastically join the cause of freedom, justice and peace, when looking upon the East–West confrontation, are left with no reasonable choice except to call 'a plague o' both your houses'.

Implicit in the limited Western perception of the East–West confrontation there are clearly militaristic overtones, which are sounding the alarm with every pacifist and are bound to cause his protest. Indeed, the West, by concentrating almost exclusively on containing and deterring the potential Soviet aggressor, is bound to emphasise its military capacity to keep the Soviets at bay. This in itself excites suspicion since it is doubtful whether it is at all possible to draw a precise borderline between the defensive and offensive usages of military strength. But even if it were accepted that the military power of the West is nothing but a pure deterrent against the Soviets (which it has been very effectively so far), the situation created by this purely military response of the West to the Soviet threat is extremely worrying to any pacifist (and even to any not necessarily pacifist but simply peace-loving person). For, to make a military deterrent credible, one has to be and also to be seen to be determined to put it into practice when necessary, i.e. one has to be really ready to engage in a fully-fledged nuclear war with the Soviet Union if it commits an act of aggression against the West (and what is to be deemed as such an act has yet to be defined). This determination cannot provide an adequate foundation for a policy of peace in the full sense of the word acceptable to the pacifists and thus makes the actual Western policy into one not of peace but only of effective deterrence and defence. It begs at least one question, namely: what values are worth defending to the point of risking a nuclear war?

The West, because of its limited, unideological perception of the confrontation with the East, has not yet found an answer satisfactory to the pacifists and thereby has driven them into opposition to the whole set of Western policies regarding the USSR. However, the supporters of the Western officialdoms and their pacifist opponents have both misunderstood the very nature of the East—West confrontation. If only the West had lived up to the Soviet challenge and adequately realised its role of defender and preserver of the liberal—democratic principles of the universal world order, it would have become clear to all who are sufficiently objective, including some of the most dedicated pacifists, that the West's surrender to the Soviets is even more lethal than nuclear war itself. The only way to avoid both surrender to the Soviets and war, is for the West resolutely to resist Communist totalitarianism not only by deterring it militarily, but primarily by combating it ideologically on a global scale until it absolutely and irreversibly collapses from within. But the West has not yet lived up to this challenge and oddly finds itself under attack from its own peace-loving people – a situation whose tragic implications are difficult to overestimate and which has to be altered decisively.

5

In the practical world, however, we are still faced with the fact that the pacifists, by opposing the Western policy of deterrence and defence, are, consciously or otherwise, actively backing the totalitarian, Soviet side of the East—West confrontation. Again, this is due to the utmost neglect by the West of the ideological dimension of its confrontation with the East, as well as to the enterprising ability of the Soviets to fill the ideological vacuum left by the West with their own relentless ideological offensive.

Indeed, ideology and propaganda are the primary weapons of Soviet expansionism and it is their skilful use that is primarily responsible for all the USSR's successes in international politics.

The Soviet ideological offensive, which has been conducted relentlessly and without much change of its content (though it differed in its extent, emphases and forms throughout the past decades) from the beginning of the Soviet state in 1917, has a two-tier structure. The first tier is the close Soviet association with and its unequivocal support for the Communist parties and their revolutionary activities, as well as anti-Western national liberation movements all over the world. There is at the present time no country in the entire world where the Soviet Union, due to this tier of its policy, has not acquired a relatively strong and committed (though, as a rule which has few exceptions, only a minoritarian) 'inner constituency' whose aspirations to acquire political power are entirely dependent on Soviet support and which therefore becomes 'clientelised' by the Soviet Union and used by it for the promotion of Soviet foreign-policy goals in the area in which it operates. By assisting such constituencies to obtain power, the Soviet Union has acquired a dominant influence in the countries now under its control and continues to acquire it elsewhere whenever an opportunity offers itself. At the same time, the presence of these Soviet constituencies in every country of the world not (yet?) under Soviet control, enables the Soviet Union to 'penetrate' all of them in sufficient depth so as to have much better knowledge than any of its rivals of what goes on and how the developments should be used to Soviet advantage. This is indeed a unique asset for a power conducting a truly global policy since, under these circumstances, this policy can be conducted not only in an effectively knowledgeable way but also subtly adapted to the specific conditions in various countries and regions of the world.

The second tier is expressed in the relentlessness of Soviet propaganda efforts to present the USSR's foreign policy as being totally and unequivocally committed to the 'struggle for peace'. This is a very special device aimed at encouraging as many 'peace-loving' Westerners as possible to oppose the Western policy of 'hostility' toward the USSR. Thus a force is created which assists the Soviets to undermine from within the resoluteness and ability of the West to resist them effectively and stop their expansionist drive.

Since the Soviet leadership is only too conscious of the ideological dimension and goals of its confrontation with the West and is trying to create another, much wider layer of its Western constituency, it is keen to do everything in its power to cater for the pacifists' sympathies and to enhance and strengthen pacifism in the Western realm. No effort or expenditure is spared for this purpose, nor any opportunity missed.

First of all, the Soviets do not simply identify themselves with the inherent pacifist discontent about 'Western militarism' but greatly contribute to its amplification, especially by providing the pacifists with systematic anti-militarist arguments, logically conceived alternatives to militaristic policies and aptly designed programmes of political action aimed at impressing their point upon the general public and the particular Western government.

Secondly, the Soviets regularly (on average about twice a year) launch various 'peace initiatives' specially designed to impress the pacifist and to enable him to endorse them as his own cause. Total nuclear disarmament, the undertaking not to use nuclear arms first, proportional reductions in military budgets and conventional forces stationed in foreign territories, the simultaneous abolition of both NATO and the Warsaw Pact — these are examples of initiatives that come first to one's mind.

Thirdly, the Soviets have initiated, organised and financed some sections of the international peace movement and, in order to keep them going, are continuing to provide them lavishly with all the necessary facilities. As the Soviet-backed peace organisations are in comparison with other pacifist bodies the richest and best organised, they try, not entirely without success, to play a dominant role in the peace movement as a whole and to provide it with, among other things, an overall coordinating umbrella. For this purpose, the Soviets regularly organise huge peace assemblies (the most recent of which was held in Prague in 1983) to which all independent peace bodies are invited and where most of them participate in some capacity (for example, the CND sent 'observers' to the Prague assembly). Soviet and other Communist 'peace officials', who pose as independent 'fighters for peace', are also accepted by international peace organizations and conferences as their equal and legitimate members and just by their presence sometimes ensure the pro-Soviet stance of these bodies.

This is how, oddly enough, the Western pacifist is swayed today to support the totalitarian Soviet side of the East—West confrontation and objectively becomes one of the main instruments by which the Soviet Union tries to confuse the West, to undermine its defences and its general guard against Soviet expansionist moves. Of course, this second tier of Soviet penetration into the 'enemy camp' has nothing to do with safeguarding peace. Its ultimate aim is to disarm the West from within and to create favourable conditions for the activation of the first tier which will 'peacefully', without a shot being fired, deliver to Soviet domination one Western country after another.

The Soviet 'peace message' has also another addressee, and one no less important than the Western pacifist — the average Russian person at home.

There is one thing which is common to all Russians, and which is of paramount importance insofar as Russian public opinion is concerned: it is the ardent desire of the people to live in peace and to be sure that their country will not involve itself in yet another war. Indeed, if there is one political issue about which the Russians as a people feel very strongly, it is, without doubt, the issue of peace; one could say that all sections of Russian public opinion − from the utmost loyalists to the fiercest opponents of the Communist regime − consider the maintenance of peace their highest priority. The Soviet government, if it wants to avoid serious domestic political trouble, must honour this political sentiment of the masses by constantly confirming its full commitment to peace, international security, disarmament, etc., and must thoroughly camouflage by means of propaganda the true expansionist nature of its foreign policy.

The average Russian senses the inconsistencies of Soviet foreign policy and needs constant reassurance about his government's peaceful intentions. One of the most important devices providing this reassurance is the Western peace movement. The fact that quite significant peace-loving sections of the presumably well-informed and independent Western public, with many prominent non-Communist intellectuals among its members, express their solidarity with the Soviet policy of peace, vehemently opposing at the same time the warmongering policies of their own governments, proves to many Russians, who are only too well aware of their lack of information, that their suspicions must be wrong and that their government is probably genuinely committed to peace. One should not forget that the Western peace movement is given a disproportionately prominent coverage in the Soviet media and appears from it as the most important and powerful movement in the Western world. Thus the Western pacifist performs unawares for the Soviets yet another crucially important political task: he helps them to keep the mainstream of the ill-informed public opinion at home convinced that the first and uncompromised priority of the Soviet government's foreign policy is really the commitment to world peace. If this conviction were shaken in any significant way, the consensus between the Soviet regime and the Russian people would be irreparably damaged, and that would spell for the Soviets so much extensive domestic political trouble that the regime's grip on power and even its ability to survive could be severely jeopardised.

6

As mentioned above, one of the West's most important and urgent tasks is to try to break the pacifists' odd alliance with the official USSR by winning them back to the Western side of the East–West confrontation. It would probably be unrealistic to demand of the West that it should at once drastically change its predominant perception of the nature of the East–West confrontation, acquire a fully-fledged ideological stance and respond to the Soviet challenge in kind. This is perhaps also not necessary for the limited task of altering the pro-Soviet, anti-Western position of the pacifists. What, however, must be done to this effect, without further delay, is to take the necessary measures in order to transform the Western policy of mere deterrence and defence into a credible policy of peace.

It is high time for the West to elaborate, to propagate, to put on all negotiation tables and to present to all international conferences a fair, comprehensive, and convincing peace plan which no true pacifist could dismiss as provocative or false. The West has not as yet bothered to come up with such a plan, probably for two main reasons. First, its traditional policy of deterrence and defence has been, and still is, sufficient in terms of commanding the support of the majorities of Western nations, and thus for winning elections. In other words, no prospective party of government has experienced the political need to alter or even enlarge the frame of this policy and the inherent conservatism of all big political establishments has kept it in its original, though inadequate, shape. Secondly, there have been no pragmatic reasons in foreign policy for drawing up such a peace plan since it has been clear in advance that it would not be accepted by the Soviets; for the pragmatic Western political mind the idea of wasting time and effort on something that could have only a propagandistic value is so alien that not only has such a plan probably never been seriously considered but even less general and down-to-earth Western peace initiatives have been extremely scarce.

This problem should be approached in a new way by carefully drawing up a Western peace plan and proposing it for consideration not with a view to it being accepted by the Soviet side but of being *acceptable* in terms of the national, international and human interests of the West and East alike and, thereby, of the rest of the world, too. The mere existence of such a Western plan, if it were conceived as the cornerstone of Western peace strategy, continually presented to all possible international bodies and thus able to get sufficient publicity, could change the situation in the world quite drastically.

A plan like this, if endorsed by the pacifists (and it should be so designed that any honest pacifist could not refuse to endorse it) and rejected by the Soviets (which in the beginning it most certainly will be), would significantly diminish the influence in the West of Soviet constituencies and thus of the Soviet Union itself. Moreover, transmitted by radio and other means of communication to the Russian public, this plan could win its full-hearted support too. Exposed to these new pressures the Soviet side would have to do something about improving its own peaceful image at home and abroad, and, who knows, would even have to make some concessions to the West by at least partially yielding to some of these Western proposals.

Hence, a properly conceived propaganda document may, in the end, acquire also a very significant, if not decisive, pragmatic political value. It would be criminal to miss such an opportunity by simple omission.

I do not entertain high hopes that such a fair and comprehensive peace plan could be initiated by Western governments. I rather expect such a plan to be drawn up by independent peace-loving people, with non-partisan experts and unbiased academics taking the lead in this process. If such a plan — whoever takes the initiative to produce it — were to gain wide public support in the West, the Western governments would have to bow to the pressure of public opinion and, in the end, would be forced to take it up too.

The problem is how one transforms the general idea into its practical implementation. I would like to make only one, though in my view, crucially important, suggestion.

7

The very core of any peace proposal is disarmament and therefore any peace programme should start by proposing positive and concrete steps leading to it. It is, however, an extremely tricky and delicate matter. For disarmament, if not properly conceived, can be a method, only a less expensive one, of achieving the same results as the arms race, namely military superiority of one side over another. In this respect disarmament can prove even more dangerous than the arms race, not only because unequal or, even more so, unilateral disarmament can easily destroy the precarious balance of power, which is still the main and most reliable deterrent against the outbreak of war, but also because it demonstrates foremost the lack of will of the party that is disarming unilaterally or too speedily to defend itself against aggression. Thus disarmament of this kind is only likely to encourage the potential aggressor and, literally, invite it to launch actual aggression against the 'disarmer'.

This shows how wrong and misleading the view is that disarmament is a good thing in itself and that one should proceed with it for its own sake regardless of the consequences. Disarmament is good only when it is part of a larger peace programme and is strictly subordinated to the task of achieving a more reliable state of world peace.

Any such 'peace-minding' programme of disarmament has to spring from at least the following principles:

1. It should be presented in the form of an overall long-term plan for *total and comprehensive* disarmament, so that the final purpose of the whole enterprise would be clearly stated from the outset. The problems of East—West disarmament should constitute only a certain part and stage of this plan, however a part and a stage which are no doubt of central and of primary importance. So, the East—West (NATO—Warsaw Pact) disarmament process should be presented in the plan as its starting and most significant point on whose success the future of the whole enterprise depends entirely.

   In the first place, the plan should foresee a *significant reduction of armaments and armed forces* on both sides of the East—West divide. This reduction should proceed gradually, stage by stage, and be expressed for each stage, as well as generally, in absolute figures and precise dates. The aim of this process must be to reduce the military forces of the East and of the West to such a level that, although they will be still superior to the military forces of countries outside the two camps, they will nevertheless not be sufficient for either side to be able to launch a successful attack on the other. Only then is one ready to proceed to the next stage of the process, which already includes all countries of the world and aims at the gradual achievement of total and comprehensive disarmament on a global scale.

2. The main guideline according to which the gradual reduction of armaments and armed forces should proceed is the achievement of *equality of military strength* of the opposing sides at each stage of that process.

   This means that the principle of proportional reduction of forces, the one that the Soviet Union so insistently puts forward in all its 'peace initiatives', should be rejected from the outset. This must be done for the simple reason that proportional reductions make the stronger side still stronger and the weaker side weaker. Thus in the process of proportional reductions the stronger side will acquire over the weaker one an advantage that could jeopardise beyond repair the balance of power and increase the danger of war. Also, it means that, when negotiating the reductions, one should reject from the outset another principle that is so dear to the Soviets— the principle of the separation of nuclear and conventional forces. For it is impossible to achieve an overall equality of strength by reducing only one part of it. For example, if one agrees to reduce, even to the level of equality, the nuclear forces of both sides, the Soviet side will obtain from this an enormous advantage since it is so much stronger than the West in conventional forces; on the other hand, the equalization of conventional forces will give a significant advantage to the West which is, in spite of all recent increases in the Soviet nuclear arsenal, in my view, still much more advanced and powerful than the Soviet Union in the nuclear field. Hence, only simultaneous reductions of both nuclear and conventional forces can produce the equality of strength at each stage of the disarmament process which is, I believe, a necessary precondition for making disarmament really serve peace.

3.   The central and most crucial point of any disarmament programme is the *full verificability* of disarmament undertaken by every side. Even today this can be reliably achieved only by establishing effective *on-site international control*, the measure which the Soviets have been most vehemently opposed to ever since this proposal was made by the West in 1962 (and regretfully never repeated) in response to one of the Soviet 'comprehensive disarmament plans', which was launched by Khrushchev in that same year. The on-site international control over disarmament has to be extended to all arsenals, military units and, most importantly, industrial plants having the capacity to produce military hardware. Without these arrangements any agreement on disarmament will not be worth the paper on which it is written, and that should be emphasised most strongly all the time.

4.   It follows that the process of East—West disarmament should be from the outset *multilateral* and conducted with the view to keeping the global balance of power intact. This means that all suggestions of unilateral disarmament, for reasons explained above, should be deemed irresponsible, dangerous and as being conducive not to peace but to war.

It is spurious to believe, as some people seem to do, that steps toward unilateral disarmament by the West will force the Soviet Union to follow suit and that the process of multilateral disarmament will thus start. Everyone who understands the nature of the Soviet regime (and in the West unfortunately only very few do) knows only too well that this will never happen, even if the Soviet government issued on this occasion a congratulatory statement and declared that it was taking reciprocal steps. Without an effective system of international control, the Soviet Union will feel free to issue any statement and do whatever it wants, including the opposite of what it had pledged itself to do in the statement issued. Hence there should be no doubt that the Soviet Union will use every advantage provided to it by the West's steps towards unilateral disarmament only to increase its military strength and to intensify further its expansionist drive.

The idea that a Western unilateral initiative is the only and ultimate thing that is needed for the Soviet Union to agree to start the process of multilateral disarmament seems to be so out of place that one wonders how supposedly responsible people could seriously entertain it at all. If the Soviet Union were really interested in disarmament, rather than in demagogic arguments about disarmament aimed at nothing else but effortlessly acquiring an overwhelming superiority over the West (and an unbiased analysis of every Soviet 'peace initiative' without exception unmistakably shows that this is the case), the multilateral disarmament process would have started a long time ago. The fact is that, as a power lacking legitimacy not only in its East European and other dependencies but also in Russia itself, the Soviet Union can ill-afford either disarmament or any other measures weakening its repressive power and therefore will never voluntarily agree to undertake them, unless pressed very hard indeed (e.g. by the existence of a viable Western peace plan, which would enjoy extensive and strong public support in both the East and the West). One has to realise and emphasise that military strength and the ability to exercise unrestricted repression are today the only assets that keep the Soviet Union intact at all. Any, even the slightest, sign of their weakening will, undoubtedly, spell the rapid disintegration of the Soviet empire and, subsequently, the collapse of the Soviet regime in Russia itself. If only the pacifists employed, in addition to their wishful thinking based on emotion, a few hard facts and made an effort to analyse them properly, they would very soon realise how spurious is their present thinking on unilateral disarmament and its possible implications.

At a certain stage the multilateral East–West disarmament should be extended and become truly *global*. Only on the global level is it safe to abolish nuclear arms altogether; only on a global level can one hope to achieve in real terms total and comprehensive disarmament for which the plan is designed in the first place. This means that a viable, peace-enhancing and realistic plan for disarmament should include at an early stage those countries (e.g. China, Pakistan, India, Libya, Israel, some other countries of the Middle East, South Africa, etc.) which either have already produced or have the potential to produce nuclear weapons and whose military strength, under the circumstances of East—West disarmament, could become dangerously excessive. This especially applies to the countries whose authoritarian governments have an adventurist record. Then, at a later stage, all the remaining countries should be included in the disarmament process too.

Hence, it is not simply multilateralism but *multilateralism on a global scale* that should be one of the foundation stones of any viable and safe disarmament process.

5. One of the most important measures in the disarmament process is the creation of *demilitarised zones* in the likely areas of a military conflict. This idea is much more fundamental than the one about nuclear-free zones propagated by the pacifists. Nuclear-free zones are unable to prevent military confrontation or war between the troops armed by conventional weapons that are stationed in these zones. And as soon as a conventional war between nuclear powers starts in all seriousness, it will almost certainly turn into a nuclear one, whether or not the zone of military operations is nuclear free. Only a total withdrawal of military forces from such zones will assure their disengagement and will thus really prevent war.*

6. It goes without saying that all the above principles of disarmament can be implemented only if a proper *international agency* endowed with sufficient authority is established to take charge of the conduct of the disarmament process. The project for such an agency should also be part of the proposed plan for total and comprehensive disarmament.

8

One could object to this plan by saying that in the present circumstances it appears as entirely utopian and that therefore it is as yet premature. What one should consider first is not such a plan but confidence-building measures, development of mutual trust between parties in conflict, and the like. Only if and when the necessary preliminary conditions are thus created could one consider, as the next step, a more or less comprehensive disarmament plan. Although this is all true, one can also look at this problem the other way around, by considering the peace and disarmament plans as powerful devices for building up mutual trust and confidence.

First of all, one should abandon the spurious hope that it is possible

---

* For more details, see Dr Morton Kaplan's paper.

for the West to achieve mutual trust with the Soviet regime whose intentions and plans are in principle incompatible with international stability and cooperation. One has to be fully aware that the Soviet Union treats its relationship with the Western world as irreconcilably antagonistic and one must never forget this when considering any of these measures. Today this Soviet attitude has nothing to do anymore with the idealistic Communist missionary zeal that was so characteristic of the early Soviet governments. It is dictated, entirely and exclusively, by the instinct of political survival of the Soviet regime and its leaders.

The real problem of the Soviet regime is that it cannot tolerate dissent. Dissent is lethal to Communist rule and, hence, must be crushed or, at least, severely restrained and kept vigorously in check. The trouble is that the whole of the non-Communist world is for the Soviet Communist rulers nothing else but a huge continent of dissent. In no way can this challenge be tolerated and therefore totalitarian Soviet-style Communism must either win, by establishing a Communist system of rule on a global scale, or perish.

However, this does not mean that one cannot equally establish mutual trust and confidence between the West and the Soviet public over the head of the Soviet government.

If the views expressed in them were acceptable to the public in both East and West, the plans for peace and disarmament discussed above could play a decisive role in bringing about such mutual trust. They could become a rallying point for bringing together public opinion on both sides of the East–West divide, insofar as the problems of peace and disarmament are concerned. Since in the end even the Soviets have to respond to public opinion if it is sufficiently strong and unanimous, one could hope that the unity of world public opinion thus established on these issues would force the Soviet government to revise its present intransigent stance and to yield substantial concessions, which could dramatically enhance the state of world security and of peace.

Part II
Peace Movements
and European Security

4 The Peace Movements and the Future of West European Security

ARMAND CLESSE

1 THE CAUSES OF THE EMERGENCE OF THE PRESENT PEACE MOVEMENTS

On 10 October, 1981, some 300 000 people demonstrated in Bonn against the NATO double-track decision of December 1979 to deploy 572 new American medium-range nuclear missiles in Western Europe (108 Pershing II ballistic missiles as well as 96 Tomahawk cruise missiles in the Federal Republic of Germany, 160 cruise missiles in Great Britain, 112 in Italy, 48 in the Netherlands and 48 in Belgium), if the negotiations on the limitation of medium-range systems would not succeed.

Even if there can be no doubt that this double-track decision and the related eventual modernisation of the nuclear arsenal of NATO in Western Europe have triggered off the frantic peace activities of these last years, it seems no less certain that the formation of peace groups, the masses that these groups brought to the streets, and the millions of signatures that were collected against the deployment of new nuclear weapons are not the result of one simple decision in the realm of defence policy. It seems rather that the double-track decision has been only the catalyst, the factor that transformed a vague mood, a hidden discomfort, into overt demonstrations.

The success of the peace groups during these last years is certainly due to a combination of factors, which reinforced each other.

There is, for instance, apart from the resistance to the planned new medium-range systems, a growing resistance to nuclear weapons of all kinds; this aversion had already become obvious in the discussions on the neutron weapon, which was considered by many people to be an especially perverse and awful weapon. But above all, people began to judge by

53

these weapons the underlying policy, which appeared to be reprehensible.

Many people suddenly became aware that they trusted neither the intentions of those who were in charge of the nuclear trigger nor the technical devices that were to control the 'nuclear devils' tools'. These people came to express more and more clearly the opinion that they did not trust the stability that these weapons allegedly had created and that, moreover, they rejected the whole concept of deterrence as immoral, since it kept only an artificial and precarious calm by threatening the political adversary with the most horrible consequences if he would not adhere to the unwritten rules of the game.

The general public's discomfort with the military policy was intensified by the politics of the new American administration under President Reagan. The apparent (because in the very first months of its government it was repeatedly proclaimed) will of that administration to drive the Soviet Union through a merciless arms race into economic bankruptcy; its sometimes wild anticommunist rhetoric; the loose talk about things that are more important than peace (cf. the former Secretary of State A. Haig), about the possibility of winning a nuclear war (cf. Secretary of Defence C. Weinberger), about the possibilities of confining a nuclear war to Europe (cf. President R. Reagan), about the necessity of being able to wage a protracted nuclear war and to prevail in such a war, aroused fear and indignation among many West Europeans. The Carter-Administration had already produced much concern with its moves on the 'neutron bomb' and the Presidential Directive 59 on selective nuclear strikes.

Many people questioned not only the moral foundations of American policies (after Vietnam and Watergate), but also, and primarily, their strategic motives and aims. Does the United States, many people in Western Europe ask, care only about the security of the West as a whole but not about the physical survival of Western Europe? Is it prepared to risk the destruction of large parts of Europe in order to prevail in its superpower contest with the Soviet Union and to remain the number one nation (as was asked for on the electoral platform of the Republicans)?

These concerns go hand in hand with a general malaise about the situation of Western Europe in the world, the state of the West European politico-strategic system, and its uncertain, unstable, unfinished order. Since the total breakdown after World War II, Europe has not found a definitive place among the world powers.

The conferences of Potsdam, Yalta, etc., created a situation, which corresponded to the existing power relations but which had neither a geostrategic nor a political logic nor a moral justification, and which could lead neither to external nor to internal long-term stability. The continued presence of the two superpowers in the strategically most sensitive parts of Europe and in fact in the whole of Europe — even if some states claim total independence and live formally without the presence of a super-power — maintains an artificial stability.

Every move of one of the superpowers affecting its commitment to Europe — whether by a loosening or a tightening of its grip — induces painful contractions in the political body of Western Europe as a whole.

Continuing uncertainty abounds because Germany remains divided and nobody knows how much the Germans want a reunification, nor how much the US is still committed to their guarantee of Western European security nor what the aspirations of the Soviet Union towards Western Europe are.

The present distrust in the Atlantic alliance parallels and reinforces the desire of many West Europeans for accommodation with the powerful neighbour in the East. This longing for accommodation is often expressed as a wish for neutralisation — neutralisation of one country (Western Germany and Eastern Germany), of Western Europe, or even of the whole of Europe. This neutralisation, which is strongly desired by large sections of the peace movements, would mean the dissolution of the existing military organisations, perhaps the creation of a large demilitarised zone or at least a nuclear-free zone and eventually the reunification of Germany.

The military thinker of the West German Greens, the former General Bastian, has stated publicly that he would regard the Finlandisation of West European countries as a desirable state of affairs.

These concerns and aspirations about security policy are further intensified by general social and political phenomena. The doubts of many people concerning the usefulness of further technical progress and unre-strained economic growth have increased during these last years. One can perceive the rejection of a purely rational form of thinking and acting, and observe a return to reliance on feelings and emotions.

This estrangement from rationality corresponds to a revolt against the traditional moral, intellectual and state authorities. Many people are un-willing to accept passively whatever they are confronted with, asking in-stead for a greater right to contribute and searching for new ways of living. Above all, they refuse to entrust matters that directly affect their lives and survival to those who were traditionally considered competent to make binding judgments on political and military questions.

This revolt is accompanied by a factor which at first seems to tend into the opposite direction but which works at least partially together with — and even determines in some measure — the first one. This is the perva-sive laxity of parts of the Western society, which manifests itself in the unconsidered striving for short-term material satisfaction, the superseding of escapism, i.e. the retreat in front of vital decisions, in place of unpleasant questions about the handling of future problems, a diminishing willingness to suffer and an increasing disposition for doubtful compromises. Cynicism and parasitism are spreading, and potentially animating ideas such as the concept of a united Europe, which formerly appeared as a possible cure for decadence are at best treated as intellectual curiosities.

2   THE DEMANDS OF WEST EUROPEAN PEACE MOVEMENTS

The most often heard and most emphatically expressed demand of West European peace movements is for the renunciation of the double-track decision, i.e. that the stationing of new nuclear missiles in Western Europe should be prevented by all means, even if the INF talks in Geneva fail and even if the Soviet Union does not dismantle a single SS-20.

They are mainly critical of the Pershing II, a ballistic missile with a range of about one thousand miles, which could reach Soviet territory after a relatively short flight time (between 6 and 10 minutes).

The peace movements argue that these weapons have, on account of their technical capacity, a first-strike capability and that, because the Soviet Union would certainly try to destroy these weapons before launching any attack against Western Europe, they would invite a preventive Soviet strike, which would annihilate large parts of a densely populated Western Europe.

This assertion by the peace groups contradicts their often repeated view that the Soviet Union has no aggressive intentions towards Western Europe. Indeed, if this last assumption is correct, how could the deployment of some hundred new nuclear missiles on the Western side (which would be more than compensated for by Soviet SS-20 warheads alone) lead to this radical transformation of Soviet foreign policy and change a peace-loving state into a bellicose one?

The peace groups are also arguing, on the one hand, that, in view of the existing 'overkill', the additional deployment of medium-range weapons on West European soil does not modify at all the overall strategic parity between the superpowers; on the other hand, and contradicting their first assertion, that the purpose of Pershing II and cruise missiles is to give the United States a strategic superiority, which the Americans would then probably use for their militaristic designs.

A striking contradiction between individual statements made by members of the peace groups is also noticeable when these members assert that the purpose of new American medium-range missiles is to confine a possible nuclear war to Europe and at the same time maintain that a nuclear war cannot be limited, and that such a war will escalate without fail to the highest possible level with the employment of all available weapons.

This last example shows that the peace movements use whatever argument fits their ideological, propagandistic objectives; they do this without considering whether these arguments are compatible or whether perhaps they are mutually exclusive. This example (as well as for instance their statements on the intentions of the Reagan Administration), moreover, shows that the peace movements use exactly those methods that they blame their political adversaries for using, namely, the thinking in 'worst case' categories. While they accuse Western officials and experts of basing their statements and analyses on the worst possible Soviet intentions, they affirm themselves that President Reagan is prepared to risk the total destruction of Western Europe for the sake of possible political and strategic gains.

Whereas major parts of the peace movements ask for a unilateral annulment of the double-track decision, other groups ask only for a postponement of this decision and further negotiations in Geneva; some groups would even favour — if there really is no other choice than to receive new missiles — the stationing of these new weapons at sea.

A large majority among the peace groups want all nuclear weapons (including the nuclear-capable bombers and fighters, the nuclear short-range weapons, the nuclear artillery shells and the atomic demolition munitions) to be eliminated from West European soil. A great number of them also want to reduce the expenditures for conventional armaments as well as for arms sales to the Third World. Some peace activists want to create a nuclear-free zone in Europe, for instance, in accordance with the proposals of the Palme Commission on a central European denuclearised zone, which would have a width of 300 kilometres, 150 on each side. There are those who seem prepared to accept a reinforcement of the conventional instruments of defence, if this would mean the renunciation of nuclear weapons and of the strategic guarantee of the United States. A few members of the peace movement even conceive of technical solutions, such as the replacement of offensive strategic systems by purely defensive systems. The dissolution of the existing military alliances and the creation of a pan-European collective security system are central to the reflections of others in the peace movements.

Some proposals on security policy coming from the ranks of the peace movements are rather confused and contradictory as well as of a maximalistic and uncompromising character. Often, one gains the impression that the groups that are making these proposals do not care so much about their practicability as about their ideological purity; the proclamation of the ideal seems to be more important to them than its concrete realisation. Moreover, they do not take into consideration the consequences of the application of these models for the international system and for global stability, nor do they ask whether the remedy might be worse than the disease. Thus many of their proposals appear to be abstract, utopian and ideologically obdurate.

3 THE OBJECTIVES AND THE MOTIVATIONS OF THE PEACE MOVEMENTS

Apart from their short-term objective of preventing the implementation of the NATO double-track decision, the peace movements want to make it impossible for governments, even if these are backed by solid parliamentary majorities, to execute political decisions on matters that are considered to be vital by an important part of the population (even if this part constitutes only a minority) against the will of this minority. If a government were to try to act against the wishes of this minority, then such high political costs should be imposed, that it would probably prefer, on the next occasion, to abandon its intentions.

However, peace movements are not content with modifying radically the way decisions are taken, but they also want to confer a completely new quality on the security policy itself. They think that the debate on security and defence should be translated from the arcane and codified language of strategy into the language of the streets, and that it should be taken away from the experts and placed in the hands of the average citizen. The politics of the balance of power and the balance of terror should be replaced by a policy of ideological *détente* and by unilateral disarmament measures; the politics of antagonism and confrontation should be exchanged for a policy of adjustment or even accommodation; and the relationship based on deterrence should be succeeded by a security partnership (as is called for by parts of the German SPD under the spiritual leadership of Egon Bahr), whose organic links would consist of economic and cultural interpenetration with the former adversary.

A new international order should be built on this basis, an order in which the traditional patterns of thought about bloc categories, about spheres of influence, about GNPs and numbers of missiles would cease, and in which the system of unilateral dependencies, of protectorates, of hegemonies and predominance inside as well as outside the structures of the alliance would come to an end. New values should be evolved:

neither fear nor greed should be any longer the determining forces of future policy, but instead mutual respect and aid. Before one peaceful world can be created, the capitalistic structures of the West as well as the state-bureaucratic ones of the East must disappear; a new form of coexistence based on the creation and rediscovery of elementary links of solidarity; a grassroots democracy; completely decentralised pools of economic production; a policy of generous help for the Third World, etc., ought to be initiated.

Of course, the peace groups express these objectives in rather diverse ways in accordance with their individual national, political and ideological backgrounds.

There are those who are inspired by a religious or almost religious impetus: the visionaries and missionaries, who defend high moral ideals, who fight against evil in the world and for a better, juster and more peaceful world. It is difficult to tell exactly who belongs to this part of the peace movements – the Christian churches, the West German '*Aktion Sühnezeichen*', those who fast for peace, people perhaps like Bruce Kent or Mient Faber, Erhard Eppler or even Petra Kelly?

There are those who have a more or less precise political project in relation to the peace activities, as for instance, E.P. Thompson who wants to give Europe a status of neutrality.

But there are also groups, perhaps under the influence of a strong minority, whose most important aim is to change the political and social system. Among these are the communist groups and the groups heavily influenced by communists, as for instance the so-called '*Autonomen*' and '*Anti-imperialisten*' in the Federal Republic of Germany, who want above all to destroy the '*Schweinesystem*'. Some former RAF-fellow-travellers (RAF = *Rote Armee Fraktion*, a West German group of left-wing terrorists) and even some former RAF members belong to them.

In their wake one can find demonstrators who are not motivated by specific issues but who take part in every rally because such a demonstration calls into question the establishment. This heterogeneous group of '*Anarchospontis*' represents a useful infantry for other groups.

Finally, there are those people who want above all to improve their personal profiles, to gain or regain influence in a group, or who want to be able to determine, using new concepts, the direction of a political party. Among these are the West German politicians Lafontaine and Eppler (who for years had to remain in the rear because their party hoped to keep the power with H. Schmidt and his Realpolitik).

What strikes the unbiased observer about many members of the peace movements is their self-righteousness. Most of these people are convinced that they possess the absolute truth and the monopoly of all means of grace. They consider themselves as morally good, their political and intellectual opponents as morally bad, and they want to impose their moral standards on everyone else. They hardly listen to the arguments of the opposing side and accept no compromises (for instance no interim solution for medium-range missiles, nor any form of nuclear deterrence). Their ethical eclecticism, indeed opportunism, entangles them sometimes in contradictions: some Green Peace fighters, for instance, praise life as the highest good and at the same time defend abortion (cf. the Green politicians Petra Kelly, Marie-Luise Beck-Oberdorf, Thea Bock), or they boast of their democratic way of thinking but collaborate with communists.

Since most of the leading figures of peace groups do not have the slightest doubts about what they believe and profess, they have an important psychological advantage over the experts who have not similarly committed themselves and who are aware of the contradictions and the limits of their understanding, whose objective is scientific truth and not indoctrination, who handle facts and figures with care, who are cautious in their statements and conclusions, who insist more on nuances than on generalisations.

Moreover, members of peace groups become very irritated if they are confronted with, what seems to them, unpleasant facts about the past and the present. If one observes their demonstrations, meetings and addresses one obtains the impression that these members want to hear again and again the same slogans and arguments, which corroborate their convictions and that they suppress all eventual doubts. So they always sing the same political verses at their rallies, repeat the carefully studied mottos like a litany, listen wistfully to the voices of the 'saints' of the peace movement, the Thompsons, Epplers, Kellys. This behaviour reinforces the impression that most members of the peace groups do not strive for understanding but for redemption.

That the leading people in the peace groups do not want to enlighten but to indoctrinate is also proved by the way they handle the results of polls on the NATO double-track decision. Analyses of these polls have shown that their value is very limited because the result seems to depend above all on the way the question is formulated. In a poll for the (German) televised magazine 'Panorama', the West German institute for public opinion research Emnid asked people: 'If the negotiations (at Geneva) between the USA and the Soviet Union remain unsuccessful, new atomic missiles are due to be deployed also in the Federal Republic. Are you in favour of or against this deployment of new missiles?' Sixty-six per cent pronounced themselves against the deployment.

A poll by the same Emnid-Institute, commissioned by the West German defence ministry at about the same time, which stated: 'The West must remain strong enough in face of the Soviet Union. Therefore it will be necessary to deploy modern nuclear weapons in Western Europe if the Soviet Union does not remove its medium-range missiles' and then went on to ask whether one did rather agree or rather not agree with this opinion, found that 58 per cent did agree.

Despite the fact that the speakers of the peace movements know exactly how controversial these polls are and how limited their findings, they refer exclusively to the highest figure of opponents to the double-track decision ever discovered and do not even mention the existence of different figures.

This way of handling the truth shows that the objective of the peace groups is not to disseminate reasonable arguments, based on scientific efforts, to the citizens, but that they want above all to have propagandistic bludgeons for the protracted ideological struggle. But it also shows that fundamentally they are not, as they claim themselves, moralists but quite normal machiavellians.

4 THE TACTICS OF THE PEACE MOVEMENTS

In order to obtain an acceptance of their view of affairs by large parts of the population and to approach their political objectives the peace groups use many tactical tricks. Their aim seems to be first to destroy the reigning minimal consensus on external security affairs by causing confusion, by sowing doubts and by arousing unrest in the minds of the public as well as the political decisionmakers.

With mass rallies (300 000 in Bonn, 350 000 in London, 400 000 in Amsterdam) — where the figures given by the organising groups are always far higher than those given, for instance, by the police — and mass appeals (e.g. more than 5 million signatures for the 'Appeal of Krefeld' against the double-track decision in the Federal Republic of Germany) they want to make people believe that large parts, if not the majority, of the population support the objectives of the peace movement. To lend their cause more prestige, prominent personalities of public life such as priests, trade-unionists, writers, singers, Nobel prize winners, etc., are used. Deserters and converts are particularly welcome, especially if they have formerly been with the military (Bastian, Pasti, LaRocque), with an intelligence service (cf. ex-CIA men invited by the Greens to the 'Nürnberger Tribunal') or if they have served in a government (McNamara, Vance, Scoville), i.e. people whom one normally would not forgive their previous activities.

The peace groups are adept at using the media whose attention is focused on whatever is new, spectacular, impressive. In their propaganda, they use single statements quoted out of context, concentrate upon a few sentences spoken by 'nasty boys' such as Weinberger and Haig and ignore all other explanations and all other officials. Thus they defame their political opponents by repeating insistently one controversial point of their biographies. Peace activists also try to play off one opponent against another by juxtaposing apparently contradictory statements by different members of a government. They do not – or only grudgingly – mention the activities of the Soviet Union in the realm of foreign and military policy (Afghanistan, Poland for instance), so that those of the United States (50 military advisers in El Salvador) appear even more reprehensible, nor do they willingly admit the existence of Soviet weapon systems such as the SS-20. In fact, peace lobbyists concentrate their critique of Western defence policy often on one single weapon system (for instance the Pershing II) in order not to overwhelm the intellects of their partisans and in order to conceal the overall balance of forces.

The final political objective is not attacked vigorously and openly, but in a rather discreet and almost imperceptible way. As if they were applying a 'thousand needle stitches', the peace activists attack single vulnerable points, one after the other.

With this tactic, they aim to weaken progressively the defence capacity of the establishment by innumerable demonstrations, sit-ins, die-ins, fasting actions, blockades, acts of sabotage until in the end it capitulates.

The escalation of violence, which these countless small 'non-violent' actions, as well as the reactions of the state-organs, could provoke, is exactly what the most radical of those among the peace groupings desire, because then the 'fundamental brutality' of these organs could be denounced and protesters could acquire the image of martyrs. Thus, according to these peace extremists, the state will be obliged to react in exactly the way that they have always predicted. The endurance of the state must be harrassed until it retaliates in an unconsidered way with sheer violence or until it surrenders.

5.   POSITIVE AND NEGATIVE ASPECTS OF THE ACTIVITIES OF WEST EUROPEAN PEACE MOVEMENTS

5.1   Possible Positive Aspects and Effects

The peace movements can increase the sensitivity of all members of society to the problems of a defence posture based on arms of mass destruction, uncertain operational conceptions and often questionable political premisses.

They can exert some pressure on those people with political responsibilities in order to persuade them to give more weight to means of preventing war and of increasing stability (for instance, through arms control measures); to be more restrained in public utterances about peace and war; to be more careful in strategic and operational planning; and to become aware of the fears and hopes of political rivals and more conscious of their own limitations.

The often inconvenient questions raised by the peace groups could bring about a useful, constructive, wide-ranging debate on the foundations of West European and Western defence in general. Indeed, the Atlantic Alliance has often evaded questions that are of vital importance to its future. NATO has often procured weapons without asking what purpose they would serve; this is particularly true for the tactical nuclear weapons (TNW) accumulated in Western Europe: official experts have begun only now to realise that these systems do not really make sense either for deterrence or for defence.

The central strategic questions of the Western alliance have never been tackled in the right way. We have not really tried — except in some curious constructions such as the MLF, i.e. the project of a multilateral Atlantic sea-based deterrent — to solve the fundamental dilemma of how, at a time of strategic parity between the superpowers, to maintain the security guarantee of the USA for Western Europe in such a way that Washington would not have to renounce its exclusive control of its nuclear weapons based in Europe, while at the same time not allowing the European doubts — or rather fears — about the possible negative effects of this guarantee to prevail.

The debate that should be initiated through the questions raised by the peace groups could lead to an improvement of transatlantic relations and even to a new partnership. It could force the partners involved to look for new policies both for armament as well as for disarmament and to strive for the formulation of strategic concepts and for the adoption of weapon systems that could create a greater stability, i.e. diminish the danger of an (unintended) nuclear war. Indeed, we have too many rather destabilising elements, such as the ever increasing number of warheads (MIRV) on one launcher; the growing precision of these systems (CEP of less than 100 or even 50 metres); the possible deployment of strategic systems in space; the progress made in the techniques of anti-submarine warfare; and the concentration on cruise missiles (these rather inconspicuous systems can be stationed on all kinds of carriers and platforms so that a verifiable arms limitation agreement could become virtually impossible).

5.2   Possible Negative Aspects and Effects

If the peace movements were to gain further influence, rational discussion of political decisions would certainly be made far more difficult: pragmatic, unbiased analysis could be replaced by an idealistic, emotion-ridden approach to foreign and security policy. Long-term planning could become even more uncertain. A plebiscitary form of democracy could emerge whereby the opportunities for demagogic politicians (like Lafontaine) would increase and the pathological traits of democracy be intensified. There could be a partial paralysis of the institutions for democratic decision-making; as it could eventually become impossible to execute decisions even with a considerable parliamentary majority, these decisions would come to depend on the moods of the population, on emotional, irrational and unpredictable elements.

6.   A SPECIFIC DANGER FOR THE SECURITY OF WESTERN EUROPE: NEUTRALISATION

6.1   How This Development Could Come About

The increasing influence of the peace groups on the decision process about security policy could, however, also lead to a rather direct and almost palpable weakening of the West European and therefore Western defence position. This weakening might be provoked through:

1.   The prevention of adequate defence spending.
2.   The elimination of one kind of defence (e.g. all or some of the nuclear weapons).
3.   The lowering of the morale of the Western armed forces.

The peace movements are also able to induce an important political development, namely the neutralisation of Western Europe; large sections of the peace movements strive quite deliberately for this development which might come about as follows:

In a first stage, the peace movements could provoke the cancellation of the NATO double-track decision, i.e. prevent the deployment of new American medium-range weapons on West European soil, even if the talks in Geneva on the limitation of these systems fail.

This could make the United States lose some of its interest in the defence of Western Europe; the Americans could become convinced that the defence of Western Europe had become too risky, not only because the

Soviets might interpret the West European refusal to deploy new weapons as a sign of irremediable weakness, but also because the United States would have to react to an exploitation of this perceived weakness by the Soviets. However, if the Americans were to retaliate strategically to a Soviet act of aggression in Europe, that would immediately expose their own homeland.

To sum up this line of reasoning: the non-execution of the double-track decision could lead to

1. A more adventurous, more aggressive Soviet behaviour.
2. A strategic decoupling by the United States.

These consequences become even more probable if the more general demand of the West European peace movements that Western Europe or the whole of Europe (which does not mean the whole of the Soviet Union) or at least Central Europe should be free from all nuclear weapons was realised.

The Americans would no longer be able – or so their reasoning would go – to counter either superior conventional Soviet forces or the use of TNW by the Soviet Union. The Soviets could use, with a minimum of risk, their battlefield nuclear weapons, because they would have to fear neither a corresponding American reply nor a strategic American retaliation (indeed, nobody believes that the United States would respond to a Soviet battlefield use of nuclear weapons by exerting a strategic retaliatory strike).

In the opinion of most Americans, rather than risking, in a hopeless fight, the lives not only of Western Europeans but also of American soldiers in Western Europe, it would be wiser to opt for a total retreat from Western Europe and to limit themselves to the defence of their homeland.

6.2   The Consequences of This Development

The neutralisation of Western Europe would destroy the existing balance of power in the world, which relies on the participation of West European countries in the Western defence.

The Soviet Union would be able to obtain a position of undisputed hegemony; Western Europe would lie exposed without the slightest opportunity of counterbalancing this supremacy. Thus, Western Europe would be at the mercy of the two superpowers: it would have to live with an adversary who would no longer have to respect its illusory strength and without any real ally who would be linked to it by treaty and organisation.

If Western Europe were to become neutral, a confrontation between the superpowers could be fought on European soil: indeed, the Soviet Union would no longer have to fear either a military reply from Western Europe or retaliation by the United States, since the United States would no longer be obliged to risk the existence of its own nation for the sake of Europeans who had rejected American protection.

The Soviet Union would be able not only to extend directly or indirectly its rule over the whole of Europe's territory, but also to turn its attention exclusively towards China and the United States — or in the event of a rapport between the Soviets and the Chinese — towards the United States alone.

The United States would become a second-class superpower and would either have to retreat into isolationism or turn to new regions in order to contain or repel the Soviet influence.

And, finally, neutralisation would reinforce the phenomenon of decadence in Western Europe and accelerate the loss of its historical vitality.

7   LIVING WITH THE PEACE MOVEMENTS

It certainly is not adequate to condemn in their entirety the objectives, the arguments and the activities of the peace movements. To confront them in a rational manner seems to be more appropriate and useful. Whoever wishes Western Europe to maintain a solid defence position should endeavour to thwart the plans of the peace movements, whenever these plans endanger the foundations of West European security. However, if some elements in the demands of the peace movements can be integrated into Western defence policy without imperilling the substance of this policy, then we should try to integrate them. The peace movements could even contribute to the search for new Western defence policies where they have obviously reached an impasse.

Those who are in charge of defence policy as well as those who support this policy politically or intellectually should not remain anxiously on the defensive and be content with parrying attacks against this policy, but should resolutely take the offensive. Thus, they should not only explain very clearly and without polemical overtones the potential dangers that result from certain demands and activities of the peace movements, but also expose in a frank and, where this appears to be necessary, critical way existing security policy, and show to the citizens the vital necessity of a strong, but by no means, aggressive defence capacity. At the same time they should seek to attract new adherents, especially among young people, and they should try to start a dialogue with all the political groupings, with the churches, the women's groups, etc. Indeed, it is the lack of dialogue and of collaboration, together with the resulting misunderstandings and anger that have certainly contributed to the success of the peace movements.

To be satisfied with designating the members of the peace groups as muddle-headed, as revolutionaries or agents of the Eastern bloc, and to try simply to contain their influence and to reject *a priori* all their criticisms and suggestions could in the long term prove fatal. It could reinforce the sclerosis of the concepts and structures of Western defence, accelerate the manifest political, military and strategic decay of the Western Alliance, and favour in a decisive way the upsurge of tendencies towards West European neutralisation and American isolationism.

The peace movements have laid bare pathological developments in the Western defence system and thus have challenged those responsible to take initiatives in improving the existing situation. The way this challenge is handled will probably decide whether Western Europe will be able to remain an autonomous actor in the international system.

5 Alternatives to Current Security Policy and the Peace Movements

HYLKE TROMP

The sudden appearance of the peace movements, in particular in Western Europe and the United States, has prompted a reconsideration of alternatives to the official security policy. While debates about security policy have filled libraries in recent decades, public attention has been very slight. Proposals put forward by individuals or groups have never been debated seriously and, despite their merits, they have always remained merely intellectual exercises. The peace movements changed all this almost overnight, not so much because their proposals had new and exciting merits, but because they seemed to embody political power. It is political power that counts; in politics power always dominates arguments or rationality.

This contribution, however, is not concerned in the first place with the how and why of the peace movements, nor does it attempt to explain and analyse their sudden and unexpected emergence on to the political scene. They may as suddenly disappear into political irrelevance and the main reasons for their disappearance would be that their proposals are not convincing enough, that their strategy fails, and that what they want is not acceptable to the decision-makers in the establishment. Of course, these 'alternatives' (a general description for their proposals concerning another security policy) are only one side of the coin that the peace movements have dropped; on the other side is their fundamental criticism of current security policy, which has given the world almost 60 000 nuclear 'devices', stockpiles of chemical weapons, the promise of biological weapons, the promise of environmental war as well as war in space in addition to a continual proliferation of nuclear weapons (to states and non-state actors). From a psychological point of view, the value of their critique is not as relevant as the merits of their (counter) proposals. Therefore, the focus here will be on the suggestions and proposals put forward in recent years, sometimes as the product of 'brain-storming' within the peace movements, sometimes produced by individual scholars and later adopted by the peace movements, and sometimes published by individuals and adopted by nobody at all.

1 CURRENT SECURITY POLICY

First of all, I shall give a probably very subjective and therefore highly controversial review of the fundamentals of current security policy. However, anyone's summary of this security policy would be debatable, for it will always be subjective, omitting elements considered irrelevant by the author and probably highly relevant by others, and it will never be authoritative, because no one can authorise such a summary. Nevertheless, there is not much doubt about the essentials: official security policy is based on an implicit theory about human behaviour. The theory holds that human behaviour can be influenced and even forced in a certain direction by threats, such as the threat to kill or the threat to destroy. The underlying assumption is that man is essentially rational and that he will calculate, under all circumstances, what the costs of a certain behaviour will be compared to its benefits; then he will draw the line and find out what he should do. Therefore nuclear war will never happen; no rational man will start it if it is clear that the costs of a certain policy or a certain course of action will be nuclear destruction. The whole deterrence theory stands if this assumption is true; it collapses when it is wrong.

The assumption that man is rational and is so under all circumstances is unproved: there is much evidence confronting it. Revolutionary movements, for example, do not calculate or act properly according to standards of rationality. Certain political leaders have been known to be unable to propose any rational policy at all, not because they were stupid, but merely because their guiding light was not so much rationality as some brand of ideology (or religious fervour). Even more problems arise when one starts to examine the assumption more closely. The main problem is credibility. If the Soviet Union were to close the highways to West Berlin, would the threat to destroy the Soviet Union with nuclear weapons then be credible and therefore effective? (and, furthermore, would it eventually legitimate the nuclear destruction of the Soviet Union?) If the other side takes one small step over a fictitious line that we have drawn somewhere (perhaps without even having told the other side beforehand), does that legitimate (morally, but also in terms of cost-benefits) the sanction of nuclear destruction in particular under the conditions of 'MAD' (mutual assured destruction)?

There are clearly several flaws in the theory on which security policy is based. First, the basic assumption about human rationality is challenged by historical evidence, empirical psychological studies and even by common logic. There is no general standard for measuring or even for defining rationality: it is a floating concept with different meanings for different people, or even different meanings for the same people at different times. The price of war may be too high in one 'rational' calculation; but, at another time, or in a calculation made by other people, the rational outcome may be that certain values are priceless and worth defending. Secondly, even in rational analyses errors may occur, miscalculations can be made and wrong assessments of relevant factors may influence the outcome. This is precisely the case in international relations, where there is an almost infinite number of factors influencing the situation, varying from Cleopatra's nose (which allegedly changed Roman history) to the unexpected effectiveness of the machine gun (which was the main factor in colonising Africa). Furthermore, the private ideology and (in)competence of decision-makers in political establishments are ranged against the political pressures coming from domestic public opinion, financial and monetary institutions, or vested military—industrial interests. Finally, specific threats may work in a very specific, well-defined situation (the 1962 Cuba crisis may serve as an example here), but most political crises are not well defined, either in scope or in geography. By nature threats cannot be too precise, and there is, furthermore, the formidable problem of possible misinterpretations and misperceptions, especially if the parties in a conflict have different cultures and values, or if the communication channels are insufficiently equipped to deliver the message unequivocally.

These points of criticism have been pointed out repeatedly in recent years.[1] More interesting is the fact that everybody is well enough informed to realise that revolutionary and ideologically motivated movements have their own brand of rationality and do not act according to standards of rationality which are alien to them. Most people who can remember the Second World War realise (or are able to realise) that political leaders have not always remained rational in their policies and have even started out with a political programme that could not be defined as rational at all. Nevertheless, the assumptions underlying the current security policy, which are clearly confronting historical evidence, seem to have been generally accepted — which once again proves that even if man is able to think rationally, there is no assurance that he will do so all of the time and under all circumstances.

The current security policy was not accepted on the basis of unproved assumptions alone, but began with the 'hard facts': the availability and the (proved) effectiveness of nuclear weapons.[2] It is highly probable that the theory followed the facts; in other words, that the assumptions underlying the current security policy were rationalised and legitimated from the facts, reinforced by repetition without contradiction since 1945. (A theory remains credible until evidence destroys it; the destructive evidence in this case would not only blow up the theory but everything else as well.) All the same, at one point the theory of 'deterrence' needed rethinking: it was when 'mutual assured destruction' ('MAD') had been reached. In fact, there was no 'point': it took a considerable time before the United States and the Soviet Union realised that retaliation (a 'second strike capacity') was in the power of both of them, as is illustrated by the period of time that elapsed before they reconsidered and changed official descriptions of nuclear strategy from 'massive retaliation' to 'flexible response'.[3]

Still, the main structure of deterrence theory has remained the same, but the mathematics needed in 'rational' policy-making that involves the threat of nuclear destruction have become much more complicated because the emphasis has changed from 'assured destruction' (which is fairly easy to calculate) to concepts such as 'credibility'; instead of a cost—benefit calculation, it is now necessary to elaborate educated guesses about how the enemy will react to a certain threat (if, in other words, the threat is 'credible' enough). The threat of suicide, for example, never has a high credibility if the threat is made as a move on what is supposed to be the chessboard of world politics, since this threat is only credible as a clearly irrational move, out of desperation, stress, and psychological pressure. The threat of genocide is total madness, and therefore not quite 'credible'. Nevertheless, this is precisely what MAD means: the destruction of territory and the mass murder of all inhabitants on both sides if the threat becomes reality.

Since MAD was established, several developments have taken place, among which is a *change of strategy* (at least officially, in the West). Another development was institutionalising the *'Arms Control' negotiations*, especially on strategic nuclear weapons, which clearly indicates that both sides realise the danger inherent in the present situation. These negotiations, however, have nothing to do with disarmament. Their main purpose is to diminish the risks of nuclear war, and to keep the arms race under control. A third development is the almost hidden effort (probably on both sides) to *establish military superiority*: a military superiority that will be nothing else but a 'first-strike capability'. These efforts seem to have continued during the last decade, after the first failure (the Anti-

Ballistic Missile defence). A 'first-strike capacity' is achieved when it is possible to destroy the enemy's entire retaliatory capacity, or when a defensive system is developed which makes it impossible for the enemy's weapons to destroy their targets. Technological progress has been made in both directions. The proclaimed 'window of vulnerability', which has been front-page news since the Reagan Administration took over, has much to do with the increasing accuracy of intercontinental ballistic missiles and, in theory, they could indeed be destroyed in their silos, if the attacking missiles are accurate enough. On the other hand, the detectability of nuclear submarines (so far regarded as the most invulnerable part of the so-called triad in strategic weaponry) has increased too, so that, in theory, all nuclear submarines could be wiped out in a first strike if it were possible to detect their location or to keep track of them continually. Finally, the long-range bombers have become outdated as weapons (in the same way as battleships are outdated): their defences against ground-to-air missiles are regarded to be insufficient and the development of new bombers is probably a waste. On the defensive side, several suggestions have been made, the most remarkable being Reagan's 'Star Wars' speech.[4] The development of lasers has given rise to the hope that they may be built into powerful weapons in space, which will be able to eliminate all attacking missiles. Probably other more advanced and highly technological equipment is being developed and a major breakthrough on either side is not impossible. Until now, the 'MAD' situation has continued and there is not much evidence to show that a major change will occur in future years. This has led, finally, to a *qualitative change in the perception of weaponry*. Instead of being weapons for eventual use in certain conflicts, they have become *symbols of political power or political superiority*. The symbolic use of weapons is not new. Armies, soldiers and weaponry have always had this symbolic value, and they have always had the function of impressing opponents into early capitulation, before the fighting would really start. Military uniforms as well as military parades and manoeuvres still perform this function, and symbolic gestures have always had a place in the arsenal of political moves: sending a cruiser to Agadir, a flotilla into the Caribbean, an airforce squadron to a border, an army division into manoeuvres, or even mobilising troops, are gestures intended to influence the enemy. Security policy in the 1970s and 1980s has gradually become more and more symbolical, and it may continue in this way.[5] This may have dangerous implications because the four developments mentioned before cannot be separated. They interfere with each other, making it very difficult to discern what is actually intended — not only for the adversary, but also quite often for the actor too, because political steps are always the outcome of a complicated decision-making process in which several parties with conflicting or competing interests participate. The examples are abundant:is the five-year increase in defence expenditure in the United States really intended to achieve military superiority, or is it merely a symbolical gesture in order to communicate that the United States will remain the leading power, or is it the end of all arms control achievements, and how does it relate to 'counterforce' strategy?

In summary, current security policy is in a mess because it continues to create less security at higher costs. Although the risks inherent in the policy are known, nothing is done to diminish them. According to some experts the arsenal of nuclear weaponry is growing with the addition of one 'nuclear device' every 20 minutes.[6] The world has already deployed almost 60 000 nuclear weapons, yet conventional political thinking concludes that this is still not enough.[7] It is clear, certainly to the experts, that this 'security policy' approaches madness. The military know, certain politicians know, some civilian experts know, and foremost, the scientific community — especially the nuclear scientists — knows. The Pugwash movement was founded as long ago as 1957, and since then, scientists have never stopped trying to attract the attention of governments as well as the public for what is nothing less than a matter of survival. The net result of their efforts is virtually zero. Quite suddenly, however, the peace movements have appeared and have soared into political prominence within a few years. They give the impression that they are trying to change security policy fundamentally. Is this true?

2   THE PEACE MOVEMENTS

There are several explanations for the sudden emergence of the (Western) peace movements, and probably all of them are true, even if some of the explanations refer only to certain specific circumstances. In general, one can say that the peace movements (in particular the institutionalised protests against armaments policy, the arms race and its rationalisations) are long overdue. Still, this does not explain the fact that in the Netherlands, Western Germany, the United Kingdom and the United States enormous mass movements have been mobilised within a few years, nor does it help to explain why these movements are not to be found in France and Italy, in Canada and in other NATO countries. (Here the question could be raised: why not in Eastern Europe either? To deal with this question requires much more space than is available here.)

The development of the current peace movement may be explained as follows. The peace movement in the Netherlands has been the catalyst, in particular the movement that was founded by the Churches as early as 1966. In 1976, this peace movement (the Interchurch Peace Council, IKV) decided to change its approach, since it was dissatisfied with what little it had achieved in raising public consciousness as well as changing policy between 1966 and 1976. It deliberately chose another strategy: it simplified its goal into one sentence ('Free the world from nuclear weapons, start with the Netherlands'), and stepped up its efforts to inform the public, which meant educating the public to grasp the complexity of the problems involved. Moreover, it decided to persist with this strategy for ten years: a remarkable idea, in comparison with the spans of time that peace movements usually have in mind when they are planning (usually a period of days or sometimes weeks until the next demonstration). In 1977, the IKV's information programme, which was first of all intended to narrow the gap between what people know and what they ought to know, was helped by overt political discussions on the decision about which type of jet-fighter should succeed the Starfighter. For once, public interest in an armaments decision was very high and when the public is interested the media tend to respond with more coverage, which raises public interest still further. In 1978, NATO's ill-advertised decision to deploy 'neutron bombs' increased the scope and level of this interest as well as the intensity of the discussions, which were now the subject of editorials, columns and letters to the editor in almost all papers. In the middle of this debate, the Dutch Minister of Defence Dr J. Kruisinga resigned in protest against the N-bomb. Dr Kruisinga was a member of the Christian-Democratic Party, whose members are supposed to have great affinity to the IKV and because it is at the same time a very conservative political party, the impact of his resignation was increased. Against this background, it was not at all surprising that NATO's decision in 1979 to deploy 572 new 'Intermediate Nuclear Forces' (as they are now called; other names are: Long Range Theatre Nuclear Forces, Long Range Tactical Nuclear Forces, European Nuclear Forces, Intermediate Range Nuclear Forces — INF, Euro-missiles or Eurostrategic Missiles, grey-area weapons) encounter-ed an unexpected opposition. The year 1979 was entirely dominated by the discussions on this 'modernisation'. Of course, in the meantime the IKV's campaign had continued, and this issue began to overshadow it. The net result was that at the end of 1979 a clear parliamentary majority was against the INF decision, that a general awareness of security policy and the intricacies of its problems had come into existence, and that the peace movement was regarded as being a relevant political force. Nevertheless, some members of parliament — following party discipline — voted in favour of the government's proposal to endorse the INF decision, which saved the government and the INF decision, even if NATO had to accept some conditions or restrictions added by the Netherlands to the ('unanimous') decision.

In December 1979, however, the picture was still very bleak concerning the existence of peace movements in other countries. This changed quite suddenly in 1981, when the peace movements in the United Kingdom — especially CND — were revived from their political deaths partly by chance and partly as a consequence of political changes. The historian E.P. Thompson reacted very strongly to the Government's brochure (about what should be done in the event of nuclear war) entitled *Protect and Survive*. Without his reaction, this pamphlet would have probably been filed, unread, in archives and libraries, as many Government information pamphlets. His reply (*Protest and Survive*) stimulated a widespread public debate, as well as the European Nuclear Disarmamant Campaign (END). However, the rise to political power of Mrs Thatcher, together with some of the armaments decisions her government made, did not anger only the pacifists; many military men of high esteem also felt the decisions to be completely wrong: in particular, the 'modernisation' of the British navy (which, to many, seemed to amount to its demise — with the exception of the nuclear submarines) was hotly debated. It is not unusual to find that, once a discussion has started, new arguments are continually brought in and to the surprise of many people, who had been complacent about security policy for decades, NATO's strategy was suddenly condemned as being 'suicidal' and 'naive' by military and civilian experts alike, who had always been held in high esteem by NATO and vice versa. To a certain extent, this demolished the belief in authority that the security policy had relied on for its acceptance; when the authorities in the field are fighting each other, they lose authority. The consequence of this was that people had to start thinking for themselves and immediately there was a swift increase in the support for the peace movements.[8]

Even more surprising was the emergence of the peace movements in Western Germany. In January 1981, practically nothing worth mentioning existed but, by the end of that year, the support for the peace movement had grown to millions of people. Once again, only a few incidents seem to have given an immense impetus to subsequent developments. The publication by the weekly magazine *Der Stern* of a map showing all the nuclear sites (or targets) in Western Germany severely shocked a public that ostensibly did not know any of this and now suddenly realised that Western Germany was the territory with the greatest density of nuclear devices and thus the greatest number of targets for destruction in a nuclear war.[9] Then, shortly after this publication, the public was appalled by the way the Chancellor and his Minister of Defence talked about nuclear affairs and defence in the *Hamburger Kirchentag* — which once again illustrates the gap which existed between the experts and their way of thinking about security matters, and the ignorant public. The result was an increasing support for the peace movements. The fact that former NATO generals (in particular Bastian) played a prominent role in these movements also indicated that experts had become divided and it is not surprising that the public started looking for guidance from others.

Finally, the United States followed suit. As elsewhere, an enormous peace movement quite suddenly came into existence, which within a few years even obtained a majority in the House on a proposal to 'freeze' the arsenals of nuclear weapons. The Catholic bishops in the United States almost simultaneously became quite outspoken on the issue (the Dutch and the West German bishops also published forceful letters). The same pattern already revealed in the Netherlands, the United Kingdom and Western Germany became discernible in the United States. Members or former members of the political establishment and the military elite suddenly made it clear that they had serious doubts about official security policy, or came forward with proposals to change it.[10]

There is, however, one specific factor directly responsible for the emergence of the peace movement in the United States (and probably in Western Europe too) that has not been mentioned so far. The Reagan administration, which started distorting reality with unfounded accusations about the 'vulnerability' of the US and the superiority of the USSR, proceeded to reduce all other government expenditure in order to increase the defence budget (to a degree that seems to have horrified even some military men). It accompanied these steps with sometimes belligerent, sometimes openly provocative public utterances about the possibility of winning and surviving a nuclear war and about the possibility of limiting nuclear war to the 'theatre' (Western Europe), and with the preparation and publication of outspoken plans for 'fighting' a nuclear war. Instead of achieving public endorsement for his views and his plans, the American president 'mobilised' the peace movements. We may ask whether there would have been even a single important peace movement nowadays without Ronald Reagan's provocative and alarming statements and policies.

This very abbreviated and impressionistic sketch of the emergence of the peace movements reveals nevertheless an unmistakable pattern. In all four countries comparable developments seem to have occurred:

(a) A *growing interest and concern of the public* in general accompanied by an increasing coverage by the media and a greater amount of information.

(b) *Public statements of renowned experts and (former) high-ranking officials* in government, expressing not only concern but serious doubts about the content and the direction of official security policy.

(c) A gradually increasing *pressure on institutionalised social forces* such as churches, trade unions and political parties to take a stand on the issue.

(d) A *sudden development of 'categorised' groups* concerned with the prevention of nuclear war (such as the Physicians for the Prevention of Nuclear War, the Union of Concerned Scientists, Women for Peace).

(e) Finally, the 'common sense' of several *proposals* of the peace movements and others in comparison with the intentions of the official security policy.

These developments are all discernible in the Netherlands, West Germany, and the United Kingdom as well as in the United States, although there may be differences in degree. In an interview published in the *Los Angeles Times* and later in his book *With enough Shovels*, Robert Scheer comments at the end: 'What is so scary about this. . . . I've interviewed hundreds of people who end up using words like, "They are crazy!" or "Madmen!".. But how did this happen? McNamara: "Because the potential victims have not been brought into the debate yet, and it's about time we brought them in. I mean the average person. The average intelligent person knows practically nothing about nuclear war – the danger of it, the risk of it, the potential effect of it, the changes in the factors affecting the risk".'[11] There is no reason to doubt McNamara's statement: it is perfectly true. For decades, people have been educated in ignorance as far as nuclear weapons, deterrence theory and security policy are concerned: and in the absence of knowledge, opinions and attitudes (whose origins could be found anywhere and which have virtually nothing to do with the problem) fill the gap[12] What is even more dangerous is that people tend to vote for politicians who seem to share their opinions *and* their (insufficient) level of knowledge. If they achieved anything, the peace movements started to change this. The help which the peace movements received from unexpected quarters was as important as their own actions: the fact that many military, civilian and scientific experts started to voice doubts in public by making proposals for a 'real' security policy, legitimated the opposition of the peace movements to government policy. It became no longer possible to dismiss the peace movements as Communist-orientated, Moscow-inspired and KGB-financed. The reality of the problems which the peace movements had raised was endorsed by the sudden appearance of rifts between members of the establishment, which primarily and as a whole bore responsibility for the state of security policy. The attempt to discredit the peace movements was of course repeatedly made, sometimes even by the American president himself; mostly it seems to have backfired. Another common strategy has been to discredit persons whose public positions and arguments on a political issue are difficult to debate (the *'argumentum ad hominem'*).[13]

The third point mentioned indicates the effect as if of a stampede of the peace movements: political parties had to make clear their position on the issue, and this began to change them almost overnight. As could be expected, the conservative parties remained relatively unharmed, since they depended for their support on voters who remained aloof from the issue as much as possible, adhering to ideological bias instead of factual knowledge: and quantitatively speaking, this is nearly always a majority of the voters. On the left, this development was a disaster in the short term. In the Netherlands, the discussions almost split up the Social-Democratic party, as well as the Christian-Democratic party. The latter has always been quite conservative, and was particularly so on this issue: the fact that the Interchurch Peace Council and the Christian-Democrats addressed the same people, inevitably led to a continuing debate whose outcome is still unsure. The Social-Democratic party finally accepted and endorsed the substance of the IKV's proposal, but before the party was unified on this, the elections were lost and subsequently the Socialists were kept out of government — the main reason being their opposition to the INF-decision.

In Germany, the picture was even more complicated. Chancellor Schmidt is regarded as one of the architects of the INF-decision (although in recent statements he denies having had a prominent role). But after that decision was taken and endorsed by his Socialist—Liberal coalition government, the development of the peace movements and the strong opposition to that decision split the Socialist party in all but name ('Vote SPD: with Schmidt and Eppler *for* and *against* nuclear weapons, with Schmidt and Klose *for* and *against* nuclear energy reactors': this ironical advice, produced by the new party 'Die Grünen' which came into parliament mainly on the security issue, summarises that split succinctly). It is not clear to what extent the turmoil in the SPD played a decisive role in the sudden collapse of Schmidt's government. The small Liberal party under Foreign Minister Genscher, which was needed for a parliamentary majority, simply changed sides in 1982, and survived the subsequent elections in 1983. Since then, the SPD has been moving quietly in the direction suggested by the peace movements, but West Germany has a government that is strongly in favour of the INF-decision, higher defence expenditure (even during an economic crisis) and more weapons. Simultaneously, a consistent majority of the German voters now seems to be against the INF-decision, which makes governing not as easy as the parliamentary majority suggests.

In the United Kingdom, the revived interest in security policy stimulated by the peace movements almost destroyed the Labour party too. First, several leading members left the party in order to found another party, which allied itself to the Liberals (among them the former minister for Foreign Affairs, David Owen). Then the Labour party was torn apart by internal disputes, in particular about security policy. The outcome was the same as in the Netherlands and West Germany: in its programme, the Labour party made an enormous move towards the position of the peace movements and in the power struggle, it was kept out of government and, in 1983, defeated in the elections.

In the United States the results were different, and the developments are to a certain extent incomparable to those in European countries. In the first place, the peace movements appeared on the scene *after* Reagan's election and their influence so far has been hardly measurable in terms of changes in government. Secondly, the central idea of the American peace movement is a very modest one. A 'freeze' on the arsenals of nuclear weapons is not a revolutionary suggestion at all and, if it is proposed as a bilaterally negotiated freeze, it may be acceptable to everybody, even to the hawks, who know that these negotiations could take as long as the SALT negotiations (more than 10 years) and that, in the meantime, no unilateral freeze would have to be considered. Therefore, a small victory at the political level was no revolutionary breakthrough. On balance, the main effect of the peace movements in the United States so far may have been to increase the amount of public information and knowledge as well as the concern about nuclear warfare and deterrence theory. The final battle, in other words, has not been fought; it could still take years before even the order of battle is discernible.

In this process the 'categorised' groups play a very important role. The 'Physicians for the Prevention of Nuclear War', 'The Union of Concerned Scientists', 'Ground Zero', etc. may in 3 years have informed the public more about the dangers and consequences of nuclear war than the Pugwash movement was able to in over 25 years (even taking into account that Pugwash always tried to address the governments in the first place). Another interesting development is the public 'dissidentism' of retired and sometimes active generals and admirals.[14] Not easy to categorise, but very important too is the 'Women for Peace' movement; and the 'Pugwash Declaration on the Dangers of Nuclear War', signed by almost 100 Nobel

Prize winners (1982), may have had an impact too.

Finally, there are the 'proposals' put forward by several groups, individuals, and institutions. To the 'average citizen' whom McNamara mentioned, they must make some sense and to the well-informed citizen they may look invariably better than current security policy. Their 'credibility' is high, and that contributed to the rise of the peace movements too. The question to be asked is: if these proposals are accepted, will they really solve the security problem and prevent nuclear war?

3   PROPOSALS TO CHANGE CURRENT SECURITY POLICY

Suddenly, proposals and suggestions for other approaches to security policy have emerged (and are even published on the front pages of papers). Some of these proposals are old and may have been published in the sixties in scholarly studies, which at that time never caught the attention of policy-makers. Others have been tried for some time – such as Osgood's GRIT proposals, which in retrospect seem to have been accepted by the Kennedy government and practised in the last 6 months before his death.[15] Some are new, some consist of no more than bare ideas, and others have been presented in elaborate detail. In summary, the picture is confusing. Nevertheless, there is a distinction between proposals based on or within the conventional framework of enhancing military security and proposals starting from quite different viewpoints. It may be helpful to introduce the word 'paradigm' here in the sense that Thomas Kuhn used it in his *The Structure of Scientific Revolutions (Weltanschauung, Weltbild)* or, in a more psychologically oriented phrase, a 'set of beliefs' or a 'belief system'. This recalls the 'Great Debate' in the theory on international relations, where a change of paradigm has been hotly discussed several times, and it is precisely because every solution to security problems depends on the 'paradigm' that is used (or in other words, on the way the problem is recognised and defined) that the concept is extremely relevant here.[16]

Military security policy belongs to the traditional paradigm in international relations, that accepts as the starting point for its theory the independence of the state and in consequence the inevitable anarchy of the international system of states. Moreover, it assumes that security policy has priority on the agenda of every state and accepts the threat or use of force as a normal and acceptable answer to security problems. Within this paradigm, however, there may be different approaches to the solution of security problems and the participants in the continuing debates may agree on their '*Weltanschauung*', but differ on the best strategy that should be followed within the framework offered by that paradigm. It is important to note here that the participants are hardly aware of being the captives of a 'paradigm'. To them, the paradigm represents the indisputable, essential, and unchangeable elements of reality, which cannot be exchanged in any way for another set of elements. They may differ therefore on how to use threats, or when or where; they may have disputes about which military strategy should be used, which weapons should be part of that strategy, which military posture is necessary, in what direction military efforts should proceed; but fundamentally, they accept the world view that is essential in this paradigm: each state is responsible for its own security and this security can only be achieved or assured by military power. Of course, this may include the building of alliances and it does not exclude cooperation, trade and other ties with states. But essentially, the state is the sole actor and the world is nothing more than an international system whose elements are the states. However, in the theory about the development of international relations, for a long time, attention has been focused on developments that seem to be independent of the guidelines derived from the traditional paradigm. In essence, they refer to the emergence of powerful non-state actors in the international system and the existence of international relations on levels other than those that kept the attention in traditional thought. Instead of focusing on the *independence of states* (and deriving theories on how to proceed in international relations from this point of view), the attention of some scholars has been drawn to the assumption of *interdependence between states* and the consequences for internal autonomy as well as the freedom to execute foreign policy. Growing interdependence is not a hypothetical construct: it is an empirical fact, and its consequences for the theory and practice of international relations are so far, for politicians as well as for scholars, a blank space on the map of knowledge and research.[17]

Therefore, it may not be surprising to find that almost all recent proposals for alternatives to current security policy have been formulated *within* the framework set by the traditional paradigm. They may be divided into two groups:

1. Proposals to change the arsenals.
2. Proposals to change the (military) strategy.

3.1 Changing the Arsenals

3.1.1 Diminishing the Nuclear Arsenals

The abundant existence of weapons of mass destruction does not at first glance indicate a high level of rationality in political and military decision-making in recent decades. It is therefore not surprising that in recent years several proposals to *diminish the arsenals unilaterally* have been made. George Kennan, in his 'Modest Proposal' for a unilateral 50 per cent reduction of the strategic nuclear arsenal of the United States, pointed out that this does not make any difference to the 'stability of deterrence' and that mutually assured destruction is not endangered. The same conclusion had already been reached in 1979 in *The Price of Defense*, published by the 'Boston Study Group' (and recently re-published as *Winding Down*). US strategic nuclear weapons should be reduced to 7000 warheads, tactical nuclear weapons with 20 000, and finally to zero.[18]

Such proposals have been made before, and generally, their aim is to establish a *'minimum' or 'minimal' deterrent*. There is another argument implicitly present here, namely, that this unilateral step may have some influence on the antagonist's perception of the situation, and may stimulate him to follow with comparable unilateral steps; the net result could be a diminishing of tensions and in the end a step towards 'normalisation' of international relations. This argument is dominant in several proposals. They are mirroring the arguments that are used to increase weapon arsenals and military expenditure. Changing the arsenals of weapons is intended as a means of communication being simultaneously a symbol as well as a signal. So far, the political decision-makers do not seem inclined to look closely into this kind of proposal. It does not seem to have reached the attention of the media, nor of public opinion. It has not been adopted by a peace movement that has a central position in the political debate. For practical purposes, it is dead.

3.1.2   *'Freezing' the Nuclear Arsenals*

This was proposed first by several scientists and other experts, and then by a huge part of the political establishment in the United States; probably the majority of the American public endorses this proposal. It is both simple and convincing, and it is easy to explain and to defend – basic virtues in a field where ignorance, prejudice and beliefs dominate over knowledge and insight.[19]

There are at the same time several points of criticism. First, a distinction should be made between a *unilateral* freeze and a *bilateral* freeze to be negotiated with the Soviet Union. A unilateral freeze would on all accounts probably be a step forward, in a psychological sense, even if its real effects would not be comparable to those of creating a 'minimum deterrent'. Still, the consequences in reducing tension and taking the heat off the arms race would probably be the same, even if on this point too several doubts may be voiced. Since politicians are not well-versed in practising psychology, they do not find it easy to predict the psychological and behavioural consequences of unilateral steps. Misperceptions may arise, particularly in a situation of mistrust; cultural differences may lead to reactions totally different from those expected, owing to the fact that predictions about other people's behaviour are based on one's own behaviour under the same circumstances.

A bilateral, negotiated freeze, on the other hand, is a virtually useless concept. It would take at least five years to negotiate such a freeze up to the point of ratification, which would leave ample time to implement the weapons procurement programme of the Reagan administration, including building another 17 000 new nuclear weapons. Then, during the five years something might happen comparable to what happened with the SALT II Treaty. That this bilateral freeze proposal is still favoured by ostensibly the majority of Americans, has only one virtue: because of it, they may have started to think about the whole issue of (nuclear) war and peace.

3.1.3 Creating Nuclear-Free Zones

There is at present one treaty which creates a nuclear-free zone: the Treaty of Tlatelolco. This treaty does not guarantee that Latin America will remain nuclear-free, taking into account the provisions made by Brasil and Argentina and subsequent developments.[20] Nevertheless, this proposal has received much attention in recent years, especially in Europe. Proposals have been made for a nuclear-free zone in Scandinavia, in the Balkans, in the whole of Europe (from Poland to Portugal) as well as for a 300 km zone along the East—West border. To a degree the Soviet Union made several steps indicating its willingness to free certain parts of Europe officially from nuclear weapons. The proposals are to be regarded 'under consideration' in the West, which usually means that they are buried to be forgotten. It is interesting to note that in any case Scandinavia is nuclear-free. There are no nuclear weapons on the territory of Finland, Sweden, Norway and Denmark. Nevertheless, it has not been possible (for reasons which remain unclear) to legitimate that state of affairs in a formal treaty. The fact that Norway and Denmark are under obligation to allow nuclear weapons on their territories in time of war does not seem to be convincing: in time of war, all treaties have a limited value, if any value at all. The fact that the Soviet Union has extensive nuclear installations on its own territory (next to the Finnish border in the north) does not seem to be a sufficient explanation either.

Even more intriguing is the proposal of the Palme Commission — especially because it was drawn up and agreed upon by an 'independent' group of politicians and experts from Eastern and Western Europe as well as the United States. The whole proposal seems to be superfluous. According to official Western sources the Soviet Union has never seen any need for deploying nuclear warheads in Eastern European countries (which does not exclude the launchers however). As a consequence, Eastern Europe (with the exception of the Soviet Union) has always been nuclear-free. This may change however, as one of the side effects of NATO's implementation of the INF-decision; it has already been suggested that, in answer to this, the USSR will deploy nuclear missiles in Eastern Europe (even if it remains unclear whether or not the warheads will be stored there too). On the NATO side, it would be very unwise to have nuclear warheads stored within 150 km of the border; if anything, this would otherwise mean an increase of the danger to be faced with an early 'use them or lose them' dilemma. Consequently, the proposal of the Palme Commission seems to be running after the facts: the 300 km zone is probably already nuclear-free. Still, even proclaiming a de facto nuclear-free zone officially nuclear-free seems to be impossible in the present political climate.

Interestingly enough, the best proposal is to be found in the same Palme Report. It is formulated by the West German expert Egon Bahr and it is simple as well as logical: nuclear weapons should be withdrawn to the territory of the countries that own the weapons (the United Kingdom, France and the Soviet Union). This has been too much even for the members of the Palme Commission: it indicates once again the barriers that have to be surmounted before anything relevant to changing the arsenals (or in this case the location of the arsenals) can be achieved. Proposals for other 'nuclear-free' zones have been voiced, and the problem of inspection has been raised in connection with these proposals. Inspection could pose insurmountable problems if the seas (such as the Baltic Sea) are to be included. The main point about nuclear-free zones still is that they may change the location of the arsenals, but that not one single warhead will be disarmed. Changing the location of the arsenals moreover will probably result in quite unexpected and to a certain extent unforeseeable developments, such as a change of military strategy which could create a need for other and new weapons systems. Reduction of tension may, or may not, be another result; and the value of its other achievement, freeing the territory of priority-targets during a nuclear war, should not be exaggerated. Sufficient targets will be left to destroy the same territories by nuclear war. In this connection it should be pointed out that the whole process of decision-making and sharing the responsibility for firing nuclear weapons is probably more relevant than the question of where the weapons are to be stationed. For the adversary, the countries that share the responsibility for firing may be regarded as much open to counter-attack with nuclear weapons as the countries that own the first-strike weapons.[21]

3.2 Changing the Strategy

3.2.1 Towards 'Defensive Deterrence'

Several times, and in particular in 1971, 1974 and 1976,[22] proposals have been made to change the official strategy of NATO into an unmistakably defensive strategy. The purposes of this change are manifold. First, if it could be proved that NATO's military posture (including arsenals and strategy) would not enable her to attack, it would demonstrate that NATO is really a defensive alliance. It was hoped that that would defuse, at least to a certain extent, international tension. Secondly, a basic assumption is that this 'defensive' posture would be more credible, because it would not mean threatening with common suicide, but building a real defence instead of doubtful deterrence. Since then, several operational versions of this idea have been proposed while several others are in preparation, and to a certain extent the general idea has received benevolent nods in official circles.

This is not the place to go into the merits of the operationalisations. At this level of the analysis, the idea could be compared with other ideas which are proposed as fundamental changes in security policy. Once again, there is reason for severe criticism. Firstly, whether a military posture is defensive or offensive is in the eye of the beholder. It is a subjective view, and whatever is said of the objective analysis, the decisive element here is the subjective perception of the party that is supposed to perceive a change from more or less offensive capabilities to unmistakable defensive capabilities. There is no reason whatsoever to expect such a change to be implemented convincingly. It has been tried before. The first instance is already found in the writings of Thucydides, who pointed out how Sparta felt compelled to start a pre-emptive war to prevent Athens from building defensive and invincible fortresses around the city, which would have made Athens invulnerable to an attack and, consequently, much more threatening than before. Almost the same kind of reasoning is applied many centuries later to proposals to reinforce civil defence, and to build anti-ballistic missile systems. At first glance, they seem to be convincingly defensive. On second thoughts they appear to be a crucial prerequisite for conquering the world.

Several basic ideas are floating around. A prominent one is that a 'defensive strategy' is in the first place a *'territorial'* defence, the inability to attack the antagonist's territory but the perfect ability to defend one's own territory. Secondly, a distinction has been made between *defensive and offensive weapons*. A 'territorial defence' however is difficult to organise convincingly as a 'territorially bound' defence, and it is probably even more difficult to convince people that certain weapon systems cannot be used to conquer territory, or in other words, in a military offensive; and that includes specific examples, such as anti-tank weapons instead of tanks. A military force can always be used for an offensive, if it is mobile. As long as a soldier can walk carrying his weapons, a force composed of these soldiers may be perceived as potentially aggressive. Still, there are examples of clearly immobile and therefore almost unmistakably defensive postures, such as the French Maginot Line; this example shows how difficult it is to accomplish a really 'defensive' posture. In the first place, the Maginot Line was not conceived to be part of a specifically defensive strategy at all: it was epitomised as a condition for the decisive attack (one is again reminded of Thucydides' story). Secondly, it was immobile and 'invincible'; nevertheless, the war in which it was intended to play a decisive role was lost within 6 weeks.

These remarks however are not meant to be a final verdict on the whole idea. They are only intended to indicate the serious doubts about the prospects of *'defensive deterrence'* or *'inoffensive deterrence'*, and in consequence, about the priority which should be given to exploring alternatives. There is another important objection to this idea of 'defensive deterrence': it does not sufficiently take into account what is known about the factors that direct, stimulate and dominate the arms race. Official acceptance of a 'change of strategy' in the direction of 'defensive deterrence' would in all probability result in another arms race of 'defensive weapons'. In addition, the existing arsenals would still remain available – just in case. The net result would then be an increase in defence expenditure, in the arsenals of devices of mass destruction and (taking into account some propositions on how to implement 'defensive deterrence') in the 'militarisation' of society as a whole. Still, the expected result (measured in terms of a qualitative change in threat-perception and consequently, in international relations) would not be ensured. What could be ensured however is a more credible defensive posture. But that has been pointed out to be dangerous too: if war may be waged, it will occur sometimes, and the central idea in (nuclear) deterrence has always been that it should be made clear that the costs of war outweigh its benefits. On balance, the merits of the idea of 'defensive strategy' are not clear although its dangers are.

3.2.2 'Conventionalise' Defence and Deterrence

There is a close relationship between the ïdea of establishing a defensive strategy, and reinforcing a conventional defence. In both cases, nuclear weapons play no role at all, or at most a secondary role. In both cases the need for new, conventional weaponry is established. In neither case is it clear whether, as a consequence of its acceptance, other weapons will be disarmed or dismantled. Recently several proposals have been made and all of them seem to have one thing in common: they try to minimise the role of nuclear weapons by enhancing the role of conventional defence. A difference from other ideas mentioned before is that it is not specifically or explicitly a 'defensive' conventional strategy that is proposed here; and the most important feature of these proposals is that they seem to make war thinkable again.[23]

Once again, the idea has several setbacks. First, the last few decades have seen a pendulum-movement between emphasis on conventional or nuclear war preparation and warfare, and the revival of this idea seems to indicate once again that there is a change of emphasis. Basically, this pendulum-movement derives from the inconsistency of the theory underlying current security policy which has never made the important distinction between 'deterrence' with nuclear weapons and deterrence in the old-fashioned military sense. The first idea (deterrence with nuclear weapons) precludes the possibility of real defence. Instead comes the threat of annihilation; and with that, instead of manipulating defence capacities, changing strategies and building weaponry, comes the manipulation of psychological concepts as well as speculations about credibility and rationality. Although military deterrence in the classical sense includes the threat of military defeat (and some destruction) too, it is in the first place concerned with a credible potential for fighting and winning a war. The difference between these two concepts of deterrence has been pointed out repeatedly, but in practice, the emphasis in official strategy and in arguments to produce and deploy weaponry has been oscillating between the first and the second meaning of deterrence. The result is a continuous ambiguity, in which arguments belonging to the nuclear deterrence domain suddenly appear in the military defence context, in a hopeless attempt to integrate both concepts into one general framework. Nuclear war therefore has become gradually more and more 'thinkable'. Nuclear weapons have been devised to be used in warfare, and the question whether a nuclear war can be fought and won is no longer anathema: for several 'experts' the answer is already that it *can* be won.[24] On the other hand conventional warfare and defence have never been totally neglected. Especially when mutual-assured-destruction was a fact of life and flexible response had become official NATO-strategy, emphasis on building conventional forces gradually increased. Under the pressure of the peace movements, which almost without exception stress the urgency of preventing nuclear war and of abolishing nuclear weapons, an acceleration in this process of changing emphasis seems to have taken place.

There is another setback that has gone almost unnoticed so far. Analysts seem to care much less about the effects of a conventional war than about the effects of a nuclear war. The basic assumption underlying all efforts to 'conventionalise' defence seems to be that whereas nuclear war is too destructive to wage, this is not so for a conventional war. There is much to support this thesis. For example: at least two hundred wars have been fought since 1945 with conventional weapons; every day at least three wars are going on, and the resulting destruction may be unacceptable for those who suffer it, but is certainly not endangering the survival of a whole society or even mankind. But this kind of reasoning fails to take into account the fact that these wars, almost without exception, are internal struggles with foreign intervention, and in particular, that they are fought mostly in developing countries. A different picture emerges when the future battlefield concerns Europe, where no major war has been fought since 1945. Since then, Europe has accumulated an enormous arsenal of destructive conventional weaponry. The *destructiveness* and effectiveness of these weapons have been perfected in a continuing process since 1945. What is even more important, the *vulnerability* of Europe has increased dramatically because of, for example, the increase in chemical industries and the building of nuclear reactors, not to mention the vulnerability of energy and transport systems, pipelines, food chains, etc. Still, war is implicitly seen as manageable without the unacceptable risks of destroying society and committing genocide.

In the third place, the argument still holds that enhancing conventional capabilities may help in preventing a conflict from crossing the nuclear threshold but that at the same time it may increase the probability of a political conflict developing into a military conflict. Having achieved this first (violent) stage in what is commonly perceived as being an inevitable escalation process, the nuclear phase becomes even more thinkable. The purpose of avoiding nuclear war may in the end be defeated by the means that are used, i.e. creating a greater potential for conventional warfighting.

Changing military strategies to avoid nuclear war is, to say the least, not a very convincing way of dealing with the problem. All variations of this theme, creating defensive capabilities, territorial defence, non-provocative defence and in all cases, a conventional war-fighting capability, meet the same objections: they will probably result in another arms race in conventional, defensive weapons and they will not abolish the existing stockpiles of nuclear weaponry. At best, their location will be changed — which is most probable with short-range tactical nuclear weapons; and in the end, security will still be in the same shape as it is now, or even worse, at higher costs.

3.2.3   Non-Military Defence

There is, however, still another proposal to change strategy. It has been proposed long before the introduction of nuclear destruction devices, and its roots are very different. In short, it is a proposal for a *nonviolent, non-military defence strategy*. A wide range of names as well as definitions are used for it, but the main elements are already present in the words used before: *nonviolence*, as well as *non-military*. The non-military part has found another transcription in the widely used term *'civilian defence'* (not to be misinterpreted as civil defence). In another definition, which focuses on the main elements of the strategy, emphasis is laid on the fact that not the defence of a territory but of a social system prevails: *'social defence'*.[25]

This idea, which has its roots in Gandhian philosophy, in Christian pacifism as well as in socialist anti-militarism, and whose strategy and tactics have been invented and developed in non-violent struggles against colonial oppression, against military intervention and usurpation as well as against internal *coups d'état*, has, however, never been translated into applicable proposals. Occasionally, governments or the defence community of some countries have been intrigued by the idea, and several times some tentative steps in investigating its potential were taken. Already in 1966, no less a person than the famous nuclear strategist Thomas Schelling described the potential of 'civilian defence' in clear terms: ' . . . the potential of non-violence is enormous. . . . In the end it could be as important as nuclear fission. Like nuclear fission it has implications for peace, war, stability, terror, confidence and international and domestic politics, that are as yet not easy to assess . . .'.[26] Since then, the governments of several Western European countries (such as Sweden, Denmark, the Netherlands) have officially taken some steps to investigate its possibilities;[27] and to a certain extent, elements of this 'strategy of civilian defence' are integrated in the defence posture of countries like Yugoslavia.[28] Still, official interest has never led to any kind of operationalised concept of a nonviolent defence system, and proposals to introduce it as an alternative (or, at least, a complement) to traditional, military defence, have so far not encountered an encouraging response. Nevertheless, the idea seems worth pursuing: if not as an immediately applicable proposal, at least as an idea that under certain conditions may be successful, provided that strategy, tactics and preparations have been further developed. This development, however, is not the immediate concern of conventional wisdom as expressed by political establishments and the sole hope here seems to reside in the scientific community (perhaps endorsed by experts from the military side: one of its first proponents after the Second World War, for example, was the British Commander Stephen King-Hall).[29]

This is not the place to summarise the present stage of theory and practice of such a system of defence; such summaries can easily be found elsewhere.[30] It is mentioned here only because several groups in the peace movements have been interested in the idea to the extent that they have more or less vigorously tried to get endorsement for proposals to replace nuclear weaponry, as well as conventional defence, with a system of 'social' or 'civilian' defence. If a change of military strategy is not a solution to the problem, the same may be said – at this moment – of the proposal to scrap military defence and to introduce civilian defence. It simply does not exist, yet. There is nothing like a detailed, operationalised plan for a strategy of civilian defence, as there are many such plans for a strategy of military defence. But if the consequences of warfare defy all of its purposes and everything that could be gained by it, there is an instant need to develop other means for winning or resolving human, social conflicts *beyond* war and the use of political violence.

4   CONCLUSION: A CHANGE OF PARADIGM?

Changing the number, the quality, the location of nuclear and other means of destruction of human life is – in conclusion – *not* to be regarded as a real alternative; nor is changing the strategy to fight eventual wars, defend one's own territory or culture, or win social conflicts with military means. It may be an almost trivial conclusion: but then it is embarrassing that in the discussions at the beginning of the 1980s, only proposals in these directions have generally been taken seriously as real alternatives to the nuclear arms race, or at the least, as the first steps necessary to end it. Such proposals merely demonstrate the intellectual poverty and the insufficient grasp of the problem under consideration that seems to be the common characteristic of their proponents. There is a serious underestimation of the internal as well as external factors that stimulate the arms race. Proposals to change the arsenals or to change the strategy could easily be integrated into the mainstream of military and political developments — or in other words, into the arms race itself. A fundamental difference exists between focusing attention on the *ways* and *means* to handle a conflict, and focusing attention on attempts to solve the conflict itself. So far, the proposed alternatives deal with ways and means, and they accept the conflict as both inevitable and unsolvable, and therefore as eternal. When this definition of the problem remains the basis of conventional wisdom and conventional politics, which so far it is, the 'final solution' is clear: nuclear war becomes then as inevitable as conventional war already is.[31] It is then only a question of time until one or more nuclear weapons will be used somewhere, and one can only wonder how far escalation will go and what its consequences will be.[32]

It may be possible, however, to change the definition of the problem, and thus to discover solutions or alternatives that until now have been beyond our scope or imagination, more or less comparable to the way old and unsolvable problems in physical science came into the grips of scientists as a consequence of their changing the way in which they defined or 'saw' them. In this sense, a *'change of paradigm'* describes aptly what is needed. As a consequence of such a 'scientific revolution'[33] it could be imagined that a social and political revolution would take place, something which is necessary according to Albert Einstein who changed the paradigm in physics. The development of nuclear weapons changed the world, but not our way of thinking about that world and 'seeing' that world; and these nuclear weapons were fitted in the old patterns of the independent-state–world system, with horrendous consequences.

A change of paradigm, although not the topic of this contribution, should be mentioned, if only to start thinking in this direction. The problem can be summarised as one of *perception of reality* more than anything else. The world is seen (perceived) as a world of virtually independent states, who have the rights and the means to defend their independence, defined according to their own definition. It is the paradigm (paradigm is to be interpreted here as a 'generally accepted' definition) of *independence* which needs urgent and immediate revision. Developments, particularly since 1945, should have changed the perception in the direction of an *interdependent world*. If this would have been the common framework (the "dominant" paradigm) in science as well as in politics now, other rules would have been invented to resolve conflicts, and other norms, values and behaviour-patterns would have developed in consequence, diminishing the role of military means and of war, and of political violence and the threat of annihilation, to almost zero.

The interesting thing is that this has happened to a certain extent, almost without anybody noticing it to the extent that such consequences were drawn. Western Europe, for centuries the foremost battlefield between England, France, Germany, Spain, Italy, the Netherlands, Belgium, Portugal and even the Scandinavian countries fighting each other in different alliances, seems since 1945 to have become interdependent and integrated to such a degree that the idea of war between these still 'independent' states is now far beyond imagination. Similarly, peace between France and Germany, who fought each other in 1870, 1914, and 1939, now seems guaranteed: not by a military balance, nor by an arms race, and these means were not even tried. It is guaranteed by their interdependency. The thought is intriguing and should be pursued.[34]

NOTES

1. For example: Karl Deutsch, *The analysis of international relations*, Englewood Cliffs, NY, Prentice-Hall 2nd edn, 1978 (1st edn, 1968!), pp. 154–62; Anatol Rapoport, *Strategy and Conscience*, first edition 1964, New York, Harper & Row; Philip Green, *Deadly Logic: the Theory of Nuclear Deterrence*, Ohio State University, 1966; Dieter Senghaas, *Abschreckung und Frieden*, Europäische Verlagsanstalt, Frankfurt a/Main, 1969.

   The interesting point about these books is that they were written in the 1960s; the arguments used in current public debates add virtually nothing to what was already written then.

2. There is some doubt about the 'proven effectiveness'. The general assumption now is that the Japanese Government decided to capitulate as a direct consequence of the destruction of Hiroshima and Nagasaki by nuclear weapons. This assumption is the basic argument for the subsequent integration of nuclear armaments in military strategy and politics in general. More recent evidence however casts some doubts on the value of the assumption. The Imperial Japanese Government seems to have been divided already *before* the bomb was dropped, in two fractions. One wanted to end the war, the other wanted to continue it. The nuclear weapons on Hiroshima and Nagasaki did not change this division at all. The members of government who wanted to continue the war did not change their minds. There was a stalemate between the fractions, which was somehow ended by the intervention of Emperor Hirohito who let it be known that he was in favour of ending the war.

Subsequently, the fraction that wanted to continue the war attempted a *coup d'état*, which failed. If this story is true, there is not much left of the 'proven effectiveness'. The opposite has been proved again: people will under certain circumstances pursue their policies or their behaviour regardless of the consequences, and even disregard rational calculations about them. We have known this for a long time: revolutions, e.g. could not start otherwise.

3. An excellent history of the development of strategy is Lawrence Freedman, *The Evolution of Nuclear Strategy*, London, Macmillan Press, 1981.

4. See President Reagan's speech of 23 March 1983 on *Ballistic Missile Defence* commonly known as 'Star Wars Speech', *Survival*, May–June 1983, pp. 129–30. In scientific circles, however, there is severe scepticism about the whole idea. For an introduction to the subject, see Herbert Scoville Jr. and Kosta Tsipis, *Can Space Remain a Peaceful Environment?*, Occasional Paper, Muscatine, Iowa, The Stanley Foundation, 1978.

5. Weapons have become symbols. See Wolfgang Panofsky, 'La Science, la Technologie et l'Accumulation des Armements' in Pierre Lellouche (ed.), *La Science et le Désarmement*, Paris, Institut Français des Relations Internationales, 1981, pp. 47–65.

6. For an overview of what is happening now and what is already there, see *SIPRI Yearbook 1983*, in particular Appendix A (pp. LI–LVI): 'All in all projected nuclear warhead production in the U.S.A., from now until the mid 1990's, may involve the production of about 37,000 new nuclear warheads, of which about 23,000 will be constructed by about 1990.' *World Armaments and Disarmament, SIPRI Yearbook 1983*, London, Taylor & Francis, 1983, p. LV.

7. In addition to what is done by the nuclear powers (see again *SIPRI Yearbook 1983*), several states are requiring nuclear capabilities and are developing – or have already developed – a number of nuclear weapons. This proliferation of nuclear weapons will continue, probably with a sharp upward trend during the next years.

8. In fact, the first doubts were voiced by military men already a long time ago; an interesting example is the British Commander Sir Stephen King-Hall, who already in the fifties opposed the idea of a 'nuclear defence' (*Defence in the nuclear age*, 1958; *Common Sense in Defence*, 1960.) Since then, a long list of quotations could be made voicing doubts about the official nuclear strategy coming from leading military experts such as Lord Mountbatten, General Steinhoff, Rear-Admiral Gene LaRocque and Field Marshall Lord Carver. Former Secretary of Defence Robert McNamara starts his already famous article on 'The Military Role of Nuclear Weapons: Perceptions and Misperceptions', in *Foreign Affairs*, Fall 1983, quoting such experts on strategy. It may be noted that the value of their criticisms in this context is not so much the content of what they say, as well as being who they are while saying it.

9. *Der Stern*, no. 9, 19 Feb. 1981, p. 33, reprinted in Dieter S. Lutz, *Weltkrieg wider Willen*, Hamburg, Rowohlt-Aktuell, 1981, p. 334.

10. For example: George Kennan, 'A proposal for international disarmament' in H.W. Tromp and G. LaRocque (eds.), *Nuclear War in Europe*, Groningen, University Press, 1981; Henry Kissinger, *NATO, the Next Thirty Years: Remarks on the NATO-Conference*, 1 Sept. 1979, Center for Strategic and

International Studies, 1979, as well as 'A new Approach to Arms Control', *Time*, 21 Mar., 1983, pp. 18–20; Robert McNamara, 'What the U.S. can do' in *Newsweek*, 5 Dec., 1983.

11. Robert Scheer, *With Enough Shovels: Reagan, Bush & Nuclear War*, New York, Random House, 1982, p. 219.

12. Particularly relevant here is H.W. Tromp, *Political Attitudes and Political Behaviour — Decision-Making In Crisis*, Polemological Institute, Groningen, 1976 (in Dutch).

13. See for example the story on William Colby, former head of the CIA and now in favour of the Freeze-proposal.

14. For example, *Seven recommendations for realistic NATO policies*, signed by former generals Gert Bastian (B.R.D.), Johan Christie (Norway), Francesco da Costa Gomez (Portugal; former president of Portugal), Georgios Koumanakos (Greece), Michiel von Meyenfeldt (Netherlands), Nino Pasti (Italy), and Antoine Sanguinetti (France), and published in *Nuclear War in Europe*, op cit., pp. 235–50.

15. C.E. Osgood, *An Alternative to War or Surrender*, Urbana 1962, and Amitai Etzioni, 'The Kennedy Experiment', in *Western Political Quarterly*, 1967, pp. 161–380. Osgood's ideas on *Grit* (abbreviation of Gradual Reciprocated Initiatives in Tension Reduction) have been republished several times; see for example A. Newcombe (ed.), *Peace Research Review*, vol. 8 (1979), nos. 1, 2.

16. The extensive debate in the philosophy of science as well as the sociology of science is relevant here, and it has its extensions in the paradigm-discussion on international relations. Some significant references are: Thomas S. Kuhn, *The Structure of Scientific Revolutions*, Chicago, 2nd edn., 1972; Robert K. Merton, *The Sociology of Science: Theoretical and Empirical Investigations*, Chicago, 1973; M.J. Mulkay, *The Social Process of Innovation — a Study in the Sociology of Science*, London, 1972; A. Lijphart, 'International Relations Theory: Grand Debates and Lesser Debates', *International Social Science Journal*, vol. 26, no. 1, 1974; Johan Galtung, *Towards a definition of peace-research*, UNESCO, Peace Research Trend Report and World Directory, Reports and Papers in the Social Sciences, no. 43, 1979; Hylke Tromp, 'Changing Perspectives in Peace Research', in *UNESCO Yearbook on Peace and Conflict Studies 1980*, Paris, UNESCO, 1981.

17. There is however an increasing interest. For an introduction to the subject: J. Sassoon, 'Interdependence in the international system: a survey of the literature', in *Lo Spettatore Internazionale*, 1981, no. 1, pp. 29–55. The leading journal in this field is *International Organisation*, University of Wisconsin Press.

18. *Winding down the Price of Defence*, the Boston Study Group, San Francisco, W.H. Freeman, 1982.

19. Jane Sharp, 'Restructuring the Arms Control Process', in *Nuclear War in Europe*, op. cit., pp. 163–71, gives an early announcement of the ideas behind the Freeze-proposal. The official proposal is outlined in Edward M. Kennedy and Mark O. Hatfield, *Freeze! How You Can Help to Prevent a Nuclear War*, Bantam Books, April 1982. It may be mentioned here that the idea of a freeze was already proposed by President Carter to President Brezhnev in November 1980, during their meeting in Vienna to sign the SALT II Treaty. According to President Carter (in a TV-interview in Sweden several years

later), the USSR response was negative. Since then, the idea seems to have been adopted by the USSR, while the American government which succeeded the Carter administration, has firmly opposed it. For Carter's story, see *The International Herald Tribune*, 8–9 May 1982.

20. See Jozef Goldblat, *Arms Control Agreements*, London, Taylor & Francis, 1983, in particular pp. 282–4 about these reservations.

21. For an excellent review and summary of such proposals: Sverre Lodgaard and Marek Thee (eds), *Nuclear Disengagement in Europe*, SIPRI, London & New York, Taylor & Francis, 1983. In addition, see Barry M. Blechman and Mark R. Moore, 'A Nuclear Weapon Free Zone in Europe', *Scientific American*, April, 1983, and *Common Security – a Programme for Disarmament* (The report of the so-called Palme Commission), London, Pan books, 1982.

22. C.F. von Weizsäcker (ed.), *Kriegsfolgen und Kriegsverhütung*, Carl Hanser Verlag, 3rd edn., 1971, and later books of the group who undertook this study, such as Horst Ahfeld, *Verteidigung und Frieden – Politik mit militärischen Mitteln*, and Emil Spannochi & Guy Brossolet, *Verteidigung ohne Schlacht*, Munich, Carl Hanser Verlag, 1976; Horst Mendershausen, *Inoffensive Deterrence*, Rand Corporation, Santa Monica, 1974; B.V.A. Röling 'Defensieve afschrikkingsstellingen', in *Transaktie*, 1978/2. See also his 'Feasibility of Inoffensive Deterrence', *Bulletin of Peace Proposals*, 1978/4. These titles are only examples: Röling has published extensively on the subject in Dutch. I mention these titles only to indicate that the idea is not as young and innovating as it sounds in current public debates.

23. McNamara's proposals (see note 8) are criticised in certain circles, because they may lead in this direction. Recently, several studies dealing with the question of conventional deterrence have appeared, such as *Strengthening Conventional Deterrence in Europe*, Report of the European Security Study, NY, St. Martin's Press, 1983; John D. Steinbruner & Leon V. Sigel, *Alliance Security: NATO and the No-first-use question*, Washington, DC, Brookings Institution, 1983. Particularly relevant in this book is William W. Kaufmann's contribution, 'Non-nuclear Deterrence'. The NATO supreme commander, General Rogers, has endorsed (in several interviews) the need for – and the possibility of – such a conventional deterrent.

24. The most famous article here is by Colin Gray and Keith Payne, 'Victory is Possible', *Foreign Policy*, no. 39 (Summer 1980).

25. A few titles from the extensive literature on the subject: Adam Roberts (ed.), *The Strategy of Civilian Defence – Non-violent Resistance to Aggression*, London, Faber & Faber, 1967; Johan Galtung, 'Non-military Defence', in *Essays in Peace Research*, vol. II, Christian Ejlers, Copenhagen, 1976; Gene Sharp, *The Politics of Nonviolent Action*, Boston, Porter Sargent, 1973; Hylke Tromp, *Sociale Verdediging*, XENO, Groningen, 1981.

26. In Adam Roberts, *The Strategy of Civilian Defence*, op. cit.

27. Resulting in several studies by Adam Roberts for the Swedish Government, such as *Total Defence and Civilian Resistance: Problems of Sweden's Security Policy*, Stockholm 1972; in a study by Anders Boserup and Andrew Mack written for the Danish government: *War without weapons*, London, 1974; and finally in still continuing discussions and several ongoing research projects in the Netherlands, commissioned by the government since 1976.

28. See Adam Roberts, *Nations in Arms: the Theory and Practice of Territorial*

Defence, London, International Institute for Strategic Studies, 1976, in particular ch. 5.

29. See note 8.
30. See the literature mentioned in note 25.
31. According to several studies, the amount of conventional warfare is not to be underestimated: the average is ten to eleven wars every year, and since 1945, on each day almost three conventional wars were going on. The use of violence for political purposes is one of the facts of life: and the spectre of this type of violence ranges much further than 'conventional war' as defined by criteria as death-toll (usually at least 1000) and participation of regular armies. The real amount of political violence is, in fact, still a matter of guessing: studies dealing with this problem normally confine themselves to violence defined according to criteria as mentioned above. The consequences are sometimes confusing. In one of the most quoted studies on warfare since 1945, nothing is to be found on – for example – the mass-murder in Indonesia following the 1965 *coup d'état* (estimated death-toll 300 000–600 000) nor do the criteria permit to take into account serious political conflicts as the Warsaw-Pact invasion of Czechoslovakia in 1968. Francis Beer (1982) estimates 3500 known major wars in history; more than 1250 of these were fought in Europe. Moreover, he counts at least 14 000 'incidents of world major and minor violence' since 3600 B.C., killing one billion people, 800 million of them in Europe. In 1983, at least 40 armed conflicts were being fought; according to a report of the Center for Defense Information (Washington) in the last three years, six new wars have started while only two have ended, more than 4 million people have been engaged in combat and 54 of the world's nations are involved in these wars. Francis A. Beer, *How much war in history: definitions, estimates, extrapolations and trends*, Beverly Hills, Sage Professional Papers in International Studies, vol. 3, 1974; Francis Beer, *Peace Against War: The Ecology of International Violence*, San Francisco, W.H. Freeman, 1981; Istvan Kende, 'Wars of Ten Years: 1967–1976', *Journal of Peace Research*, vol. 15, no. 3, pp. 227–41; John Keegan (ed.), *War in Peace: an Analysis of Warfare Since 1945*, London, Orbis, 1981.
32. In most studies about the consequences of nuclear war, emphasis is laid on the disastrous consequences of all-out nuclear attack, even if that attack is limited to a certain part of the globe. It is more probable, however, that the next time nuclear weapons will be used, it will be done under the same circumstances and with the same logic behind it as in 1945: in a conventional war, where one of the two sides decides to take advantage of its nuclear-development stage and to drop one, or two, nuclear bombs. This prospect may have been one of the reasons for the Israeli attack on the nuclear-energy factory in Iraq: to prevent the development of a nuclear weapon that could be used decisively against Iran, and so establishing superiority in the Middle East.
33. See references made in note 16.
34. The idea is not at all new of course, and was mentioned as a solution to the problem of war already before the World War I. For the same reason, it may be argued that it is a 'great illusion': there was increasing interdependence between the states who started and fought the World War I, and this inter-dependence increased further in the period before the World War II. Never-

theless, these wars took place. Still, the idea that increasing interdependence may finally change the methods of conflict resolution *qualitatively*, in the direction of *nonviolence*, may be a sound one. There are several reasons why increasing interdependence did not prevent the world wars, or even other wars. At first glance it may be that a certain, until now unknown, level of interdependence must be reached before such a qualitative change occurs, and this has probably happened now in western Europe, where the prospect of war has declined to zero since 1945 whilst interdependence and integration have grown. Moreover, increasing interdependence does not decrease conflicts: probably it results in even more conflicts, which may escalate to armed conflict. Finally, one has to take into account that there is always a difference between *reality* and the *perception of reality*. In reality, waging war to win a conflict may be a disastrous decision, but in the perception of the political decision-makers it may still be a worthwhile solution to their problems. Of the several studies which could be mentioned here I refer to only two: Robert O. Keohane & Joseph S. Nye, *Power and Interdependence — World Politics in Transition*, Boston/Toronto, 1977; James N. Rosenau, *The Study of Global Interdependence. Essays on the Internationalisation of World Affairs*, London, 1980.

6 Are the Peace Movements Pace-Setters or Pitfalls for Peace?

GERARD RADNITZKY

INTRODUCTION

For a rational discussion of the problems that the 'Peace Movements' raise for political philosophy and for politics, it is necessary to understand what makes it possible to integrate into a peaceful order individuals and groups that pursue different ends. Reflection upon the development of order and peace and on the mechanisms that maintain a peaceful order contributes to the improvement of our image of man and to our understanding of contemporary society and politics. This understanding is a prerequisite for coping with the problems raised by the 'Peace Movements'.

PRE-SUMMARY

1   The Evolution of Order and Peace

1.1   The two routes to sociality in *biological* evolution: the semi-sociality achieved by non-human primates, baboon hordes, etc.; the social insects' route to ultrasociality.

1.2   The route to human ultrasociality opened up by *cultural* evolution: the rise of a civilised order. The development from the human tribal horde, the face-to-face community, to the mass society, the anonymous society. This development is made possible by the replacement, in the public–political sphere, of the norm system fitted to the tribal horde by the abstract rules that make possible the mass society. The process of cultural evolution yields spontaneous order, complex order among interacting individuals. The primacy of spontaneous order over design is due to epistemological factors. The market order (F.v. Hayek's catallaxy) is a precondition of the development of an order of peace under law and, hence, of the possibility of an open society.

2   Attempts to Construct Human Sociality by Design

These attempts are seen as efforts to reverse the cultural evolution that extended the order of peace beyond the small groups pursuing the same ends, and to return to a state where a common purpose is required for establishing and maintaining a peaceful order.

2.1   Efforts to return to the norm system that fitted the tribal hordes: socialism.

2.2   The *'tentation totalitaire'*: efforts to model human ultrasociality upon the social insects' sociality.

3   Situational Analysis of the Relationship Between the Two Superpowers

The assumption that both parties are rational agents; the stylisation of their relationship in terms of the Prisoners' Dilemma; particular historical conditions.

4   The Modern Phenomenon of the 'Peace Movements'

The problems raised by their presence. What attitude it is rational to adopt towards the 'Peace Movements' — by a totalitarian regime and by a liberal democracy. On the likely consequences of their activity for international relations, and in particular, for the Western democratic system.

5   Conclusion: on the Future of the Open Society

1   THE EVOLUTION OF ORDER AND PEACE

1.0   BIOLOGICAL AND CULTURAL EVOLUTION: THE ROUTES TO 'ULTRASOCIALITY'

The following skeleton outline is based, as far as biological evolution is concerned, on recent, in part as yet unpublished work, of Donald T.

Campbell. As far as cultural evolution is concerned, I am departing from Campbell and basing myself on the recent work of Friedrich von Hayek.[1] Grouping can be achieved by mechanisms developed in the course of biological evolution (section 1.1) or by mechanisms developed through cultural evolution (section 1.2) — and also by design (section 2). Biological and cultural evolution have in common the selection principle. Whereas in biological evolution the unit of selection is the individual or the gene, in cultural evolution it is the group or rules and customs. Cultural evolution operates much faster than biological evolution and the differentiation it achieves within a species is considerably greater.

1.1   The Routes to Sociality in Biological Evolution

1.1.0   A species trapped in an ecological niche that makes grouping necessary either develops the required mechanisms or disappears. I shall outline two different routes leading to two very different types of sociality. They will be used as a foil for reflections on the human route to sociality.

1.1.1   *The Semi-Sociality Achieved by Baboon Hordes, Monkey Bands, and Non-Human Primates*

Multimale social groupings of baboons, Rhesus monkeys, etc. trapped into group life for mutual defence achieve semi-sociality. This may be explained by the selection over time of traits, dispositions, behaviour patterns or 'rules', which have greater survival value than others. They are stable because of their value in promoting survival and genetic propagation and hence, behaviour is fairly predictable. It is doubtful whether group selection (of kins or structured demes) can fully explain the phenomenon of semi-sociality. Acts which are 'altruistic' in the sense that they benefit others more than the actor will be eliminated through natural selection. The evolution of such behaviours is impeded by absolute or relative costs in fitness to those who have the disposition to act 'altruistically'. This situation is parallelled in economics in the 'free rider' problem. At any rate, these group-selection mechanisms are not sufficient to overcome genetic competition among cooperators. Hence, ultrasociality cannot be achieved by this route.

The expression 'altruistic' just used — in shudder quotes — reflects the fact that the behaviour is often interpreted in analogy to human moral conduct. Keeping in mind that the behaviour is instinctive, these 'as if' interpretations have heuristic value. Thus, we find that these hordes have evolved a 'clear-cut facultative polymorphism of dominance and submission' (D.T. Campbell). This manages internal conflicts and secures internal peace so that 'contributive justice' is combined with enough peer equality: food and information about food is shared in the chimpanzee horde; there is a recognition of private property so that the dominant male will beg meat from a subordinate who happens to be in possession of it (D.T. Campbell); there exists some division of labour, e.g. a sentinel and warning function. Baboon hordes, monkey bands, etc. are *more prone to internal dissension than to group fights; but the internal aggressiveness is held in check by the dispositions and the 'rule system'*. This is of great importance because these fights would reduce the group's effectiveness as a whole in group struggles. In-fights may be terminated by a dominant animal making use of protohuman 'moralistic aggression' in order to stop a fight and to restore internal peace. The monkey hordes etc. have remained in this state. Thus the plausible explanation is that there are limits to the further development of sociality which result from the continued presence of genetic competition between cooperating males.

1.1.2   The Biological Route to Ultrasociality: the Social Insects

By 'ultrasociality' is meant a division of labour that has reached such an extent that neither the group nor the individual member (perhaps with a few exceptions) could survive without it. The ultrasociality achieved by the social insects is the result of the adaptation of a species trapped in an ecological niche in which solitary or single family existence is no longer viable. The social insects successfully eliminated the factor that has prevented baboon hordes and social primates from proceeding further on the route towards ultrasociality by removing genetic competition among cooperators through the mechanism of caste sterility. The sterility of the cooperators made possible the extremes of behavioural and even anatomical specialisation that are characteristic of the social insects. If we interpret this adaptive development in terms of 'as if'-rational problem-solving and postulate that the overall 'aim' of the species is gene propagation and the maximum level of population possible with given environmental resources, then a cost-benefit analysis would yield the result that for the ant worker the utility in terms of individual fitness achieved through caste sterility outweighs the cost of own sterility. If the castes are sterile, not only is competition among individuals removed and *perfect equality* between caste members realised, but also *individuality as such is eliminated*.

The selection occurs at the level of queens and nests, which means that in group competition the effectiveness of the cooperating group will be the trait that is selected. Hence, the whole system of ant aggression guarantees *complete peace within the nest and merciless aggression towards any potential rivals of the community as a whole*. The ultrasociality achieved by the social insects appears to be the utmost that can be achieved by biological evolution: there is complete stability at the price of stagnation — a '*post histoire*' situation.

1.2 The Route to Human Ultrasociality Opened Up by Cultural Evolution: the Rise of a Civilised Order

1.2.0 The basic problem of human social systems is similar to that of the non-human primate group: *to maintain a peaceful social order* in changing situations. There will always be some conflicts. The issue is to prevent them as far as possible and to resolve them or keep them in check. If this is to be achieved, much of the behaviour must be *rule-following behaviour*. This is only possible if there is an incentive structure conducive to this behaviour.

The way of looking at human social systems that will be used here is based upon certain *assumptions about man*. All life is concerned with problem solving, and species and individuals behave 'as if' they attempted to improve their lot, their ecological niche. The general mechanism of evolution is adaptive-variation-and-selective-retention. Man is essentially a '*r*esourceful–*e*valuating–*m*aximising' being: he strives to realise as much of his goals as possible with the help of the resources at his disposal. There are always competing goals and scarce resources. This *REMM-model or 'rational choice' model of man*, this 'economic' approach to man's activities, is appropriate to the evolutionary perspective. With the help of the 'rational choice' model, it is possible to explain why, in certain spheres of activity, man's behaviour is rule-governed and, hence, why the *model of man as rule-follower* is applicable to these spheres of life. The function of rules of conduct or laws is to change the individual's expectancies, to provide incentives for law-conforming behaviour and disincentives for law-breaking behaviour. Incentives and disincentives are taken in the widest sense. Dissuasion from law breaking is achieved by fear of punishment, in general, by the expected costs of violating norms. If the norms are internalised these costs will include psychological costs such as remorse, etc.

1.2.1   The Human Tribal Horde, the Face-to-Face Community

The mobile hunter-gatherer horde with an average of 25 persons has many similarities with the non-human primate horde. Man has lived for 3 to 4 million years in this way and only about 10 000 years as a farmer. It is to be expected that the *norm system fitted to life in the face-to-face group* is deeply ingrained in our emotional make-up. F.v. Hayek speaks of 'innate moral instincts'. I prefer to call them 'quasi-innate drives and emotional responses', because 4 million years appear to be too short a time to make any genetic impact and because it appears plausible that — so far as our moral experiences are concerned — these norms are *internalised* in the decisive formative years when the child is completely dependent and hence has to accept authority unconditionally.[2] At any rate, these norms are coupled with our *emotional* responses. This, of course, does not entail anything concerning their moral validity.

The decisive breakthrough on the road from the chimpanzee horde to the hunter-gatherer horde is the emergence of language. Language makes tradition possible and transgenerational social memory increases the efficiency of learning because it enables man to represent possible states of affairs, and to run through future scenarios in order to reduce risks. In biological evolution there are many counterparts, e.g. vision makes possible a vicarious experience of locomotion and this brings an enormous advantage to the organisms concerned. Language and with it the emergence of abstract entities such as contents of thoughts, hypotheses, problems, appraisals, etc. make possible the transmission of knowledge from one generation to another and systematic learning. This in turn makes possible the enormous tempo of cultural evolution as compared with biological evolution. The economy principle that governed the substitution of vision or hearing for exploration by locomotion, of vicarious experience for risky and costly trials may now operate also on a higher level. Thus an organism acts upon certain expectations and if an expectation is disappointed, the organism is forced to correct its system of expectations. On the biological level a disappointed expectation tends to lead to the death of the individual. If the expectation is linguistically formulated and expressed by a hypothesis or theory, it can, if falsified, be eliminated while the believer, the 'carrier', can survive. Thus, men can let theories die in their stead.[3] A self-critical person can eliminate his own conjectures; scientists subject their theories systematically to severe tests, and those theories that do not stand up to the tests, are eliminated. In this way deliberate selection complements and in some areas supersedes natural selection. However, *the most important mechanism is the cultural selection of rules not involving deliberate choices of rules on the part of the agents.* A tradition or a routine relieves one from making decisions and it diminishes decision and information costs. When men rely on a tradition that makes their behaviour appear efficient, this behaviour may be interpreted *as if* they had calculated the information costs. *Cultural evolution proceeds by the selection of rival rules of perception and action, practices and institutions.* It does so by selecting competing groups; those groups that survive and grow are those that rely upon the more efficient rules and traditions. Or, to put it differently: a rule is widely adopted if it has survived the test of daily life (i.e. if it brings advantages to the group which adopts it).[4]

The norm system or moral system fitted to life in the tribal community is collectivist. The mobile hunter-gatherers represented an *egalitarian* stage in human social and economic life. (Even the low-density farmers as tribalists are still egalitarian.) The norm system is based on sharing and and caring, on solidarity. The group has a *common perception of reality* and a *common concrete purpose*. No alternatives are visible to the group members so that criticism of the common goals is not possible. Each member of the tribal community is subordinated to the common ranking order of needs: there is no room for independent action, no place for privacy. *Primitive man is collectivist, and cannot help being collectivist.*[5]

The practical recognition of the moral system by all members of the horde is indispensable for the success of the group in the process of group selection through group struggle. The individual is literally dependent upon his fellow group members — whom he *knows* and who *know* him — and he can survive only as member of a group. Hence, there is scarcely any 'free-rider' problem, because the expected costs of violating norms — expulsion from the group — are too high. In sum, the tribal horde is a tradition-governed sociality; its norm system is collectivist and egalitarian. The mechanisms for maintaining social order are *personal*. With their help *aggressiveness* within the group can be handled — one of the functions of the moral system is to suppress instinctive aggressiveness — and channelled towards rival groups that stand in the way of the realisation of the group's common purpose. However, so long as territory is not a scarce resource territorial wars rarely occur. The sociality is stable but also stagnant and its norm system can be replaced by another norm system only if the face-to-face group is transformed into an impersonal society, into a mass society.

1.2.2 Human Ultrasociality Achieved by Cultural Evolution: from the Tribal Horde to the Abstract Society and to the Possibility of an Open Society

1.2.20 All systems capable of increasing adaptive fit — such as progress in knowledge, efficiency, material well-being, etc. – require mechanisms for variation, selection and retention. Hence, for an evolving sociality the general problem is how to maintain social order while simultaneously allowing for the possibility of innovation. The tribal horde is collectivist, conformist, and stable. Dissidents and innovators are bound to be banished. Therefore it appears likely that a change is possible if some of the banished 'innovators' manage to take with them a few members of the original group and if their innovation proves to be beneficial to the new group, so that the group not only survives but also expands and the innovation is adopted by others. In the foregoing section it was asserted that cultural evolution proceeds by the selection of competing groups via their rules and practices: the evolution of rules through cultural selection. *The rules that are selected and survive in the competition of rules and norms, are those that offer the group which adopts them more benefits than costs.* Until fairly recently in human history, the basic advantage gained by a group through the adoption of a particular rule was that it allowed that group to multiply more rapidly than competing groups. Size was the decisive advantage in group competition through group struggle. Only fairly recently the factor size appears to have been replaced by other factors, particularly by a nation's 'possession and management of "human capital"'.[6]

The process of cultural evolution yields spontaneous orders, i.e. complex orders among interacting individuals. The spontaneous orders have properties which are not derivable from knowledge of their elements, and which could not have been predicted from knowledge about previous stages: in other words, emergent properties. Cultural evolution has gone further in differentiation than biological evolution. The structure of modern society and economy is made possible by *people being different*, and having different and complementary capacities. This fact made specialisation rational and, thus, division of labour, private property and trade have existed at least since the Archeolithicum (Old Stone Age). Cultural evolution is a gradual accumulation of adaptive recipes for action and practices 'achieved by an uninsightful blind variation and selective retention'.[7] F.v. Hayek emphasises that *for a group to be successful* because it has adopted a certain rule, practice, tradition, or institution, *it is not necessary that anybody in the group understands why it is successful* or how the tradition or the norm system has arisen. Hence, many of the basic norms had to be rationalised and legitimised by shared superstitions. From the earliest times, we find striking examples of human credulity for group-shared beliefs of a supernatural kind. 'Superstitious tribes can acquire beliefs that – at the functional level – are wiser than the individuals transmitting them.'[8] This obviously holds not only for tribal socialities. In this way, D.T. Campbell implicitly supports F.v. Hayek's thesis of the *primacy of spontaneous order over deliberate design*. Man has been civilised much against his will.

1.2.21   The institution or tradition that is the driving force underlying the development from the face-to-face group to mass society is the *market order*. F.v. Hayek proposed for it the term '*catallaxy*'. It is derived from the Greek verb '*katallattein*' which 'meant, significantly, not only "to exchange" but also "to admit into the community" and "to change from enemy into friend"'.[9] 'The decisive step which made such peaceful collaboration possible in the absence of concrete common purposes was the adoption of barter or exchange.'[10] The market order increases the chances for peace although, of course, it cannot by itself secure peace. A catallaxy is the special order brought about by many individuals – who need not and normally do not know each other – adjusting to each other, through the barter or market process, within the rules of the law of property, tort and contract. It not only reconciles different purposes but also makes it possible for members of the anonymous, mass society to benefit from each other's effort in spite of and often even because of the difference in their several aims.[11] The tribal horde needs a common purpose, but abstract society does not need any. Catallaxy enabled the group which adopted it to support a much greater population than it could have done without it. Finally, it made possible mass society. Mass society has no common purpose, apart from the purely instrumental aim of its members to secure the formation of an abstract order that will enhance for all the prospects of achieving their respective purposes. Because *mass* society must be an *anonymous* society, the mechanisms used for maintaining social order and peace must be impersonal and the rules must be abstract rules. Hence, the label '*abstract society*' is aptly chosen.[12] The legal framework necessary for catallaxy made it possible to restrict coercion to observance of the *negative* rules of just conduct and thus enabled individuals and groups which pursued different ends to be integrated into a peaceful order. Through this restriction it made *possible* a society of *free* men: the Open Society. Of course, it cannot by itself bring about a pluralistic free society under the rule of law and with limited government, but *it is one of the preconditions of a free society*. If the catallaxy is destroyed, individual freedom will also be destroyed.[13]

The primacy of spontaneous order over deliberate design is due to epistemological factors. The market order is basically a discovery system, which tells man to serve the needs of people whom he does not know in order to serve his own interest. The knowledge that underlies the market prices 'is not only the practical knowledge possessed by the millions of dispersed market actors; it is also knowledge possessed by none of them individually'.[14] In this sense each of the market participants knows more than he can ever say. Hence, for a centralised authority it is impossible — for *epistemological* reasons — to recover that dispersed knowledge that is utilised by markets, let alone to handle it. This reflection unmasks the constructivist hubris of central planning.

The market order arose as a spontaneous order which brought with it the gradual discovery that *in order to live together in peace it is not necessary to agree on a common purpose*; that men can benefit each other in the absence of such consent; and that *it is possible to extend the order of peace beyond the small groups held together by a common purpose.* In the abstract society the situation with respect to aggressiveness is similar to that in the tribal horde and the non-human primates horde and it stands in sharp contrast to that in the social insect sociality. In the abstract society aggressiveness oscillates between civil and foreign conflicts. However, in order to make people engage in warfare one needs every encouragement of propaganda and mass redirection and this can be effectively done by persuasively projecting some common purpose.

The abstract society has many advantages. Even if in the context of ultrasociality everyone is, by definition, dependent upon the functioning of the division of labour, the individual is not dependent upon the goodwill of particular persons. He can ensure his survival and welfare by exercising a function or he can buy services and this has increased his freedom. Even in the event that he is unable to support himself the social security steps in. A society based on catallaxy can easily afford to support those of its citizens who are unable to support themselves. For example, through a negative income tax — an issue which has nothing to do with taxation policies in the service of egalitarianism. The abstract society with market order has made possible the open society, which for the ordinary citizen has brought a measure of personal freedom unimaginable in all other known forms of society.

What about '*costs*'? Neither the abstract society nor the open society can satisfy the 'instincts' fitted to the tribal horde and the moral responses and emotions internalised in early childhood because they leave an emotional vacuum. Those who cannot fill it on their own will long for group membership and for the elation which we may sometimes feel by identifying with a group or with a 'cause'. Of course, face-to-face groups are interspersed in the abstract society: family, circle of friends, and so forth; but apparently for many this is not enough. The strength of this longing for the emotional atmosphere of the tribal horde is beautifully expressed by F.v. Hayek: 'It shows itself conspicuously when sometimes even the outbreak of war is felt as satisfying a craving for such a common purpose; and it manifests itself most clearly in modern times in the two greatest threats to a free civilisation: nationalism and socialism.'[15] Both are motivated by atavistic impulses. They desire to *reverse* the cultural evolution that extended the order of peace beyond the small groups pursuing the same ends and to return to a state where a common purpose is required for establishing and maintaining a peaceful order. Both nationalists and socialists are susceptible to the *'tentation totalitaire'* (J.-F. Revel's phrase), and socialists are particularly prone to constructivism.

2   ATTEMPTS TO CONSTRUCT HUMAN SOCIALITY BY DESIGN

2.0   By *'constructivism'* F.v. Hayek means in essence *the belief that social life can be the outcome of rational design*. This belief is usually taken to entail that it is always possible to improve institutions by design. It is closely connected with 'holism', which leads to hubristic attempts to implement synoptic reforms of society *as a whole*. Constructivism shares with some variants of sociobiology the erroneous belief that the instinct and the disposition needed to deliberately calculate cost-benefits are the only sources of social order. Underlying the constructivist position is a foundationalist position in epistemology (*Begründungsphilosophie*). Only those who believe themselves to be in possession of guaranteed truth about the functioning of society can also believe that design is the genuine way to solve societal problems. The more comprehensive the planned transformation of society is, the more comprehensive and perfect the knowledge of those attempting to bring it about would have to be. When discussing the primacy of spontaneous order, we have already mentioned that constructivist hubris underlies the attempts at rational allocation of resources and central planning in the socialist economy and that these attempts are bound to founder for *epistemological* reasons. Constructivism will exert a strong pull towards totalitarianism.

2.1   Efforts to Return to the Norm System that Fitted the Tribal Horde: Socialism

F.v. Hayek sees socialism as essentially an attempt to reinstall a common purpose. The lowest common denominator of the many varieties of socialism is the desire to create a society which again has a common purpose:

'social justice' and a 'just distribution'. The idea of a 'just distribution' is explained on egalitarian lines.[16] *Socialism without egalitarianism would be just a variant of capitalism.* The elimination of the selection principle in a culture formed by group selection must stop further evolution.[17] The aim of socialism is not only to stop evolution but also to return to the egalitarian stage that is characteristic of life in the tribal horde. Socialists hope to achieve this by *reintroducing into the public-political sphere the norm system that fitted the tribal horde and still fits the 'natural instincts which are the instincts of the savage'.*[18] In the course of cultural evolution this norm system was, in the public-political sphere, replaced by the abstract rules underlying human ultrasociality. It is one of the functions of the abstract rules to suppress the 'instincts' associated with the 'solidarity' norm system of the tribal horde, in the same way that the 'solidarity' system functions to suppress instinctive aggressiveness. The 'solidarity' norm system has been retained in the various face-to-face groups, which are interspersed in the mass society. However, for the socialist this is not enough. Like the tribalist, he wishes to reduce privacy as much as possible, and tends to give a persuasive definition of 'freedom' as 'social security', and of 'justice' as 'social justice'. Socialists of good will can make these proposals only because (a) they do not understand how civilisation and a society of free men have been brought about by cultural evolution and that man was civilised much against his will (F.v. Hayek) and (b) they do not understand the functioning of modern society and economy and, hence, do not recognise that a return to the 'solidarity' norm system of the tribal horde — in the public-political sphere — would destroy the peaceful order that makes a society of free men possible: an order of peace beyond the small group pursuing the same end. They do not understand that the 'mirage of social justice'[19] is the best means for destroying the market order and with it one of the preconditions of the open society. The practical results of constructivist policies would be disastrous. 'Any attempt to make the remuneration of the different services correspond to our atavistic conception of distributive justice must destroy the effective utilisation of the dispersed individual knowledge, and what we know as a pluralistic society.'[20] The replacement of the market order by a socialist-constructivist system would mean that the economy could support only a much smaller population than that a market economy could support. Moreover, it is obvious that the socialist programme has an imminent tendency towards totalitarianism.

2.2   Modelling Human Ultrasociality on the Social Insects: Totalitarianism
— *'Real Existierender Sozialismus'*

Modern technology provided the techniques of control and domination which made it possible to turn a mass society into a totalitarian system. The totalitarian state is the result of a successful attempt to achieve human ultrasociality by construction: by modelling it on the social insects' sociality. Instead of biological mechanisms it employs institutions like the secret police and the army in order to enforce that type of ultrasociality. This development was prophetically described by Franz Kafka and outlined in Hayek's classic of 1944 *The Road to Serfdom*, which inspired George Orwell's *Nineteen Eighty-Four*. A recent comment on Orwell's classic summarises his insight as follows: 'Orwell is addressing socialism *tout court*, that socialism is stasis, an atavistic fantasy destined to resurrect the past in the future . . . In one moment of profound insight, *1984* proclaims that the model for the hegemony of political evil has already been marketed.'[21]

The two paradigmatic examples of totalitarianism in human history are Germany under National Socialism and the Soviet empire. The central thesis of Hayek's *The Road to Serfdom* is that the two belong to the same family. Many well-documented system comparisons endorsing Hayek's thesis exist, which also document the *egalitarianism* (for the masses, of course) of National Socialism.[22] To counteract the effect of such studies Marxist Newspeak has tabooed the word 'totalitarianism' and renamed National Socialism 'fascism', thereby emptying the term 'fascism' of content so that the concept it designates becomes useless as an instrument of sociological or historical study.

A central feature of the ultrasociality achieved by the social insects is the *elimination of individuality* and totalitarianism attempts to emulate this. Marx's ideal of man, the 'New Man', is a species being. National Socialism proclaimed the end of the individual in slogans such as *'Du bist nichts, Dein Volk ist alles'* (You are nothing, your people/nation is everything). It dissolved the individual into the community, into the *Volksgemeinschaft*. It vigorously denounced privacy and demanded that all life should be public-political, devoted to the common 'cause'.[23] On the Soviet system Leszek Kolakowski writes: 'On the home front it succeeded in asserting to the ultimate extent the principle of the absolute priority of the state over its subjects by trying to convert into state-ownership everything, including people, their minds and memories, and every form of their activity, economic and cultural.'[24]

In the totalitarian ultrasociality the rule of law is replaced by rule of fear. (The '*Macht des Rechts*' replaced by the '*Recht der Macht*'.) The sacrifice of the quality of life of subjects of no account (akin to the ant workers) is *legitimised* by socialist.messianism including the 'mythology' of 'proletarian internationalism'. The uniformity of belief is enforced at least in the form of lip-service or 'dissenting assent' — to use Alexander Shtromas' felicitous formulation.[25] However, the Marxist historicist myth has found a receptive market outside the Soviet Union, among 'intellectuals'. This phenomenon presents a modern example of human credulity for group-shared superstition. One reason for the popularity of the myth appears to be the socialist craving for a return to the warmth of a tribal community — something which the Marxist myth promises to realise in the context of mass society. With respect to the social insects, the question of justification is meaningless. Their route to ultrasociality proved *viable*. The socialist states have proved eminently viable, but only because they have been able to remove the selection principle. With the help of the police, army, and Gulag, they have been able to maintain order and domination, and with the help of the Iron Curtain to prevent emigration. Yet, they have one societal problem which has no counterpart in Western capitalist–pluralist societies: large groups of citizens are intent on leaving these societies whenever the opportunity presents itself, sometimes at the risk of their lives. If there was competition among states for citizens, if the citizens of the socialist states were able to vote with their feet at least, then these states would not survive for long. So far no nation has voluntarily opted for communism.

With respect to *aggressiveness* the totalitarian system has been able to reproduce faithfully the social insects' ultrasociality. Whereas the social insects ensure peace within by anatomical specialisation and caste sterility, the totalitarian system secures it by repression and, to some extent, also by successful propaganda. Just as the social insects are fiercely and mercilessly aggressive towards any potential rivals, so the totalitarian system is likewise fiercely aggressive towards all potential rivals and even towards anybody who is not a fellow-traveller or sympathiser. For, *the totalitarian system needs at least the image of an enemy*, and if there is none, it must invent one by target marking. The National Socialists invented the 'capitalist world Jewry' ('*das Weltjudentum*') as their arch-enemy and the Soviet Union nominates various 'class enemies' and can always have recourse to the fiction of 'American imperialism'. In both cases militarism was and is intimately connected with and legitimised by the state ideology. The National Socialists claimed to be a 'people without space' ('*Volk ohne Raum*'). The Soviets effectively use in their propaganda the fiction of a 'beleaguered fortress' in order to legitimate the enormous military expenditures to their citizens.[26] There are convincing studies indicating how deeply embedded militarism is in communist theory and practice and how broad its scope is.[27] The military is the main pillar of support for the *Nomenclatura*. Hence, to reduce it drastically would endanger the whole system. L. Kolakowski summarises the situation succinctly: 'The new order failed abysmally in all areas except three: army, secret police, and the huge machinery of mendacity . . . by using the massive lie . . . and thus appearing much stronger than it is, the empire really *is* stronger.'[28]

3   SITUATIONAL ANALYSIS OF THE RELATIONSHIP BETWEEN THE TWO SUPERPOWERS

3.0   The most central assumption is that both partners are *rational* agents. This is an extrapolation from history since World War II and only inductivists would consider it an inference. Nonetheless it appears extremely plausible,[29] and without it no rational discussion of the problem would be possible. It is recognised that, at present, international relations exemplify a state of anarchism, in the sense at least that agreements between sovereign states cannot be enforced. Hence, the situation exemplifies what in game theory has been christened *'Prisoners' Dilemma'*. A Prisoners' Dilemma is a two-person non-constant-sum game, in which some outcomes are preferred by *both* players to other outcomes. Thus, it is assumed that both players have the same subjective preference structure, and it is further assumed that both make the same assumption about the other's future behaviour. *The dilemma arises from the impossibility of providing a guarantee that agreements will be honoured* by both partners and moreover, from the fact that the advantage is gained by the competitor that breaks them. Hence, there is no way of rationalising that choice of action which, if taken by both players, would benefit both. The classical illustration is that of two 'prisoners' in a situation where only a confession by both or by one can lead to a conviction; if neither confesses, they can be convicted of a lesser offence; if both confess the major crime, both receive a reduced sentence; if one confesses and the other does not, the first goes free, the other receives a heavy prison term.

In a civilised order the Prisoners' Dilemma has been overcome for many types of situation because the norm system upon which the abstract society is based includes the norm that agreements will be honoured, and the state possesses the means to enforce contracts (section 1.2.2). The practical recognition of the moral system of the abstract society brings advantages to both the state and the individual since it reduces transaction costs for both. Hence, this behaviour constitutes a sort of 'collective' rationality. However, in international relations the situation is different. I claim that an account of rationalist individualism which views the situation in terms of game-theory, can throw light on the present international situation. Only against this background can one meaningfully discuss what attitude it would be rational to adopt towards the 'Peace Movements'.

3.1   Stylisation of the Relationship Between the Two Superpowers in Terms of the Prisoners' Dilemma

Let us make the following assumptions about the two players A and B: the government of each of the superpowers. (a) The assumption about A's preference structure is that the possible outcomes envisaged by A are, in ascending order of preference, as follows: (i) destruction or enslavement by B (the attitude expressed by the slogan 'Better slave than brave' is not available to a responsible government); (ii) freedom and security through deterrence; (iii) freedom and security with minimal military expenditures; (iv) elimination of any danger from B by achieving own dominance. (b) It is further assumed that A believes that the lower his deterrence potential is, the greater is the likelihood of outcome (i), whereby in the beginning B may use his superiority only to exert political pressure or to blackmail A. (c) It is assumed that B's appraisal mirrors A's. If these assumptions are fulfilled, then A and B are in a Prisoners' Dilemma situation. It could be represented by the following diagram.

		A	
		no deterrence potential or insufficient potential	high deterrence potential
B	no deterrence potential or insufficient potential	3, 3	4, 1
	high deterrence potential	1, 4	2, 2

For both A and B, '*high* deterrence potential' dominates 'no or insufficient potential'. Hence, the high expenditures continue. Deterrence means demonstrating that *if* deterrence fails, the target of aggression is capable of making the *costs* so high for the aggressor that aggressive war becomes most irrational.

3.2   This stylised picture of the situation has to be made concrete by a number of considerations of the particular historical circumstances. The rationality of an action can be appraised only relative to the agent's aims and beliefs. It is a separate problem whether or not it was rational for the agent to adopt these beliefs, considering information costs, his evaluation of risks, etc. The problem situation stylised by the above diagram would be completely changed if armament became unnecessary. The presupposition of this ideal situation is the antecedent dissolution of the dilemma. This possibility is not in the opportunity set of the agents in any foreseeable future. The idea itself is problematical, because at present no one knows how to solve the problems of peace-keeping in a disarmed world, where international problems would become police problems and any war would, *by definition*, become a civil war. Phantasies about a 'world government' are not very helpful. A review of the past record of international organisations might prompt the rhetorical question: 'How long could a civilised order survive if it embraced the East River standards of the General Assembly of the United Nations?'[30] Hence, the best available option is to attempt to mitigate the dilemma as much as possible. How? The best way is well-known: to make cuts in forces without creating imbalances which would endanger the security of either side. The plausible assumption underlying it is that there will be no war unless the Soviets believe they can win it, i.e. unless they believe that the West is unwilling or incapable to defend itself. Insofar as the 'Peace Movements' create that impression or contribute to creating it, they are very dangerous indeed.

Either side can make sure that its security is not jeopardised only if there is an *effective inspection* of forces at every stage of a mutual disarmament process – 'verification' followed by a suitable tit-for-tat strategy. If the Soviets continue not to permit inspection on the site and are not willing to accept minimal deterrence – and considering the role played by militarism in their system, it would not be rational for the rulers to reduce drastically the military sector (section 2.2) – then Western negotiating positions should be designed to demonstrate that fact. Unilateral disarmament can only throw away major bargaining positions in the negotiations whose aim is gradual force reduction. There would then be *no incentive* for the Soviet Union to negotiate at all. Hence, if one aims at peace, this policy would be the most counterproductive of any one can imagine. This is what makes some of the 'Peace Movements', particularly CND, so *dangerous.*[31]

The Prisoners' Dilemma is mitigated by any policy which helps to increase respect for the rule of law and for human rights in national and international affairs. Hence, *playing down the difference between states that honour the rule of law and totalitarian states that replace the rule of law by the rule of fear can only aggravate the Prisoners' Dilemma.* Insofar as representatives of the 'Peace Movements' propose that this difference should be played down or even ignored — 'for the sake of Peace' — they make the situation more *dangerous*. Their intentions may be the best, but this is irrelevant to the consequences of their actions.

To act rationally it is necessary to base decisions upon accurate descriptions of the situation. The Prisoners' Dilemma arises from the impossibility of making binding agreements. In the case at hand one of the partners rejects the abstract rule of catallaxy and civilised order that agreements should be honoured. I can do no better than again quote L. Kolakowski, who describes what Lenin left to his successors as an ideological legacy as the 'self-righteousness of an empire that . . . by being progressive and thus always right by definition, *had the right* to conquer any country, *to break any international agreement*, and to use any means of oppression in order to establish and to expand its area of domination'.[32] It is also necessary to keep in mind that the Soviet Union excels in the use of Orwellian *Newspeak*. As Vladimir Bukovsky pointed out in his pamphlet, *The Peace Movement and the Soviet Union* (1982), 'the "struggle for peace"' has always been central to Soviet foreign police and 'peace' is defined thus: 'As an ultimate objective, peace simply means Communist world control.' In this context 'struggle' is a total struggle: every means of achieving a successful outcome is allowed. The morally-justified and self-authorised use of force is a characteristic of Marxist-Leninist ideology which can be illustrated by this memorable and classic quotation from the Cheka-organ of 18 August, 1919: 'To us everything is permitted.' Why? The answer is provided in the same article: 'Our humanity is absolute . . . We are the first in the world who have drawn the sword not in order to enslave or to suppress, but in the name of freedom.' Marxism as a historicistic theory asserts that the believer of that theory *eo ipso* is the most 'progressive' subject in history. It explains that among the outstanding properties of this most 'progressive' of all subjects is the property of possessing this insight into the necessary course of history and the recognition of one's epistemological monopoly: of being the sole subject in history that possesses this insight. Hence, with a consistent Marxist no rational discussion is possible. If he adheres to this theory, he has to reject any criticism *a limine*, because criticisms of the infallible creed cannot be anything but a symptom caused by the fact that the critic has not yet overcome his class bias or, generally, his contingent biography. This argument runs like a red thread from Marx to the neo-Marxists such as, e.g. Jürgen Habermas and the Frankfurt School. It underlies their assertion that the claim that a particular stipulation or command constitutes a 'just' law can be *founded* ('*begründet*') through 'binding or ultimate arguments' ('*zwingende Argumente*').

4 THE MODERN PHENOMENON OF THE 'PEACE MOVEMENTS'

4.0 THE PROBLEMS RAISED BY THE PRESENCE OF THE 'PEACE MOVEMENTS'

The problems are much the same as those raised by other social phenomena, namely problems of social science and history: to describe the 'Movements'; to explain the various motivations of their participants; to explain how they arise; to describe, explain and predict the impact of the 'Movements' upon public opinion; particularly to explain why they obtain an amplification through the media which is out of proportion to their estimated strength. For example, in West Germany, the estimated strength of the 'Peace Movements' is about 2 per cent of the population, but the attention they receive from the media is impressive. Another scientific problem is to *predict the likely consequences* – intended and *un*intended – of the activity of the 'Movements'. As everywhere in science these forecasts will be hypothetical, and in this case particularly so because 'we' ourselves can influence the 'antecedent conditions'.

This leads to a different problem: how to *evaluate* the expected consequences of the activities of the 'Peace Movements'. This evaluation is an activity different from the scientific activity of describing, explaining or making forecasts. A rational discussion about an evaluation is possible only if the value system used in the evaluation is made explicit. Obviously, the result of these substantive, non-instrumental evaluations will depend upon the political standpoint adopted. However, in connection with these evaluations one cognitive problem always arises: what attitude it is *rational* to adopt towards the 'Peace Movements' given certain aims and a particular political context, and how to spell out the policy implications of the answer.

4.1 What Attitude is Rational, for a Totalitarian Regime, to Adopt Towards the 'Peace Movements'?

The answer to this question is relatively straightforward since it follows from what has been said in section 2.2 about totalitarianism. The previously mentioned persuasive definition of 'Peace' suggests that, in order to interpret correctly what totalitarians say about 'Peace', one has to keep in mind that they are using Orwellian Newspeak, and also that they are systematically using a double standard. The rationale for the double standard is expressed, e.g. by the British Marxist J. G. Crowther with disarming frankness: 'The danger and value of an Inquisition depend on whether it is used on behalf of a reactionary or a progressive governing class.'[33] The acknowledgment of the fact that the KGB is a counterpart of the Holy Inquisition provides a further clue to the hermeneutics of Newspeak. 'Being progressive' automatically confers the right to use any means of oppression, to break any agreement, to conquer any country, etc. – *to the progressive everything is permitted.*

For a totalitarian regime it is not only 'progressive', but also *rational* not to tolerate independent 'Peace Movements' within the Soviet empire, and to imprison their members or put them in a mental asylum. And it is *rational* for it to give every support to 'Peace Movements' in the free world, since they can be used as one of the means of undermining and destabilising these countries. It is an investment that is part of a rational foreign policy of an aggressive power. To make this mechanism work effectively the support, including financial support, must be given in a discreet fashion, so that the rhetorical accompaniment may be all the shriller. This policy has a venerable tradition; in the instructions that Lenin gave to his foreign minister Chicherin in 1922 (which became known only a decade ago), he stressed the necessity *'to make use of Pacifism'*, in order to undermine (*zersetzen*) the enemy, the bourgeoisie.[34] As early as 1922, Lenin proposed general disarmament expressly in order to confuse and split the 'bourgeois countries', while at the same time he was building up Russia's army. In the 1930s, Hitler proclaimed himself a champion of peace and coined the word *'Entspannung'*, the German equivalent of *détente*, and supported French and British Peace Movements.

A totalitarian system needs the projection of an enemy; its imminent aggressiveness needs a focus (section 2.2). A. I. Gavrikow, a researcher at the Soviet Academy of Pedagogical Sciences, recently summarised the official position unequivocally: 'While raising young people as fighters for peace we have no right to leave out of their moral make-up an active, irreconcilable acute hatred towards class enemies . . . This is a noble feeling, inseparable from socialist humanism.'[35] The quotation again provides a good example of Orwellian Newspeak. Combined with the above-mentioned persuasive definition of 'Peace' – 'peace simply means Communist world control' – we can see that the 'struggle for peace' as the corner stone in Soviet foreign policy means the struggle for the 'Pax Sovietica'.

4.2   What Attitude Is Rational, for the Western Democracies, to Adopt Towards the 'Peace Movements'?

4.2.0   What matters in the public–political sphere are the consequences of social actions, and more often than not the *unintended consequences* are more important than the intended ones. The agents' intentions are irrelevant: *Gesinnungsethik* is not an auxiliary of political science or of politics. Sometimes one gets the impression that the 'Peace Movements' monopolise 'love of peace'. If so, this claim is unfounded and also imper-tinent: no one in his right mind does not want peace! However, the debate centers not only on differences in belief, but also on differences in attitude and preferences. For example, the Surrender Lobby of the 'Peace Movements' appear ready to humbly sacrifice the freedoms under which they protest – not only for themselves but for their fellow-citizens as well. The slogans 'Better red than dead' or 'Better slave than brave' leave unanswered the arguments of those who would be willing to risk their lives if it would save millions of others from both death and Russian domination. Yet, in this case what is involved is a difference not only in subjective preferences but also in belief. The unilateralist implies that the alternative constitutes a dilemma. This view is wrong for two reasons. Firstly, there is another possibility: freedom in peace secured by deter-rence; and, secondly, being 'Red' need not prevent one from being dead: under the Soviet regime, based on terror, an indefinite number of 'class enemies' have been eliminated or disappear into the *Gulag*.

A rational discussion of the likely consequences of the activity of the 'Peace Movements' will focus on examining the arguments these movements put forward. However, if the criticism of an argument yields the result that the argument is invalid or that some of the premises are false, then it is legitimate to turn to an empirical problem: to explain why supposedly intelligent people believe in this argument. An acceptable explanation of why a person holds a particular belief, however, says nothing about the validity of that belief. Problems of validity and empirical problems of explanation must be clearly separated in order to avoid the 'genetic fallacy'. Here I am concerned primarily with consequences, and, secondarily, with the argumentation of the 'Peace Movements'. Hence, I will make only passing remarks about the problem of motivation, about which an extensive literature already exists.

The 'Peace Movements' are an extremely heterogeneous group. What unites them is 'meaning well'. But apart from this, is there a lowest common denominator? An undercurrent of anti-Westernism appears to pervade the 'Movements'. Insofar as this is the case, they will be susceptible to the '*tentation totalitaire*' — all totalitarians are anti-Western by definition simply because Western tradition represents the opposite of totalitarianism, and the spirit of anti-Westernism goes well with the '*tentation totalitaire*'. The hypothesis of anti-Westernism is supported by the incredible one-sidedness of the 'Movements'. The 'Peace Fighters' do not seem to be upset by the fearful Soviet war-machine, nor are they upset by the prospect of shifting the balance of power in favour of the Soviets. Rather, they appear to be people who recognise power and form their policies accordingly. In the 1930s, this mechanism worked to the advantage of the Third Reich of National Socialism; now it works to the advantage of the Soviet Union. The European inhibitions against any moves that would displease Moscow provide an indicator of the degree that the Finlandisation of Western Europe has already reached. The 'Peace Fighters' together with the proponents of unilateral *détente* play down the difference between liberal democracies and totalitarian systems. They also conveniently forget the historical factor: that the Soviet Union is an expansionist power. It appears that many of the 'Peace Fighters' must be either out of touch with reality or insincere, hard left-wingers who conceal their political aims with the slogans of a crusade for 'Peace' — that is 'Peace' in the Newspeak sense of 'Pax Sovietica'. It is important to notice that members of the 'Peace Movements' use Orwellian Newspeak, for example, they have kidnapped the word 'peace' from the English language. In Orwell, the department responsible for the prosecution of permanent aggressive war was known as the Ministry of Peace. Some observers have come to the conclusion that the concept of 'Peace' is an *Ersatz*, a substitute concept for 'socialism' in the widest sense, and that because of this fact the 'Peace Movements' can attract people from very different quarters, among them those interested in Third World problems, ecological problems, and so forth. In view of all this, the rational attitude towards the 'Peace Movement' is to expose the calculated political activism which lies behind the siren song of the 'Peace Fighters'.

4.2.1   What Are the Likely Consequences of the Activity of the 'Peace Movements' for International Relations?

Some of the consequences are obviously dangerous to peace, and even counterproductive if the goal is to preserve peace. In section 3.2 three ways in which the 'Peace Movements' are dangerous were mentioned. Let me summarise them:

(a) Whoever plays down the difference between those states which recognise the rule of law and those which replace the rule of law by the rule of fear, aggravates the Prisoners' Dilemma situation and, hence, impairs the climate for negotiations between the superpowers.

(b) Unilateralists abandon major bargaining positions unilaterally, thereby depriving negotiations about reductions in forces of any chances of success, because they remove the main incentive for the Soviets to negotiate seriously.

(c) The activity of the 'Peace Movements' may encourage the Soviet Union to perceive that the West is unwilling to defend itself. If it does so, this activity is acutely dangerous. It can be most plausibly assumed that the Soviet Union is a rational agent and that it will not wage war unless it believes that it can win it because the costs are surmountable. Hence, any suggestion that the West will not defend itself increases the chances of an event whose avoidance is the ostensible goal of 'Peace Movements': a global war resulting from Soviet miscalculations. Members of the 'Peace Movements' have succeeded in forgetting or repressing the lesson of the 1930s when the one-sided disarmament of the Western powers encouraged Hitler, who also was encouraged by the false information about the strength of French and British peace movements (whom he financially supported) that was fed to him from diplomatic sources. What makes the 'Peace Movements' acutely dangerous is that they signal not only to the Soviets but also to the United States that the people of Western Europe are no longer prepared to defend themselves at all and that all they want is to be disarmed.

Hence, the rational way to treat 'Peace Movements' is to expose the poverty of their arguments as well as the calculated political activism underlying many of those arguments, and to demonstrate that much of their agitation is dangerous to peace. Thus one will reassure the great majority of the people of Western Europe and reinforce their instinctive aversion to the 'Peace Fighters'.

4.2.2 What Are the Likely Consequences of the Activity of the 'Peace Movements' for the Western Democratic System?

Some striking features of the 'Peace Movements' are their absolute self-assurance, their dogmatism, and their intolerance of those with different views. For example, they propose simple-minded solutions to highly technical problems of defence policy with a claim to certainty. The epistemological basis, if any, of the thinking of the 'Peace Movements' is foundationalist philosophy, which is particularly strong in the German tradition. This may, perhaps, explain their extreme intolerance, although it does not justify it.

In a parliamentary democracy the voter has delegated decisions about defence policy to the elected government and to parliament, which are responsible to the whole nation, but the 'Peace Movements' simply usurp for themselves the right to interfere with the decision-making process and, finally, the right to take over the handling of defence policy. This anti-democratic conduct is camouflaged by the ploy of pretending that decisions about defence are not political decisions after all, but, in the last resort, moral decisions — and for moral decisions the only sources of authority are the 'Peace Movements'. Then these self-appointed arbiters justify their moralistic aggression by claiming that it is the 'right to resistance' which entitles the 'Peace Movements' to take these actions. However, the 'right to resistance' developed in European history in connection with delicate problems of resistance against a regime that was criminal and arbitrary. So, it is an irony of history that this right was not used by the Germans to resist a criminal government in the 1930s, when they had one, while in the 1980s, it is claimed by the German 'Peace Movements' against a state and a government which has full democratic legitimation and whose decision-making proceeds in perfect agreement with the Constitution. No wonder that among Germany's neighbours old misgivings about German irrationalist traditions have been revived. For the 'Peace Movements' acting in the name of 'civil disobedience' and with their arrogant disregard of the will of the vast majority can only undermine respect for parliamentary democracy.

The 'Peace Movements' attempt to transform concrete and highly technical political problems into moral or even religious problems. German protestant pastors even pretend that they are theological issues. What about their standing with respect to morality? A striking feature is the impertinence with which they create the impression that those who are not on the side of 'peace' as the 'Peace Movements' understand it — that means Newspeak 'peace' — are either morally delinquent or mentally obtuse. Although there are perhaps a few people on the fringes of the 'Peace Movements' who might still be open to rational argument, the general climate of these circles is that of intolerance, a climate in which moralistic posturing and moralistic aggression is preferred to rational discussion.

5   CONCLUSIONS: THE FUTURE OF THE OPEN SOCIETY

In his classic *The Open Society and its Enemies* (1945) Karl Popper examined the problems associated with a society of free men and in the previous year appeared F.v. Hayek's *The Road to Serfdom*, which inspired Orwell's *1984*. The political philosophy presented in these works constitutes the best the free world has to offer as an alternative to Marxist mythology and the pathetic fudging of the New Left. The socialist-collectivist political doctrine is deeply reactionary, because not only is it based upon an epistemological position that is untenable, but above all its view of the history of mankind is completely mistaken. Nonetheless, it has found a receptive market in the free world. Its popularity and that of the 'Peace Movements' have many causes. Among them is the process of spiritual self-mutilation by young people which we witnessed in the late 1960s and which is not yet over. The collapse of the value system that young people had inherited is caused in part by a lack of confidence among older generations in the moral standards that had been handed down. However, in my opinion, one of the chief causes is a lack of insight into the evolution and functioning of the abstract society. This insight would have indicated which ways of satisfying the longing for group solidarity, identification with a group and the craving for a common purpose are rational and which are irrational, because they attempt to realise unfulfillable demands. Those who do not understand how the social order and the open society evolved, fail to recognise that reintroducing into the abstract society the moral system fitted to the tribal horde would destroy civilisation as we know it. Hence, for them a chimera such as the Marxist idea of the 'New Man', which separates the socialist vision from all sense of reality, can function as a marketing technique in the sale of socialism as a way of life.

The open society is a rarity in history and a permanently endangered species. Whether the Open Society and our Western form of life will survive is uncertain, since there is no Iron Law of History which guarantees this. Each generation has to attempt to improve it and has to defend it, both against self-undermining tendencies and outside threats. The future of the Open Society will depend upon the willingness of each generation to do so.[36] It is certainly worth defending, and many are willing to do so, not least the Russian dissidents. The 'Peace Fighters' who combine starry-eyed naivety with arrogant aggressiveness and hardly show any sign of a pacifist spirit have to be counted among its enemies.

NOTES

1. Esp. Campbell, D., 'The Two Distinct Routes Beyond Kin Selection to Ultra-sociality: Implications for the Humanities and Social Sciences' (unpublished

MS, to the published in Bridgeman, D. (ed.), *The Nature of Pro-social Development: Interdisciplinary Theories and Strategies*, New York, Academic Press, forthcoming), with references to an extensive literature, and, e.g. Hayek, F.v., *Law, Legislation and Liberty*, 3 vols, London, Routledge & Kegan Paul, 1973, 1976, 1979, Epilogue to vol. III. The theme of the Epilogue will be elaborated in a trilogy, the first volume of which, entitled *The Fatal Conceit*, will appear in 1984.

2. Radnitzky, G., 'The Science of Man: Biological, Mental, and Cultural Evolution' in Cappelletti, V. *et al.*, (eds.), *Saggi di storia del pensiero scientifico dedicati a Valerio Tonini*, Roma, Società Editoriale Jouvence, 1983, p. 393.

3. Cf., e.g., Popper, K., *Objective Knowledge*, Oxford, Clarendon Press, 1972; 5th rev. edn, 1979, pp. 66, 122.

4. E.g., Hayek, op. cit., Epilogue *passim*; Gray, J., 'The Idea of a Spontaneous Order and the Unity of the Sciences' (unpublished MS, to be published in *Proceedings of the Twelfth International Conference on the Unity of the Sciences*, Chicago, Nov. 1983. New York, NY, Paragon House Publishers, 1985, pp. 15, 21, 23.).

5. E.g., Hayek, op. cit., Epilogue; Hayek, F.v., *Drei Vorlesungen über Demokratie, Gerechtigkeit und Sozialismus*, Tübingen, J.C.B. Mohr, 1977, pp. 25 *et seq.*

6. With this proposal I am departing from F.v. Hayek's thesis that the main advantage is the group's capacity to multiply more rapidly than others, and that this applies also in our time.

7. Campbell, op. cit., p. 41; cf. also Campbell, D., 'On the Conflicts Between Biological and Social Evolution', *American Psychologist*, 30 Dec. 1975, p. 1120; Hayek (1979), op. cit., Epilogue.

8. Campbell (1983), op. cit., MS p. 42.

9. E.g., Hayek, op. cit., (*Law, Legislation and Liberty*, vol. II, 1976) pp. 108 *et seq.* [emphasis mine].

10. Ibid., p. 109.

11. E.g., ibid., p. 110.

12. Cf. Popper, K., *The Open Society and Its Enemies*, 2 vols, London, Routledge & Kegan Paul, 1945. vol. I, ch. 10, 6th rev. edn (1962) pp. 174 *et seq.*; Hayek (1979), op. cit., pp. 162 and 168.

13. Hayek, F.v., *The Road to Serfdom*, University of Chicago Press, 1944 – the classic about totalitarianism, or, e.g. Hayek (1977), op. cit., p. 48.

14. Gray (1983), op. cit., p. 8.

15. Hayek, op. cit., (*Law, Legislation and Liberty*, vol. III, 1979) p. 111.

16. On egalitarianism see, e.g., Flew, A., *The Politics of Procrustes*, Buffalo, NY, Prometheus Books, 1981; Radnitzky's contribution to Bossle, L. and Radnitzky, G. (eds), *Die Selbstgefährdung der offenen Gesellschaft*, Würzburg, Naumann, 1982; F.v. Hayek's writings in political philosophy, esp. Hayek (1976), op. cit. The egalitarianism paradox of levellers and people to be levelled with necessary difference in political power at least, socialism hopes to be able to circumvent by the chimera of the 'New Man'.

17. Hayek (1979), op. cit., p. 172.

18. Ibid., p. 174; see also p. 165.

19. Significantly, the sub-title of the second volume of Hayek's *Law, Legislation and Liberty* is 'The mirage of social justice'.

20. Hayek (1979), op. cit., p. 169.

21. McNamara, J. and O'Keeffe, D., 'Waiting for 1984. On Orwell and evil', in *Encounter*, 59:43–51 (Dec., 1982) p. 48.

22. E.g., Kuehnelt-Leddihn 1953, Schoenbaum 1966, Unger 1974, Bracher 1976, etc. References to the literature are given also in Radnitzky, G., 'Die Verwandten aus dem Souterrain. Zum Systemvergleich von Nationalsozialismus und Sozialismus', in *Sonde. Neue Christlich-Demokratische Politik*, 12:94–112 (1979).

23. This was expressed by slogans such as 'Only sleep is private' ('*Privat ist nur der Schlaf*'), 'Private individuals no longer exist' ('*Privatleute haben wir nicht mehr*'), etc.

24. Kolakowski, L., 'A General Theory of Sovietism: a Word About Dangers and Hopes', in *Encounter*, 50:19–21 (May, 1983) p. 20. The tendency to abolish individuality is widespread. For example, utilitarianism in ethics dissolves 'individuals into collections or series of episodes of pleasure and pain'; Gray (1983), op. cit., p. 20. It has collectivist policy implications. The 'critical theory' of the 'Frankfurt School' uses 'private' and 'privatisation' in a derogative sense.

25. Cf. Shtromas, A., 'Der Propaganda-Faktor in den Ost-West Beziehungen' in Gabriel, L. *et al.*, (eds.), *Die i-Waffen: Information im Kräftespiel der Politik*, München, Herbig, 1982, *passim*.

26. Ibid.; Shtromas explains how the 'beleaguered fortress' propaganda functions.

27. See, e.g., Pipes, R., 'Militarism and the Soviet State', in *Daedalus: Journal of the American Academy of Arts and Sciences*, 109: 1–12 (1980).

28. Kolakowski (1983), op. cit., p. 20.

29. E.g., Adomeit, H., *Die Sowjetmacht in internationalen Krisen und Konflikten*, (vol. 11 of the Series published by Stiftung Wissenschaft und Politik, Ebenhausen), Baden-Baden, Nomos-Verlagsgesellschaft, 1983.

30. McNamara and O'Keeffe (1982), op. cit., p. 46.

31. Chalfont, A., 'The great unilateralist illusion: "Ignorance is strength"', in *Encounter*, 60:18–38 (April, 1983) p. 37.

32. Kolakowski (1983), op. cit., p. 19; [emphasis mine].

33. Crowther, J., *The Social Relations of Science*, New York, Macmillan, 1941, p. 331.

34. Cf. hereto Revel, J.-F., *Comment les démocraties finissent*, Paris, Grasset, 1983. (Significant title!)

35. Quoted from *Encounter*, vol. 50 (Jan., 1983), p. 11.

36. Cf. Andersson, G. (ed.), *Rationality in science and politics*, (*Boston Studies in the Philosophy of Science*, vol. 79), Dordrecht, Reidel, 1984, esp. p. 11.

Part III
Problems of the
Strategy for Peace

7 The Soviet Union and the Politics of Peace

ALEXANDER SHTROMAS

1 INTRODUCTORY REMARKS

1.1 From the very day of the Soviet state's inception, the relationship between the Soviet Union and the outside non-Communist world has been, at least from the Soviet point of view, that of unceasing and uncompromising *confrontation*. Whatever form in the course of history this confrontation has taken (or will take) — even that of direct military alliance, as during World War II, or of *détente*, as from the early 1970s until recently — its antagonistic essence has remained unchanged, and will remain so until the final victory of Communism over Capitalism.

This Soviet concept of East–West relations as of a struggle to the death (or, as the Soviet saying goes — '*kto kogo*' — 'who beats whom') between two irreconcilable parties representing opposite views of the world (*Weltanschauung*) and ways of life, should not be easily dismissed. If at least one party in the relationship is seriously treating it in this way (and all the evidence suggests that the Soviet Union does), it becomes so in reality, even though other parties in that relationship are unwilling to recognise and accept this fact. Hence, it is spurious for the West to treat East–West relations as a normal, competitive relationship between ordinary nations with differing interests and goals, which the West so readily does. Such an attitude, under the above circumstances, amounts to nothing but sheer complacency and self-deception, whose dangerous, even lethal, implications are difficult to overestimate.

1.2 Its antagonistic perception of the East–West relationship makes it only natural for the Soviet Union to attach one of its highest priorities

*Editor's note: This paper was first presented at a meeting of the Professors World Peace Academy-Europe held in Salzburg in 1981.

in the conduct of foreign policy to propaganda. This is true today as much as it was in the very beginning of Soviet history, in 1917, when Leon Trotsky, the first Soviet People's Commissar for Foreign Affairs, declared after having been appointed to that post that he 'will issue a few revolutionary proclamations to the peoples of the world, and then shut up shop',[1] thus expressing in a nutshell his government's attitude to propaganda as being the most crucial issue in its foreign policy making.

Of course today, Soviet propaganda activities on the international scene are not confined to the issuing of mere inflammatory proclamations. These activities have become incomparably more complex, much more firmly institutionalised and have become characterised by the Soviet instigation of and assistance to national liberation and socialist revolutionary movements all over the world. Using the Soviet Union as their most powerful source of support, these movements have become, though sometimes unconsciously, 'clientelised' by the Soviet Union and unquestioningly promote Soviet foreign policy goals in the areas where they are active. There is at the present time no country in the world where the Soviet Union does not have a relatively strong constituency of supporters (who at the same time are supportees) and where through these supporters it cannot acquire, in favourable circumstances, a decisive influence. At the same time, this Soviet 'penetration' into each country enables the USSR to conduct most knowledgeably and effectively a truly global policy.

1.3   The direct call upon (supported by the direct assistance to) the peoples of the world to rise against imperialism, to destroy the capitalist order and to join subsequently the Soviet socialist union-state, where each nation acquires the status of an equal and sovereign member,[2] represents, however, only one aspect of the Soviet propaganda effort directed to the outside world. The other aspect of this effort, also prominently figuring from the very day of the Soviet state's inception, is the *perpetual Soviet call for world peace.* Indeed, one of the first three decrees which gave birth to the Soviet state was none other than the Decree on Peace (26 October/8 November, 1917) in which the Soviet government, referring to the continuing World War I, pleaded for 'an honest and democratic peace' which it defined as 'an immediate peace without annexation . . . and without indemnities'.[3] Furthermore, by the Decree which declared the war 'about how to divide among strong and rich nations weak peoples captured by them' to be 'the greatest crime against humanity . . .',[4] the Soviet state, in fact, was pledged to a permanent policy of peace. This Soviet pledge, certainly in terms of propaganda, remained unswerving throughout all the following years. The more irreconcilable with this pledge the practical political behaviour of the USSR on the world stage became, the more insistently the Soviet propaganda campaign would try to justify this behaviour as expressing the Soviet government's 'sacred commitment' to the defence and strengthening of world peace. Whatever the Soviet Union undertook to do on the international scene, its propagandists (the most prominent of them speaking officially on behalf of the Soviet state) would go to any lengths to try to prove that the undertaking in question was aimed at either saving or strengthening world peace. Indeed, according to them, it was in the name of peace that the Soviet Union invaded Hungary in 1956, Czechoslovakia in 1968, Afghanistan in 1979, and one can remain assured that if an invasion of Poland is going to take place at some time (which, in my view, is still a highly probable event in spite of the superficial and, most likely, very temporary 'normalization' achieved by the Jaruzelski regime), it will also be presented as being carried out for the sake of the defence of peace 'intolerably jeopardised by the imperialist warmongers'. (Soviet propaganda never ceases to stress that whatever has remained of the oppositional activities in Poland, these represent a conspiracy of imperialist powers directly threatening world peace.)

Hence, the structure of Soviet propaganda, insofar as it tackles foreign policy issues, was from its very beginning, and remains to this day, twofold: it is aimed, on the one hand, at encouraging and supporting the change towards Soviet-style socialism in the non-Communist world; on the other, at identifying Soviet foreign policy — its basic principles, historical record and, first and foremost, its current endeavours and goals — with the policy of world peace.

According to Soviet propaganda, Soviet foreign policy, in contrast with foreign policies of the 'bourgeois' states whose ultimate end does not extend beyond the pursuit of their narrowly conceived 'national interests' (in fact, the interests of the ruling classes), is a broadly conceived global policy which consistently implements, in the interests not only of the USSR itself but of the whole of mankind, a cohesive and comprehensive programme of 'peace in the whole world'. Therefore the Soviet propagandists claim that every peace-loving human being, independently of his nationality, should be in full accord and total solidarity with Soviet foreign policy — the only foreign policy in the world which is committed not simply to national goals as such but also to the higher, global goal of the preservation and promotion of peace in which all genuine national interests coincide. Thus Soviet foreign policy claims to be really a universal policy to which not only the Communists or the Socialists but all 'honest and progressive people of the world' without exception should owe loyalty in preference to the policies of their respective national governments.

Soviet propaganda to the outside world is mounted as a gigantic publicity campaign conducted on a global scale (to a large extent by Soviet supporters among the indigenous peoples of all countries) with a view to win 'peacefully' to the Soviet side of the East–West confrontation as many people within each non-Communist nation (and, in the end, as many entire non-Communist nations) as possible. In this respect propaganda could be seen as the very core of the practical conduct of Soviet foreign policy, as an instrument of direct political action rather than as mere persuasion or justification accompanying that action. As Professor Leon Lipson once succinctly suggested, 'in Soviet intention words are not expressions, but moves'.[5]

2   DISSENTING ASSENT

2.1   The profound political changes which took place in the USSR after Stalin's death (March 1953) did not affect Soviet foreign policy in any substantial way. Nor was Stalin ever criticised for the conduct of Soviet foreign policy which thus remained, together with the Party and some other Soviet 'sacred cows', free from any sort of revision. This is not to say that nothing at all changed in Soviet foreign policy after Stalin's death. The pattern of peaceful coexistence, already established in the late 1940s (and consolidated after the failure of the Berlin blockade and the formation of NATO in 1949), was further strengthened and made substantially more reliable when the new Soviet leadership agreed to end the Korean war (immediately after Stalin's death), and to reduce tensions in some other areas of the world; and although this by no means amounted to a qualitative change marking the end of the cold war, one could reasonably argue that in Stalin's time there was more cold war and less peaceful coexistence, whereas with Khrushchev's ascendency this situation was reversed. However, the most remarkable, though least noted, change consisted of the Soviet leadership's new emphasis on making its foreign policy more acceptable to the Soviet population itself. In Stalin's days there was no need for the Soviet leadership to be much concerned about the impact which its policy or propaganda made on the Soviet population. The active terror relentlessly and unhesitatingly applied by Stalin served as an effective substitute for any sort of genuine consensus between the Soviet regime and the Soviet people. This situation changed with the post-Stalinist Soviet leadership's renunciation of rule by terror and its search for ways of establishing rule by consensus. For the post-Stalinist Soviet leadership was not only keen to stabilise the pattern of peaceful coexistence with the outside world, but also, for the first time, was trying to extend this pattern to its relationship with its own population. The effort bore fruit and by 1956 a kind of peaceful coexistence between the Soviet regime and the Soviet people was more or less established too.

I see this newly-evolved and continuing consensus between the Soviet regime and population to be by its nature one of *dissenting assent*. It is dissenting in the sense that the regime had to reconcile itself with the population's refusal to take seriously, let alone to accept and to 'internalise', the values, goals and ideals on which the legitimacy of a Communist system rests. It is assent in the sense that the people were only too happy, on this 'ideologically undemanding' basis (which implied the government's guarantee for their minimal security and its toleration of their pursuit of some of their genuine interests), to accept the political reality of their country as it was. Thus they were ready to recognise in the Communist regime the only available and viable (at least at this time) authority that they had to live with and that they as citizens should owe loyalty to.

This 'dissenting assent' type of consensus between the Soviet regime and the Soviet people (which in its essence amounts to a relationship of peaceful coexistence) can be described in the following way. The Soviet regime, in exchange for the individual citizen's absolute (though only outward) political loyalty and non-interference in governmental business, guarantees to that citizen (and thus to all politically loyal people in general):

(a) A minimally reliable state of his physical security exemplified by the regime's renunciation and abolition of the reign of indiscriminate terror.

(b) A tolerant and even encouraging attitude to his efforts to satisfy consumer and some other 'selfish' demands and needs. This is demonstrated by the regime's introduction of some substantial changes in legislation to that effect accompanied by the institution of a number of new legitimate material incentives, but most significantly by the regime's adoption of a conciliatory attitude to the country's fast growing 'counter-economy' of the black market and other illegal or semi-legal markets.[6]

(c) A state of political stability exemplified by the continuity not only of the regime's policies described above but also of its policy of peace which should satisfy him that the utmost is being done to avoid war or any other direct military confrontation with Western powers and to further enhance security and cooperation in East–West relations in general.

It is because of the latter pledge that Soviet propaganda in foreign policy matters had to undergo a certain change, so that it could be more effectively used not only for foreign but also for domestic consumption.

This change did not introduce any new elements into the content of Soviet propaganda, nor did it affect its two-fold structure. However, in order to capture domestic public opinion, Soviet propaganda was significantly intensified and underwent a shift of emphasis by stressing the commitment of the Soviet government to world peace.

2.2   Soviet public opinion is far from uniform and should be dealt with accordingly. It should be first divided into two main sections: the *Russian* and the *non-Russian*, the latter part embracing almost 50 per cent of the population of the Soviet Union (and, in addition, the whole population of Eastern Europe which could also be seen as the addressee of the propaganda effort destined for domestic consumption). Within each of these two sections of public opinion, one should then further distinguish between *uninformed mass opinion* and the *informed opinion of the intelligentsia.*

The Soviet government, which is only too well aware of these divisions, has decided to concentrate its propaganda effort on the uninformed Russian mass opinion. It would be futile for the regime even to try to influence the informed opinion of the intelligentsia in both Russian and non-Russian sections of the USSR's society. When it deals with the latter, the regime uses not propaganda but either bribery (when employing the members of the intelligentsia to serve the purposes of the regime), or intimidation, or, if the latter does not succeed, sheer repression.

The non-Russian section of mass public opinion is for the regime of secondary importance. The Soviet leaders believe that as long as their policies receive at least the passive support of the Russian mass opinion and through it the relative security for their hold on power in the Russian mainland of the USSR, the non-Russian outskirts of the realm they rule are fairly safe, whatever genuine public opinion prevails there. The Soviet leaders are well aware that by trying to identify the regime with Russia they automatically alienate all sections of the non-Russian public opinion making them even more hostile to the USSR than they were before; but they equally know that the fear of Russia's prevailing strength over each relatively small and weak non-Russian nation will force them all into full submissiveness and obedience to the USSR's regime, in spite of their essential hostility to it. (One should remember that there is no unifying pattern which could bring the non-Russian nations together in order to match the strength of Russia.) It follows that Soviet propaganda in foreign affairs, as far as it is destined for domestic consumption, is addressed in the first place to ordinary Russians. Therefore, the following analysis will concentrate on the effect of Soviet propaganda on Russian mass public opinion, as opposed to all the other sections of public opinion in the USSR mentioned above.

3   THE RUSSIAN PEOPLE'S DESIRE FOR PEACE

3.1   There is one thing which is common to all Russians, from the utmost loyalists to the fiercest opponents of the Communist regime, and which is of paramount importance insofar as Russian public opinion is concerned: it is the ardent desire of the people to live in peace and to be sure that their country will not involve itself in yet another war. Indeed, if there is any political issue at all that the, on the whole politically apathetic, Russians feel very strongly about, it is, no doubt, the issue of peace. There is something very real about this unanimous desire for peace in Russia, much more real than in many other major European countries, even in those which have experienced all the hardships of the last world war. This is because the repercussions of that war are still felt in Russia today very acutely, probably more acutely than anywhere else.

3.2   I will try to explain why this is the case.

3.2.1   In the four years of war Russia lost more than twenty million of her people, i.e. about 5 million per annum. The Russians were accustomed to a continual loss of life from unnatural causes during the years of Communist terror. For between 1918 and 1940, according to most modest estimates,[7] the number of people killed in Russia, excluding those fallen on the front of the civil and other wars, amounted to about 1.5 million people per annum on average (i.e. about 33 million altogether); however during the 4 years of collectivisation (1929-32), about 3.5 million people were killed per annum, mostly from the rural population, and during the 3 years of the 'Great Purge' (1937-9), about 2.5 million per annum, mostly from the urban population. It was of course the unprecedented scale and density of the loss of life during the war that so deeply shocked the Soviet population. But even more so, it was the fact that unlike terror, which each time was directed at a different section of the population, it equally affected all sections of Soviet society and also has been equally perceived by all of them as an unmitigated national tragedy. Official Soviet propaganda has unceasingly, through all channels (e.g. the educational system), emphasised this and has managed to create, especially among the young generations who have experienced neither the war nor the Stalinist terror (but have strongly felt the repercussions of the heavy loss of life caused by both in their immediate family environment), an impression that war has been mainly responsible for this plight which has befallen the nation.

3.2.2   Probably even more important has been the character of the loss of life caused by the war. If terror killed men and women on a more or less proportional scale (whole familes of the 'enemies of people' were usually exterminated), the war affected mainly the male part of the population. As a result, at the present time, Soviet society counts about 20 million more women than men.

Here are some Soviet official statistical data to this effect:

Year	Men (million)	Women (million)
1913	79.1	80.1 (1 million more)
1929	65.3	71.5 (6.2 million more)

(after the civil war, from 1920 until 1940, this proportion remained basically unchanged)

1950	78.4	100.1 (about 22 million more)
1975	117.5	135.8 (more than 18 million more)[8]

This disproportion seriously affected and still continues to affect the life of every Russian family, including the post-war generations, and is felt as a curse inflicted on the people by war.

3.2.3   Another factor, which is still deeply felt today, is the destruction and hardship caused by the war. Unlike in West Germany and Western Europe in general, there was no post-war economic miracle in the USSR or in any of the other Communist countries. They refused to accept the Marshall Plan; but even if they had accepted it, the rigidity and inefficiency of the socialist economic system would most certainly not have allowed them to proceed with the post-war reconstruction swiftly enough to have fully recovered even by 1980. Hence, extreme hardship (starvation, homelessness, etc.) was experienced by the Russian people for an inordinately long time after the end of the war, and severe shortages of a number of essential commodities still continue. The housing boom started only in the late-1950s and accommodation is in very short supply (the rule now in force is that a family is entitled to apply for a larger flat only if the one in its possession provides less than 5 square metres per person[9]); private cars were put on the market only in the 1960s, and by the 1980s people, even if they have the money, have to wait for 5 to 7 years to buy a car; in the 1970s, because of *détente*, imported consumer goods, as well as more facilities to travel abroad, all very much appreciated commodities, were introduced, but in such short supply that they still are prestige items rather than items of mass consumption; even food, let alone clothes, remains in short supply: meat, for instance, is very seldom available in the shops and still considered a luxury item. All this is seen by the people as the result of the destructions and hardships of the war from which the country has not yet fully recovered. Hence, today the people are still struggling very hard not only economically, but also psychologically, to overcome the damage caused by the war, and thus the war is very much alive even for those who have never actually experienced it. Everybody continues to refer to 'before the war' as the time of normality and of a tolerable standard of living, which perhaps could be matched at some time in the future if a new war would not erupt.

3.2.4   Peace has become even more precious since Stalin's death in 1953 when active mass terror was stopped by the authorities and the Soviet people at last acquired a sense of physical security. Now the only real threat to people's lives and to the present, on the whole tolerable, standard of living is war. People see it this way and therefore in Russia today peace has become the strongest political sentiment of the masses. Thus the Soviet government, if it wants to avoid serious domestic political trouble, must honour this sentiment by constantly confirming its full commitment to peace, international security, etc., and by thoroughly camouflaging by means of propaganda the danger to world peace which the expansionist nature of its foreign policy implies.

4   THE MESSAGE OF SOVIET PROPAGANDA

4.1   Official Soviet propaganda, as far as the issues of war and peace are concerned, could be described as consisting of the following main elements:

4.1.1   Since, as has been shown above, the Soviet Union claims that peace always was and still remains the main pillar of Soviet foreign policy (and even Stalin's foreign policy, according to the official Soviet view, was as much a policy of peace as Lenin's before him or the Soviet government's after him), the constant message of Soviet propaganda is that at all relevant times the USSR never has been an aggressor but invariably the *victim of foreign aggression*. The facts of history that do not exactly correspond to this claim are manipulated and interpreted so that it can be substantiated − (the Party's monopoly over the Soviet sources of information is here of enormous help even for the spreading of this message abroad, let alone domestically). The foreign intervention of 'fourteen imperialist powers' in 1918–19, and Hitler's aggression in 1941 are thus constantly emphasised in order to prove the point and, accordingly, the USSR's common aggressive venture with Hitler against Poland in 1939 as well as the war waged by the USSR against Finland, also in 1939, are deliberately hushed up;

the facts about other aggressive Soviet ventures, like the occupation of the three Baltic States in 1940, the Sovietisation of a number of East European countries in 1945-8, the invasion of Hungary in 1956, Czechoslovakia in 1968, Afghanistan in 1979, etc., are distorted so as to be presented as Soviet 'fraternal help' to the peoples of these countries, who were either defending themselves from actual (or even potential) imperialist aggression or trying to liberate themselves from capitalist-imperialist oppression, or both (and it has already been mentioned that all these actions are depicted as moves necessary to protect world peace from 'imperialist adventurism').

4.1.2   The claim that the USSR has always been a victim of aggression helps to advance another official Soviet claim, also of a general nature. According to this claim, the USSR and all socialist countries are a gross nuisance to all the *capitalist-imperialist forces*, who, in order to protect their positions of power and privilege, mortally threatened by the existence of 'real' socialism embodied by the USSR and its allies, *are constantly dreaming about waging a war against the 'socialist camp' with a view to restoring capitalism on a global scale.* Thus all imperialist governments (those of the USA, Britain, France, etc.) are treated as unashamed war-mongers, who are waiting only for the right moment to strike a mortal blow at the countries of 'victorious socialism', and whose plans for waging a war are deterred only by the redoubtable military strength of the USSR and its allies. The USSR is therefore forced to arm itself heavily, to partici-pate and even to take the lead in the arms race, because this is the only way for it to survive and, at the same time, to preserve peace. The assump-tion here is that the only possible aggressors are the Western powers and that they are only deterred from actual aggression by the overwhelming military strength of the USSR. The Party bases its policies on these 'general assumptions' and increasingly indoctrinates the population in the spirit of total distrust of 'capitalist foreigners' who, if they are not Communists or known admirers of the USSR, should be treated as possible 'enemy agents', e.g. of the CIA or the British Intelligence Service. 'Although they pretend to be friendly, most of them are our enemies actively engaged in secret operations against our country' — this is the vigilant motto that the Party constantly addresses to the Soviet people. The spirit of *isolation-ism* and *vigilance* is thus thoroughly injected and an atmosphere is created in which any unauthorised contact with a foreigner is seen as a step towards treason. All this was exemplified in the gigantic 'security operation' mounted by the Soviet authorities in preparation for the Moscow Olympic Games of 1980, as well as on a great number of other similar occasions. For the last 60 years the country has been kept in a psychological situation of a besieged *military camp* under a permanent threat of attack. This was and remains absolutely necessary so that the authorities can justify strict regimentation, the absolute dictatorial rule of the Party apparatus and of its masters — the self-appointed clique sitting in the Politburo and posing as the nation's leaders. Hence, Soviet propaganda on international affairs serves also to legitimise the entire Soviet political system and the way the USSR rules the countries under its control.

4.1.3   The Soviet authorities willingly admit that the imperialists are afraid of the Soviet Union (and therefore are very keen to destroy it and its allies, e.g. by means of war if that would not be too risky) with good reason. They always openly stress that as Communists and therefore revolutionaries, the Soviets and their allies in the 'socialist camp' are fully committed to the fulfilment of their *internationalist duty* in helping all the anti-imperialist forces in the world to get rid of their oppressors and to establish in their respective countries the same sort of social and political order that already reigns in the Soviet Union. Hence, another pillar of Soviet foreign policy, already identified above, supplementary to, but also of superior significance in comparison with that of peace, is *international solidarity with all forces of national and social liberation* who are acting within the capitalist world for the destruction of capitalism and the establishment of Communism or, in other words — the expansionist promotion of Communism on a global scale. That is why the renowned peace researcher, Professor Johan Galtung, defines Soviet foreign policy as that of 'social imperialism', thus contrasting it with the traditional imperialism of the capitalist West whose motivations are not social but economic and strategic.[10]

Both aims of Soviet foreign policy, the 'social–imperialist' one and peace, in the long run, coincide, because in the Soviet official view capitalism is incompatible with peace anyway. Peace can be firmly established only on the basis of a uniform Communist world order and therefore the struggle against capitalism and imperialism is at the same time the struggle for a stable and permanent peace.

All this is expressed in a nutshell in the Soviet Constitution of 1977. Here is the relevant extract of its Article 28:

The USSR steadfastly pursues a *Leninist* policy of peace ... The USSR's foreign policy is aimed at ensuring favourable international conditions for building Communism in the USSR, protecting the Soviet Union's state interests, *strengthening the positions of world socialism, supporting the peoples' struggle for national liberation and social progress* ... and consistently implementing the principle of the peaceful coexistence of states with different social systems.[11] [emphasis added]

Anybody who knows anything about Leninism also knows that a *Leninist* policy of peace is not exactly the peace policy that people genuinely resenting war would be keen to pursue. Far from being pacifist, this policy distinguishes between 'just revolutionary wars' — wars aimed, ultimately, at the transformation of the world into a global communist society — of which it is in favour, and 'unjust imperialist wars' — wars waged in defence, let alone for the promotion, of capitalism — which it totally condemns. But not many people know, and even more do not want to know, what it is all about and are happy to swallow these 'peaceful' proclamations only to reassure their wishful thinking and reluctance to face the uncomfortable reality of the world's situation. The Soviets with their emphasis on propaganda have really mastered the art of encouraging the natural tendency of people to pursue an 'ostrich policy', which apparently is the most convenient policy at any given moment in time, whatever the disastrous results it might entail in the long run.

4.2   This is roughly the view that Communist officialdom wants the people in the USSR, and the world at large, to accept as their own and which it tries effectively to shape by its propaganda efforts on a worldwide scale. Communist officials are especially eager to make the Soviet people acquiesce to this view and thus to swallow the idea that the policies of peace and Communist expansion are inseparable from each other and should naturally be seen as going hand in hand.

The Russian public at large, however, senses the inconsistency of the official Soviet policy line. Accepting the commitment to peace totally and without reservation, it resents the other commitment to support the friendly governments and revolutionary movements acting in the outside world. First of all it resents this policy for purely economic reasons. The argument goes as follows — 'we are hungry, almost naked and badly housed ourselves and here we spend millions of roubles every day helping strangers for some strange reasons about which we could not care less'. But also, because of the 'strangeness' of these reasons, they wonder whether these policies are not undermining the first pillar — that of peace. Why should one antagonise the Americans and the West Europeans, why should one make them want to destroy the Soviet Union and other socialist countries? Is it not better to find a *modus vivendi* with them by being less ambitious with our foreign commitments and plans? This sentiment runs very deep and causes some concern to the Soviet government, which is keen to improve its peaceful image not only in the eyes of the outside world but also, even more importantly, in the eyes of the Russians themselves. Here are a few examples of how the Soviet authorities are going about the business.

4.2.1   The whole enterprise of *détente* − an obvious concession of the USSR to the West expressed in the Soviet readiness to arrange for a status quo maintaining peaceful settlement in Europe, e.g. the stabilisation of the situation in Germany − was originally conceived by the Soviet leadership as a bargain for acquiring a free hand in its dealings with China (the price that the West was supposed to pay for *détente* consisted of its guarantee of benevolent neutrality to the Soviets in the event of a Soviet attack on China.)[12] In 1971, when Nixon's forthcoming (1972) trip to China was announced and it became clear that this plan had failed to materalise, the Soviet leadership reluctantly chose nonetheless to stick to the policy of *détente*. There were a number of reasons for this decision, but among them the domestic ones − aimed in the first place at satisfying the peaceful sentiments of the Russian people − played probably the decisive role. It was, by the way, not a unanimous decision. The Politburo was divided into 'doves' and 'hawks', but the more flexible and pragmatic 'doves', led by Brezhnev, carried the day and as a result the 'hawks' (Shelest, Voronov, Polyansky) were dismissed from the Politburo just before Nixon's visit to Moscow in May 1972.

4.2.2   The international movement for peace which the USSR initiated after the war and attentively cultivates by trying to get into it as many foreign people as possible, above all prominent Western intellectuals, is another such example. One of its main domestic functions is to create among the Russians an impression that the independently-minded people of the world, if they are seriously concerned about peace, are expressing their full solidarity with Soviet foreign policy and are vehemently opposing the warmongering policies of their own imperialist governments. Thus Soviet foreign policy acquires some significant international credentials and credibility, which − in the relentless efforts of Soviet authorities to convince the Russian people that, in spite of all its inconsistencies, Soviet foreign policy is first and foremost committed to peace − are assets whose importance is difficult to overestimate. Indeed, when prominent Western intellectuals such as Sean McBride and Frédéric Joliot-Curie, Cyrus Eaton and Isabelle Blume, Dominique Pire and John Bernal, C. P. Snow and Eric Burhop, Philip Noel-Baker and Eugenie Cotton, as well as many others of comparable reputation, are identifying their views on peace with those of the Soviet government, it is most reassuring for the Russian people. The Russians assume that these prominent intellectuals, mostly non-Communists, are well informed about the realities of the political situation in their part of the world and must know what they are doing. Hence, if they approve of Soviet foreign policy, it must really be peaceful, whatever doubts the Russians with their lack of information might have. One should bear in mind that the peace movement obtains front-page publicity in the Soviet media and is presented by it as the most important mass movement in the world acting unanimously in support of the Soviet policy of peace. Although some Russians are convinced that most leading figures in the international peace movement must be paid agents of the USSR, the overall propagandist effect of this movement on the positive assessment by the Russians of their government's foreign policy is quite considerable.

4.2.3   Regular Soviet 'peace initiatives' serve the same purpose. Each year, and sometimes twice a year, the Soviet government propagates some seemingly constructive proposals about disarmament and other similar issues, or projects some unilateral steps — which have been either necessary anyway, or have never been implemented — as significant peace initiatives.

Among such 'initiatives' one should name the following:

(a) Some unilateral actions, like the withdrawal of 20 000 troops from East Germany before the invasion of Afghanistan, or the proclaimed, but never realised, withdrawal of SS-5 missiles and their replacement by SS-20s. Everybody in the West wondered why the SS-5s remained in service where they were, with the SS-20s simply being added to them, but no one realised that all this fuss about the withdrawal was mere propaganda for domestic consumption to show to the public at home how peaceful its government was.

(b) Total nuclear disarmament.

(c) The undertaking by all nuclear powers not to use nuclear weapons first.

(d) Proportional reductions of military budgets (10% to start with).

(e) Proportional reduction of conventional weapons and of foreign troops present in other countries.

(f) The abolition of both NATO and the Warsaw Pact.

All these proposals only seem to be peaceful. If implemented, however, they would gain very substantial military advantages for the Soviet Union and thus, by encouraging the Soviet expansionist drive, increase the probability of war. The acceptance of both proposals on nuclear weapons (b, c) would leave the West totally helpless against the Soviet military machine, which, in terms of conventional weapons and the number of troops, is overwhelmingly superior. Moreover, the Soviets are not even prepared to consider the establishment of international on-site control over the production of nuclear weapons. This refusal renders any treaty on nuclear disarmament unverifiable and thus void of any meaning since it only provides the Soviet Union with an opportunity that the West, because of the less secretive nature of its society, free press, etc., does not have. As for the next two proposals (d, e), they would be acceptable only if instead of the suggested proportional reductions, they stipulated equalisations. Proportional reductions always favour the stronger side, and the Soviet side in both these respects (military spending and the number of conventional weapons as well as of troops stationed abroad) is much stronger than the West. (It is, by the way, worthwhile to note that the Soviets have never proposed a proportional reduction of nuclear weapons.) Of course, even if these proposals were about the equalisation of forces, they would be acceptable only if accompanied by a reliable system of verification, which in Soviet initiatives has never been forthcoming. Finally, the proposal about the liquidation of NATO and the Warsaw Pact boils down to the unilateral liquidation of NATO, since NATO is a genuine pact, which can be either maintained or abolished, whereas the Warsaw Pact is a simple cover up for Soviet domination over Eastern Europe, which will not be affected by any changes in formal arrangements, e.g. by abolishing the Warsaw Pact.

No wonder that all these Soviet proposals are constantly rejected by the West. The Western powers are pragmatic and not too much concerned about sheer propaganda. That is why they do not care to make a point of explaining properly to the public the motives for these rejections. As for the Western media, it is looking for real news, not for reports about debates concerning some unviable proposals serving obscure, image-boosting propaganda aims. This lack of explanation of motives unfortunately applies also to the Western broadcasts in Russian and other languages to the USSR and Eastern Europe, and thus keeps the peoples of the Communist realm in the dark on the issues they hear so much about via their own media. Thus the Soviets take full advantage of the lack of concern of the Western media about propaganda and are, because of it, quite successful in clouding the unsophisticated minds of the general public at home and even abroad, by using Soviet 'peace initiatives' to present the Soviet side as a genuine advocate of peace and the Western rejections of these initiatives to depict their opponents as warmongering partisans of confrontation and the arms race.

4.2.4   The Soviets, in order to project a peaceful image of the USSR do not mind using straightforward, unashamed lies in their propaganda. For example, in 1968, they explained the Soviet-led Warsaw Pact intervention in Czechoslovakia by stating that had they not invaded Czechoslovakia, the West Germans, with the support of the USA, would have done so. (Hence, theirs was a pre-emptive strike against the aggression by the other side.) In the case of Afghanistan (1979), Soviet propaganda claimed that the USSR moved its troops into that country to help it fight against a trilateral — American, Chinese and Pakistani — intervention. Although Western broadcasts, which people in the USSR eagerly listen to, refute those lies, some doubts remain. After all, how can the people know the true situation when they are faced with such contradictory versions of the same events? Of course, they know that the Soviet propaganda is constantly lying and are quick to discover the lies when something involving their direct experience in domestic matters is concerned. But in remote international affairs it is quite different: here they have no direct experience which could help them to distinguish the lie from the truth. There are also doubts about the trustworthiness of the Western media. If the Soviet propaganda lies, why should the Western one be so much different in matters of serious concern to the West? They could lie as well. Moreover, in the ordinary Russian's view, there is nothing illogical about, for example, the Germans planning to invade Czechoslovakia. After all, they lost the war and now, strong and prosperous again, must want some compensation for that defeat. Or why should the Chinese, who are generally disliked and held in suspicion, not invade Afghanistan? Are they not Communists and do they not seek to spread their own brand of Communism as much as the Soviets theirs?

'The more unashamedly you lie', Joseph Goebbels used to say, 'the more convincing your propaganda is.' This is exactly the way that Soviet propaganda works. People do not usually think that things can be totally invented: one can exaggerate, not tell the whole truth, hide essential parts of the information, but there must be at least a grain of truth in what is said. Hence, all these lies have a certain impact in spite of the fact that the Russians are fully aware that in no way can they trust their own media. Of course, to a large extent, this impact is self-imposed because it is more comfortable to live believing that you are on the right side and your government is doing justifiable things than the other way around. After all, this is a part of the established consensus and there is no sufficient evidence around to convince people that it is not properly observed. The inclination to adopt an attitude of ostrich-policy (always asking for more evidence) is very strong indeed and it expresses itself in very many different, sometimes most unexpected, ways and forms.

4.2.5 One of the more recent Soviet lies is most characteristic of Communist propaganda and is very revealing. I have in mind the official Soviet declaration in June 1980 about a partial withdrawal of Soviet troops from Afghanistan. The Soviet media tumultuously announced this withdrawal and explained to the public that the situation in Afghanistan was about to revert to normal and thus hinted that the Soviet military involvement in this country was soon to come to an end. No doubt, this was done in response to the growing worries of the Russian people about the situation in Afghanistan and its implications for the maintenance of world peace. (It was clear anyway to the outside world that this was not a straight withdrawal, but a replacement of some troops by others — by those better trained and more suitable to the conditions of war in Afghanistan.) It shows how sensitive the Soviet government is to the shifts in Russian public opinion, how diligently it tries to dispel doubts about the peacefulness of Soviet policy, as soon as for one reason or another they start growing stronger. Since this declaration, the Soviet mass media regularly carries reports about Afghan governmental troops (not Soviet) liquidating, one after another, small (though extremely vicious and bloodthirsty) pockets of anti-governmental resistance by foreign-hired and armed gangs of bandits; thus trying to convey to the Soviet public the message that the armed struggle in Afghanistan is a rather marginal affair, which, if not for the persistent support and instigation from abroad, would have come to an end a long time ago.

Another characteristic sign of this sensitivity is the way that the Soviet authorities drafted the 1977 Constitution. I have already quoted its Article 28 and indicated that the latter's ambiguity was met with suspicion by many members of the Russian public who found the constitutional commitment to support national liberation, socialist and other 'progressive' movements in the world too pronounced. In order to reassure people on this account by showing them that the Soviet government's commitment to peace prevails over its commitment to support revolutionary changes abroad, the authorities, at the very last moment, decided to include in the text of Article 28, the following amendment to the list of the aims of Soviet foreign policy given in this article: '. . . achieving general and complete disarmament'.[13] These words were absent in the original draft of the Constitution published for a general discussion several months before[14] and appeared only in the final text published on the day of the Constitution's adoption by the Supreme Soviet of the USSR.[15] The balance between 'peace' and 'expansionism' was thus re-established and the bid for reassurance won.

On the whole, all these strenuous propaganda efforts manage to keep the consensus between the Soviet government and the Russian people in a more or less viable shape. The mainstream of uninformed Russian mass public opinion is still prepared to accept that the Soviet government's foreign policy is basically peaceful, which enables the latter to remain in control without much trouble being caused by the former, at least for the time being.

5　THE RUSSIAN MASS PUBLIC OPINION: THE EFFECTIVENESS OF SOVIET PROPAGANDA

5.1　The premisses established above allow me to give the following summary of the uninformed Russian mass public opinion:

5.1.1　There is no doubt that the Russians on the whole deeply resent everything to do with proletarian internationalism, foreign aid and Soviet global involvement in general. In this sense one could say that there is a fundamental disagreement between Soviet official policy and Russian mass public opinion.

5.1.2　Nevertheless, this disagreement does not amount to total rejection by the Russian masses of Soviet foreign policy, because they continue to believe that, despite this involvement, the Soviet government is pursuing basically peaceful policies and will not allow itself and the Russians to get involved in a major military confrontation with the West. This belief is, however, not very firm and far from stable. It is a very shaky and very assumptive belief, which, if some effort were made, could be swayed quite drastically. That is why the Soviet government is so keen to keep a lead in the propaganda war and every so often goes out of its way to confirm, as strongly and as plausibly as possible, its peace pledge.

5.1.3　The attitude of the uninformed Russian mass public opinion to the West and its policies on war and peace is one of uncertainty. On the one hand, the masses do not believe that the Americans or NATO as a whole will suddenly launch an attack against the USSR; on the other hand, however, they are inclined to think that the Western powers could be tempted to do so if the USSR was weak and improperly armed. They know only too well what a nuisance the Soviet government is and suspect that the outside world is as much annoyed with it as the Russians themselves. Although there are many Russians who would like to see their country occupied by Western powers in order to be civilised by them, like Japan or West Germany were, a war seems even to them, let alone the others, too high a price to be paid for that. Hence, every ordinary Russian is opposed to the West waging war against the USSR and probably everyone is in agreement that it will be much better for Russia to be left alone to sort out her domestic problems and finally get rid of the Soviet-Communist regime imposed upon her by her own devices. Thus the general popular consensus in Russia is for peace and against direct military interference from outside, whatever the possible benefits of such interference might be. People are only too well aware of the horrors of war, they are also quite well informed of what a nuclear holocaust would be like, and therefore rightly think that it is the worst option — one which should be avoided at all costs.

5.1.4   This leads to another consensus view in the Russian mass public opinion — that Russia should be militarily strong because this is the only reliable deterrent against possible American and West European temptations to interfere in Russia's affairs and to destroy Soviet Communism by the means of war.

5.2   This reasoning in favour of the maximum development of the country's military strength is powerfully backed up by the genuine fear of China, shared by almost all Russians, including the members of the intelligentsia. One could try to formulate the Russian consensus attitude towards China in the following terms:

(a) The Sino-Russian conflict is real, not only ideological as with the West, because of the genuine territorial disputes involved. In this conflict Russia is entitled to defend her territorial integrity by all means in her power.

(b) China is practically invincible because of her huge population. One cannot totally win a war against China even if one possesses a substantial nuclear superiority over her. Hence, one should not wage an aggressive war against China with the view of bringing her back to the Soviet fold but one should be ready to counter any aggressive move on China's part.

(c) China is a genuinely Communist country, a mirror image of Russia in the days of Stalin's terror, whatever the effect of the latest moves towards liberalisation may be. Everybody knows how determined and ruthless Communists are in the pursuit of their goals, and nobody in Russia wants the restoration of a genuinely ideological Communist regime of the Stalinist kind which the Chinese will inevitably seek to introduce and, if necessary, go to war for. Hence, China is considered by the Russians as a likely aggressor, much more dangerous to Russia than any other aggressor might be, and thus a potential adversary in a war worth fighting, as the Russian saying goes, 'to the bitter victorious end'.

(d) Therefore, Communist China, in the Russian view, is the real 'bogey man' and the only genuine enemy of Russia. There is no doubt that in the case of a direct Sino-Soviet confrontation ('Chinese aggression against Russia' as it will inevitably be dubbed and believed to be), or even of fully-fledged Sino-Soviet war, which the Russians believe the Chinese are very likely to provoke, the Russian people will firmly stand by their government. A preemptive strike against China, before it is too late, with the view not of conquering or subduing China but either of destroying her potential to wage a war against Russia or of preventing an imminent Chinese attack against her, would also be welcomed by very many Russian people.

(e) There is an element of racialist 'anti-yellowness' in the Russian attitude towards China. The Russians are proud to consider themselves to be the vanguard of the white race in containing the threat of 'yellow domination'.

5.3   The suspicions about the intentions of the West towards Russia have increased recently because of the Western association with China, which has so rapidly and so worryingly grown stronger ever since 1972. The ordinary Russians are seriously worried that China can easily draw the West into an adventurous military enterprise against the USSR. Against this background, the Soviet invasion of Afghanistan was more readily accepted by the Russian people, since officially it was presented as the first common Sino-Western venture directed against the USSR, and many people believed that this was true (in general the Russians tend to believe all the nasty things that one can say about Communist China are true). In the Russian people's view every venture like this one must be strongly resisted and prevented from developing further by showing steadfast determination rather than timidity and unresoluteness. In other words, the USA, and the West in general, by moving closer to China provided the Soviet leadership with an invaluable asset for its relentless propaganda campaign and thus significantly halted its fading efficiency.

6   THE DISSIDENT COUNTER-PROPAGANDA

6.1   The informed opinion of the Soviet intelligentsia, with the exception of those few of its members who work in the Soviet Foreign Office, the KGB, and other similar agencies implementing the goals of Soviet foreign policy, can be identified with dissident opinion. Even many officials of the above kind, those who are not total cynics (though most of them are), have to justify, at least to themselves, their close cooperation with the regime by motives that have nothing in common with the proper aims of the latter. Some of them flatter themselves that they try, as much as this is possible, to use their influence within the regime in order to defuse international tension and to make peace more reliable than it would otherwise be; others invoke patriotic considerations and say that under the disguise of working for the Soviet regime they actually work for Russia's prosperity and glory and would stop all this cooperation as soon as they felt that the regime was putting genuine Russian national interests in jeopardy.

6.2   The fields of consensus of different segments and shades of views of the Soviet dissidents on international affairs and Soviet foreign policy,[16] which are highly representative of that of Soviet (e.g. Russian) intelligentsia as a whole, are definable in the following points:[17]

6.2.1   The Communist Soviet regime forcefully established in Russia in 1917 is inherently expansionist. In the past it was committed to spreading Communism throughout the world and to working for the world Communist revolution out of ideological zeal. By now, this has gone, but expansionism remains unaffected, as it is the only policy which can assure the regime's survival and the continuity of its grip on power in the USSR itself. The Communist ideology has never been popular with the masses because, among many other propositions which were either directly unacceptable to them or too abstract and 'scientific' to be properly comprehended (let alone taken to heart) by them, it demanded from all people the sacrifice (voluntarily or by coercion) of their immediate 'petty' gains in exchange for the gains of the whole of mankind in the more distant future. Therefore, all 'expedient' ideologies capitalising on people's instinctive drives for immediate gratification, if allowed to compete with Communism, could tempt people to side with them against Communism. Hence, the nature of the Soviet Communist regime is such that it cannot tolerate dissent. Dissent is lethal to Communist rule and, hence, must be crushed or at least severely restrained and kept vigorously in check. The trouble is that the whole non-Communist world is in the Soviet Communist view nothing else but a huge continent of dissent – dissent which is extremely formidable and powerful since it demonstrates its ability to provide people with a much better standard of living and quality of life than Communism could ever dream of providing. In no way can this challenge be tolerated and therefore totalitarian Soviet-style Communism must either win, by establishing a Communist system of rule on a global scale, or perish. It is akin to what could be called the 'Dracula phenomenon'. Maybe Dracula would have preferred to live without sucking other people's blood but unfortunately for him as much as for other people, there was no other way that he could keep himself alive. The same applies to the USSR and explains the inherent expansionism of Soviet foreign policy.

6.2.2   This does not mean that the Soviet leaders are eager to wage a war against the West and do not mind risking a full-scale nuclear confront-ation. On the contrary, being extremely cautious and unadventurous politicians (which makes them so different from Hitler and his Nazis), they do their best to avoid taking any steps that could put at risk the survival of their system of rule. And after all, why would they need a war if they can successfully proceed with the 'peaceful conquest' of one pro-Western country after another, simply by capitalising on the success of their propaganda campaign backed by the constant readiness to give their full and unequivocal 'fraternal support' to the constituencies of Soviet followers in every non-Communist country in their bid for ascendancy. The Soviet leaders have the advantage of ruling a closed society, impenetrable for any outside forces, and at the same time of confronting open societies which can be easily penetrated from outside. All that the Soviet leaders need to do in order to successfully advance their expansionist plans is to use this advantage to its full extent. They heavily arm themselves and are trying to achieve military supremacy not so much in order to fight a war as in order to be able, at an appropriate time, to intimidate the 'adversary powers' sufficiently for the purpose of obtaining from them 'peacefully' all the concessions they deem necessary. They are convinced that no one in the West would risk a nuclear war in preference to meeting Soviet demands, however unacceptable these would be, especially since the image that the Soviet Union projects makes people in the West believe that she would readily take such a risk. The Soviets intend to take full advantage of the specific moral and psychological climate created by this situation in the West and exemplified by the ever growing popularity in Western society of the slogan: 'better red than dead'. In other words, the Soviets are feverishly arming themselves not with the view of waging and winning a 'hot' war against the West, but in order to intimidate the West into voluntarily surrendering to the Soviet Union.

This is not to say that the Soviets would not have recourse to war under any circumstances. Indeed, they would seriously consider waging a war, but only if they were sure that such a war did not entail their defeat and loss of power in Russia itself. In Georgia in 1921, in Finland in 1939, and elsewhere at different times, they proved their willingness to wage 'safe' wars and there is no doubt that in favourable circumstances they would do it again. However, in spite of the fact that the Soviet leaders do not intend to wage a 'risky' war, no one can be sure that their expan-sionist ventures will not get out of hand and go beyond the cautious limits the Soviet leaders themselves have drawn for the pursuit of their ventures. A major East-West confrontation could thus come about, especially when third parties would be involved in the dispute at stake, even against Soviet wishes. In 1962, for instance, Cuba was opposed to the withdrawal of Soviet missiles from her territory, and if the Soviets had taken a softer line towards Castro, the third world war would have started then. And who could be sure that, let us say, a Colonel Qaddafi would be as easily amenable as Castro was? Thus, in order to eliminate the imminent risk of war, Soviet expansionism should be stopped at once and, since that is impossible under the USSR's present regime, all those who are interested in establishing a reliable state of world peace must strive for political change in the Soviet Union. This is the unanimous attitude of Soviet dissidents who constantly emphasise that their struggle for human rights is a struggle for world peace and desperately appeal to Western governments and their publics to take their side more resolutely in this struggle.[18]

6.2.3 The Soviet dissidents are convinced that it is more important to ensure the survival of mankind (including their own nation) than to solve the problem of how mankind should live. Therefore, for them peace takes precedence over any political principle or ideological creed. This is absolutely contrary to the official Communist line according to which socialism is the most precious value, which must be defended at all costs (in other words, for the Soviet leadership it is better to be dead than 'not red'). Whatever the regime's declarations about the USSR's commitment to peace, its practical policy puts socialism before peace and this is resented by all dissidents, socialist and anti-socialist alike.

Hence, the dissident Russian intelligentsia, unlike the mass of the Russian people, is not simply in disagreement with Soviet foreign policy, but considers it contrary to the vital interests of Russia, and dangerous to the whole of mankind, and thus totally rejects it. This attitude leads the dissidents to blame the Western public and governments (as well as Western media and propaganda) for their lack of understanding of Soviet foreign policy and, hence, of how the Soviet Union should be dealt with.

6.2.4 The core of the problem of peace is *disarmament*. But disarmament is a delicate matter. One does not need disarmament for its own sake, one obviously needs it for the sake of achieving a reliable state of world peace.

The Soviet dissidents fully realise that disarmament can fulfil the same function that armament does — the achievement of military superiority by one side — only with no extra expense involved. Unilateral or unequal disarmament is, in their view, even more dangerous than armament since it not only destroys the precarious balance of power in the world, which still is the main and most reliable deterrent against the outbreak of war, but also demonstrates the lack of will of the party that unilaterally or too speedily disarms to defend itself properly. This in their view will only encourage the aggressiveness of the party that is either not disarming or disarming reluctantly and literally invites it to launch actual aggression against the 'disarmers'. Hence, one has to proceed with disarmament carefully and steadily, by equalising the balance of power and thus improving the deterrent, but never the other way around.

It follows from the above that Soviet dissidents are strongly opposed to Western unilateralism and consider this trend as extremely dangerous. They know only too well that their government will not even start to consider any unilateral steps in this direction and under no circumstances will follow suit if the West unilaterally takes the initiative in the disarmament process; on the contrary, the Soviet government will use every advantage thus acquired to intensify its expansionist drive. Therefore, the Soviet dissidents insist on a multilateral (moreover, global) approach to this problem. They want the disarmament process to embrace simultaneously not only the USSR, the USA and Western Europe, but also China, Pakistan, India, the countries of the Middle East, etc. And, of course, they totally reject the spurious idea of the so-called 'one-continental' European disarmament. They are also opposed to mere nuclear disarmament which would give the USSR the opportunity to use, unrestrictedly, its absolute supremacy in conventional military forces against the West.

The central point, however, on which all Soviet dissidents insist, is the full verificability of the disarmament process which, they believe, can be assured only by establishing on-site international control on all developments in arms production and armament processes. This is what the Soviet government has opposed most vehemently ever since such a proposal was made by the West in 1962 in response to one of the Soviet 'comprehensive disarmament plans' presented in the same year by Khrushchev. In the view of the Soviet dissidents the problems of ending all armament development programmes and stopping the proliferation of nuclear and conventional arms, let alone the problems of disarmament itself, can be radically and fundamentally solved only on the basis of established on-site international control over all these issues. Hence, without agreement about on-site control, there is no way that the processes of genuine disarmament can be started so that peace can be enhanced, rather than put in jeopardy.

6.2.5   On-site control, and thus disarmament itself, can be agreed upon only on the basis of mutual trust. Mutual trust, however, cannot evolve without changing the closed nature of the societies in socialist countries and without establishing a free exchange of information with, and free movement of, people of those countries.

The freedom of publication and speech, and the establishment of checks and balances in the system of government are other issues on which the reliability and implementation of all international treaties and mutual agreements heavily depend. The USSR's unreliability with regard to international treaties was demonstrated by its attitude to the implementation of the Helsinki Final Act, the Covenants on Human Rights, and other international obligations which the Soviet government officially undertook to honour. Hence, the respect for human rights in the USSR is seen by the dissidents as the most crucial issue which would also make all the international ventures aimed at disarmament and enhancement of world peace viable and agreements on them reliable. As one Soviet dissident observed, *détente* is about the right of people to dissent; without this right the whole concept of *détente* becomes spurious and amounts to a policy of appeasement, the most dangerous policy as far as preservation of peace is concerned.

6.2.6   The Western governments are not doing enough on disarmament. Knowing that none of their proposals will be acceptable to the Soviets, they do not propose anything positive at all. It is high time for the Western governments to change their purely pragmatic attitude towards disarmament and start to look more seriously at the whole set of problems of ideological confrontation (including a propaganda war) with the USSR. Although the West will not be able to convince the Soviet government that it should accept any of its proposals, it still can exert an influence on the people in the USSR. And if these proposals are fair and comprehensive (and why should they not be?) they can after all win the full support of Soviet public opinion. As stated above, even the Soviet government cannot remain indifferent to the pressures of public opinion, and will be forced to introduce some changes in its armament and disarmament policies in order to try to satisfy public opinion at least partially. It is wrong for the Western political forces to allow the Soviets to retain the monopoly in the propaganda war. The challenge of this war must be accepted by the West so that it can decisively win the arguments about peace as well as other issues.

6.2.7   The most important task of the Western peace movements is to exercise pressure on their respective governments so that they produce such proposals, rather than to side with the Soviets in their criticism of the Western policy of peace. The Western peace movements should stop campaigning for unilateralism and for uncritical support of Soviet 'peace proposals', since by so doing they are really undermining peace instead of promoting it. If they were to fail to persuade their governments to become the main agents for world peace and disarmament, they should elaborate independently-conceived proposals for peace and disarmament themselves, and insist on them being considered by all governments, including the government of the USSR. To achieve this, the peace movements of the West should employ the experts who now work almost exclusively for the governments and are very seldom associated with peace movements. Western peace movements have failed to elaborate such plans and proposals because they have so far been exclusively concerned with exercising pressure on their own governments only (this is what one usually calls provincialism). They have forgotten that there is another side to the confrontation which should be put under pressure too, and, furthermore, that the people on that other side have no freedom to put pressure on their governments independently. Therefore, it is the duty of Western peace movements to exercise direct pressure on the Soviet government too — there is today no one in the world who can do it for them. Hence, Western peace movements should stop cooperating with the agents of the Soviet government posing as 'fighters for peace'. A peace movement in which free and independent, critically-minded people of the West unite and cooperate with governmental agents of the East becomes a perversion of the concept of peace. It becomes a peace movement which advances, under the guise of peace, the interests of one side in the conflict, which, moreover, happens to be the most aggressive one. Instead the peace movements should establish their full independence of any government and produce comprehensive proposals on disarmament and peace addressed to all governments of the world, without exception, and try to win the support of independent public opinion for their proposals in all countries, but first and foremost in the USSR and other members of the Soviet bloc, where public opinion is so heavily suppressed and so deliberately misguided.

6.2.8 Mutual trust can develop when a mutually acceptable view on peace and disarmament is established. An independently conceived, reasonable and unbiased Western disarmament programme could become a stumbling block for any further successes of Soviet propaganda at home and abroad and the rallying point for bringing together under the Western aegis public opinion in East and West. World public opinion thus united on both sides of the East–West divide could become the decisive force which would consolidate mutual trust and generally overcome all the obstacles to disarmament and peace which today seem to be insurmountable but which tomorrow, if tackled properly, could fade away.

From what has been said, one can conclude that the propaganda factor in the East-West relationship is of decisive importance. If the Western governments and different sections of Western public opinion would recognise this fact and draw from it appropriate conclusions, e.g. about the necessity of winning the propaganda war against the USSR, the East-West confrontation could be resolved without a war or serious clash, and also much sooner than one would otherwise expect.

I would like to end this essay by quoting Alain Besançon who so aptly defined the main deficiency of the West in its relationship with the Soviet Union:

> I take it to be a general rule that in any one country at any one time there are rarely more than a dozen minds capable of understanding the Soviet phenomenon and of translating what they know into politically usable terms . . . Failure to understand the Soviet regime is the principal cause of its successes.[19]

The way to overcome this deficiency is through developing a proper understanding of and an adequate concentration on the propaganda factor in East-West confrontation by the Western public and governments.

NOTES

1. See L. Trotsky's *My Life: an Attempt at an Autobiography*, Harmondsworth, Penguin edition, 1975, p. 355.
2. From 1922, when the first four Soviet socialist republics (the Russian Federation, Ukraine, Belorussia and the Transcaucasian Federation which later was split into three separate republics – Georgian, Armenian and Azerbaijani) created the Union of Soviet Socialist Republics – the USSR as it is known today – the Soviet state acquired a form which made it completely adequate to the purpose of expanding into a world union of socialist states. The constitutional arrangement according to which the USSR, as a Union-state with an open-ended structure, was at any time ready to accommodate every nation 'communised' enough to join in (or, more precisely, to be joined to) as a member, remains today (i.e. after the introduction in 1977 of the USSR's newest Constitution) exactly the same as it was in 1924, when the first Constitution of the USSR was adopted. But if from 1922 to 1943 this constitutional arrangement was regularly put into practice as the only conceivable device to finalise the 'socialist transformation' of every nation turned this way (as, for instance, in the case of the incorporation into the USSR of the three Baltic states or, in 1944, of Tanu-Tuwa – the last country to be thus treated), it was laid to rest in 1945 (after and because of the Yalta agreements) and has never been used since. One should not forget, however, that this mechanism of direct incorporation into the USSR of new nations is still potentially operational and in a changed international situation can again be adopted by the Soviet authorities.

3. Quoted from the Decree's text in W. H. Chamberlin, *The Russian Revolution*, vol. 1, New York, 1935, p. 472.

4. Quoted from the full text of the Decree published in *Kommunisticheskaya partiya v period uprocheniya Sovetskoy vlasti (Oktyabr' 1917–1918): Dokumenty i materialy*, Moscow, Gospolitizdat, 1960, p. 24.

5. *The Times*, 17.2.1981 (Letters column).

6. For an apt and comprehensive analysis of the different Soviet 'coloured' markets and the 'counter-economy' as a whole, see: A. Katsenelinboigen, *Soviet Economic Planning*, White Plains, NY, M. E. Sharp, 1978, pp. 165–201. See also K. M. Simis, *USSR: Secrets of a Corrupt Society*, London, Dent, 1982. The efforts of the Andropov regime to change this situation have borne no fruit and receded already by summer 1983.

7. I refer here to a relatively recent statistical study of 'unnatural death' in the USSR under Stalin by a Soviet dissident scientist, I. Dyadkin (for a summary of the results of that study in English, see: *Wall Street Journal*, 23 July 1980. For a fuller account, see: Iosif G. Dyadkin, *Unnatural Deaths in the USSR, 1928–1954*, New Brunswick & London, Transaction Books, 1983). Dyadkin's is a 'modest' estimate in comparison with that given previously (in the 1960s) by another Russian scientist, Professor A. Kurganov, in his study of the death toll of the Soviet government's repressions during 1918–1956 (according to this study all Dyadkin's figures should be increased by approximately 30%).

8. *Naselenie SSSR: statisticheskiy sbornik (USSR's Population: Statistical Collection)*, Moscow, Statistika, 1975, p. 8.

9. This is the rule for Moscow (see: 'Rules of Distribution of Housing in Moscow' in *Zakonodatelstvo o zhylishchno-kommunal 'nom khozyaystve*, vol. 1, Moscow, Yuridicheskaya Literatura, 1972, p. 494); in other Russian cities the rule is harsher: in most cases the space allowed is three square meters per person.

10. See: J. Galtung's 'Social Imperialism and Sub-Imperialism', *World Development*, IV, 1976, pp. 153–65.

11. Quoted from R. Sharlet, *The New Soviet Constitution of 1977: Analysis and Text*, Brunswick (Ohio), King's Court Communications, 1978, p. 85.

12. For a brief and apt summary of Soviet policies towards China, e.g. of the USSR's preparation for an attack against her, in 1969–1970 (i.e. at the same time when the preparations for the East–West *détente* were at their peak) see R. Edmonds, *Soviet Foreign Policy 1962–1973: The Paradox of Super Power*, London, Oxford and New York; Oxford University Press, 1975, pp. 49–51.

13. R. Sharlet, ibid.

14. See the draft text in *Izvestiya* of 4.6.1977 and in official translation into English in *The Times* of 6 June 1977.

15. See in *Izvestiya* of 8 Oct. 1977.

16. With the exception of the Medvedev brothers who are 'independent loyalists' rather than 'dissidents'.

17. I shall draw here mostly on A. D. Sakharov's works which, in my opinion, as far as the issues of international politics are concerned, are fully representative of the views of the whole Russian dissident community. Among Dr. Sakharov's works specially dealing with these issues and, more specifically, with disarmament problems the following ones should be mentioned: the last three chapters (III, IV, V) of *My Country and the World*, (London, Collins and Harvill Press, 1975), especially ch. III on the problems of disarmament; the Nobel Lecture

1975, 'Peace, Progress and Human Rights' (full text in English published in *Index on Censorship*, vol. 5, No. 2, Summer 1976, pp. 3–9); 'Letter to the 1975 Pugwash Conference in Kyoto' (no full text in English; for the full text in Russian see *Kontinent*, no. 6, 1976, pp. 5–8); 'Letter to the York World Forum on Disarmament' (full text published in the *Guardian* of 1 Apr. 1976). This, however, does not mean that the consensus dissident view which will be presented below represents a mere summary of Dr A. Sakharov's writings only. Many of the issues which will be described in the following text have never been tackled by Sakharov directly and explicitly and should be attributed to Soviet dissident writers other than Sakharov.

18. One such appeal was addressed by Dr A. Sakharov on the 24 March 1981 to the international community of scientists. It is most impressive in argumentation and also provides a fully-fledged programme for the Western public to act in support of the Soviet dissidents' struggle for human rights and peace. (Extracts of this appeal by Dr Sakharov, 'The Responsibility of Scientists', were published in almost all serious Western newspapers during March and April 1981, but for the full text in Russian, see *Russkaya Mysl'*, no. 3365, 18 June 1981.)

19. A. Besançon, 'The End of the Soviet Mirage', *Encounter*, vol. LVII, no. 1, July 1981, p. 90.

8 The Soviet Union and the Uses of Pacifism

CLAUDE HARMEL

As a former editor — until December 1981 — of the Sovietology review *Est et Ouest* (East and West), founded in 1949 under the title BEIPI (*Bulletin d'études et d'information politiques internationales*, Bulletin of International Political Studies and Information), I adhere to the Boris Souvarine school; hence it is implicit in my approach that I prefer to speak of the international Communist movement rather than of the Soviet Union. The Soviet Government appears to me to be first and foremost a tool wielded by the Communist Party of the Soviet Union, which is itself at the head of the international Communist movement.

What is the attitude of the Communist movement towards the idea of pacifism? Communists are not pacifists. Just as they have never renounced the use of force within a country in order to seize power, create revolution and change society, so too they stop short of renouncing the use of force in order to achieve revolution on a worldwide scale. Class struggle, the vital driving force of revolutionary action, may take the form of a war between nations as well as that of a civil war. This is simply a question of opportunity. Communists do not subscribe to the view that peace is a supreme benefit to which all else must be subordinated. They would not agree with the pre-war 'total pacifists', who repeated after Bertrand Russell (of whom the Communists have since made so much use) that none of the evils which war is said to avert is as great an evil as war itself. They believe that there is a value higher than peace: Communism, and the Revolution which leads to it. The concept of peace must therefore be subordinated to the concepts of revolution and Communism. Peace is good only to the extent that it is useful to the revolution and to Communism. Moreover, what is true of peace is even more true of pacifism: Communists make use of it, but they do not believe in it.

They have taken over the classical distinction between just and unjust wars, but they have altered the criterion for deciding whether or not a war is just. We have been taught ever since Ancient Rome that war is just when its objective is self-defence, the safety of hearth and home, *'pro aris et focis'*, national defence. We regard as unjust a war of conquest, a war aiming only to establish or to extend the domination of a state over a foreign people, when the law of nations provides no justification for establishing such domination.

For the Communists, a just war is one which enables a people to free itself from capitalism, a war of liberation, a war fought for justice. This vague and elastic definition quickly became very specific: the camp with justice on its side is the one which includes the Soviet Union, the land of Socialism. The other is the camp of injustice and of unjust war.

There has been at least one example of this morality being applied to a specific situation and this was during the World War II by the French Communist Party, one of the most Stalinist parties in the world. At the beginning of the war, the French Communist Party considered it to be a war between imperialists, in which the working classes were not involved and in which they should therefore not take part. They should only seek to take advantage of the circumstances in an attempt to overthrow their own State and their own capitalism. The reason for this was that the Soviet Union was neutral (ostensibly, at least; in reality, it was assisting Germany). After 21 June 1941, on the other hand, the war became a just one. The Communists took part in it and joined the Resistance because, from that point on, the future of the Soviet Union was at stake.

We may therefore take as our starting-point this basic concept: Communists are not pacifists. They make use of peace and of pacifism when it is to their advantage, but they make use of war as well when it is necessary. War may be revolutionary. War may serve the revolution. To Communists, in other words, only one thing matters about both war and peace and that is to what extent they serve revolutionary action, the seizure of power, the expansion of the Communist empire and world revolution.

A digression is needed here. Because war and peace are to them only a means to an end, Communists have never liked *conscientious objection*, the most exalted form of pacifist feeling. Conscientious objection is an individual and personal act, and this runs counter to the Communist concept of action, which must be collective, and determined, directed and controlled by the Party. Conscientious objection is the assertion of one personality against the group, and as such is diametrically opposed to the Communist mentality and Communist philosophy.

Moreover, even if it happens that some conscientious objectors are singled out and used for propaganda purposes, a good Communist militant is not a conscientious objector. He takes Lenin's advice: 'You will be a soldier! You will join the army and learn how to handle weapons so that, when the time comes, you can turn them against your real enemies, who are in your own country, who are the capitalists and not the proletarians you will find opposite you in a war between nations.' The militant's presence in the army also makes it possible to weaken the cohesion of that army and to prevent it from acting as an instrument of oppression or repression at national level.

There are several ways of using war for revolutionary ends. There is the war of liberation, which, as Robespierre put it, brings freedom on the tips of bayonets. Examples of this may be seen in the history of the Soviet Union: in 1920, the Communists attempted to bring freedom and Socialism to Poland – on the tips of bayonets – and the Red Army reached Warsaw. In recent times, too, the Communists have not hesitated to use war for creating revolution and exporting Socialism, in Afghanistan, Vietnam and elsewhere.

A second revolutionary use of war is revolutionary defeatism and the conversion of an international war into a civil war. There is some truth in Lenin's remark that, when there is a war, the government of the country beaten by a foreign army is weakened, and from that point on it becomes easier to create revolution. It is easier to take over power when those who hold it are discredited. After all, the French Republic was born, on 4 September 1870, of the defeat at Sedan and of the resulting unpopularity and weakness of the Imperial Government. One could give many more examples.

Thirdly and finally, war between nations destabilises the established world order and thereby creates opportunities for revolution. This is an old idea, voiced by numerous political and social revolutionaries of the 19th century, and then taken up by the Communists for their own ends. At the last Communist Party Congress to be attended by Stalin, held in October 1952, Malenkov recalled that the World War I had seen the birth, in the USSR, of the first Socialist State; that the Second World War had brought the expansion of Socialism to all the countries of Eastern Europe; and that, in a third world war, Socialism would surely spread still wider. Given this idea, it is impossible to reject all war *a priori*, since war may assist the creation of Socialism. Soviet and Western Communists have not gone as far as Mao Tse Tung, who declared that a good nuclear war would usher in Socialism, but they lean in this direction nevertheless. In any event, Stalin's *Economic Problems of Socialism in the USSR* — his last doctrinal work, published in 1952 and hailed at the time as a masterpiece of political thought — contains a chapter entitled *Inevitability of Wars between Capitalist Countries*.

Here, Stalin writes:

> Some comrades hold that, owing to the development of new international conditions since the Second World War, wars between capitalist countries have ceased to be inevitable. They consider that the contradictions between the socialist camp and the capitalist camp are more acute than the contradictions among the capitalist countries; . . . that the foremost capitalist minds have been sufficiently taught by the two world wars and the severe damage they caused to the whole capitalist world not to venture to involve the capitalist countries in war with one another again. . . . These comrades are mistaken . . . It is said that the contradictions between capitalism and socialism are stronger than the contradictions among the capitalist countries. Theoretically, of course, that is true. It is not only true now, today; it was true before the Second World War. And it was more or less realised by the leaders of the capitalist countries. Yet the Second World War began not as a war with the USSR, but as a war between capitalist countries.

And Stalin explains further that:

> capitalist Britain, and, after her, capitalist France, will be compelled in the end to break from the embrace of the USA and enter into conflict with it in order to secure an independent position and, of course, high profit.

and

> to think that the major vanquished countries, Germany (Western) and Japan, will not try to get on their feet again, will not try to smash the US 'regime' and force their way to independent development, is to believe in miracles.

So, Stalin is speculating here about the rekindling of nationalism, especially in Germany and Japan; so sure is he of his ability to use the 'contradictions' between the capitalist countries to bring about a war between them that he ends the chapter thus: 'the inevitability of wars will . . . continue in force'. And he was firmly convinced that a war between the capitalist countries would make possible a further expansion of the Communist empire.

It is clear, then, that Communists throughout the world — and in particular those who lead the Soviet Union — do not reject all war *a priori* as war may be useful to the revolution.

Communists, then, are not pacifists; however, they are not warmongers either. They do not want war regardless of the cost. Just as they find some of the moral values of pacifism repugnant, so too they find some of the moral values of war disconcerting and alarming; in particular, devotion to the fatherland must not be allowed to prevail over devotion to the Party. Moreover, while defeat in war weakens power, victory in war may create a potential threat to the true, political, power in the form of military power. Even in democracies, victorious military men have always been feared; they are showered with laurels and accolades, but care is taken to make them keep their distance. In France, Foch after the First World War is an example. Similarly in the USSR, victorious marshals have been showered with medals, titles and material advantages, but they have always been regarded with suspicion, as the popularity achieved by a military leader might enable him to oppose the political power of the Communists.

This has even been observed in the French Communist Party. After 1949, Thorez eliminated from the Party leadership all those who had gained a measure of reputation or popularity in the Resistance. For one thing, there was no certainty that the struggle against the Germans had not kindled a measure of French patriotism in the Communists, and for this reason it was feared that they might put *Patrie* before Party should the day come again when they would be forced to make that choice.

A second factor was that, by admitting men who were not Communist militants into the Resistance forces, these militants had acquired in the public mind a stature, a popularity, and a political following which they did not owe to their membership of the French Communist Party; a following which was partly drawn from outside the Party and its own following. Even if in their heart of hearts they were still good Communists, might it not follow that they were, objectively, already traitors? They could attract devotees and continue in politics even if the Party expelled them. Hence they had the potential for autonomy, a basis for independence from the Party. Therefore, they were no longer fully reliable. It would be better to remove them from positions of leadership.

It should be added that war is always hazardous, and Communists only take it on when the forces involved are so unequal that they believe there is no risk of losing. This is probably a typically Stalinist characteristic. Souvarine has often quoted (e.g. in the new 1977 Champ Libre edition of his monumental *Stalin*) Hitler's remark to Marshal Antonescu, the Rumanian leader:

> Stalin was not a man to take risks. Poland is a typical example: in spite of the appeal from Germany, he did not order his units to advance until there was no danger in becoming involved. . . . Even if he had a revolver and his enemy was only armed with a knife, he would wait until the enemy had fallen asleep: he is a Goliath who is afraid of David. (Op. cit., p. 585)

Such caution is typical of Stalin, and it is typical of the Communists as well. Perhaps it derives from their materialist convictions on historical development: situations develop of themselves and human intervention should only take place when the time is ripe, only a gentle push being needed for everything to collapse. If resistance is met, this means that things are not ready. The USSR climbs down each time Western governments react to its initiatives and threats with a degree of determination. It does not give up – but it waits for a better opportunity before beginning again.

Communists, then, are neither pacifists nor warmongers. They use war as they use peace, whenever they hope to gain from it.

I should like to add a rider here: Soviet imperialism is not to be confused with Russian imperialism, as our politicians all too often do. There was, and perhaps still is, such a thing as Russian imperialism, but, if it still exists, it now has no will of its own. It is now only a tool wielded by Communist power and intended to create revolution in the world. We should never forget that the Russian people are the first victims of Communism. The Communists took hold of them, and they control them by means of any device which can control a people, including its national tradition and its imperialism if such a thing exists. This is useful for domestic purposes. It is also useful abroad, as it serves to camouflage the true nature of Soviet imperialism, which has but one aim: not to extend Russian power across the world, but to export Communist revolution throughout the globe, because, while 'Socialism in one country' may be possible, 'Communism in one country' is not. Khrushchev and Brezhnev have said as much on numerous occasions: 'Communism can be fully achieved in one country only if it is achieved worldwide.' In particular, the withering away of the State prophesied by Marx and Engels can only come about when there is no longer any possibility of conflicts between nations.

The Marxist—Leninists of the Kremlin thus see a link between the success of Communist construction in the USSR and the spread of Communism in the world. For this reason they never leave other countries of the world alone, but give at least moral and material aid — if they can do nothing more — to the Communist parties operating in each country.

How do the Communists seek to make use of pacifist feeling and turn it into one of their main weapons of war?

There are two main ways of using pacifism: the use of the organisations which represent it, and the use of spontaneous movements.

The Communists have a deep-rooted preference for organisations, as they are still greatly influenced by Lenin's dictum that 'spontaneity does not exist', and they always distrust spontaneous movements although they have learnt to manipulate them and take control of them. They prefer to operate through an apparatus or organisation, however, even when manipulating spontaneous movements. The Communist Party cannot operate by itself. This is a basic concept of Sovietology: a Communist party is a minority party, because it is tightly organised and submits to the discipline of democratic centralism, which cannot be imposed on the broad masses. It follows that the party cannot by itself rally a mass movement capable of breaking the established regimes. Were it to put itself at the head of such a movement, there would soon be nobody to lead. Its connotations of Communist revolution are too strong for it to command the support of pacifist or other movements.

In Lenin's concept of the revolutionary apparatus, this apparatus is headed by a central Party, surrounded by a whole variety of organisations indirectly dependent on it; these are known to Anglo-Saxon Sovietologists as 'front organisations' and to the French as 'satellite organisations', but it is preferable to keep the name given to them by the Communists: 'mass organisations'. These are non-Communist organisations whose aims vary greatly from one to another, and which can command the support of the masses on the strength of those aims: workers' demands in the trade unions, pacifist demands in the peace movements, tenants' grievances in a tenants' association, etc. The list could go on. Everything has its use. Any organisation which can mobilise the people is a mass organisation. It is a Communist principle to infiltrate and attempt to seize control of organisations capable of mobilising the people, regardless of the aims of those organisations.

One example in France is almost comical. The movement known as MODEF (*Mouvement de défense des exploitations familiales*, Family

Farms Defence Movement) existed to defend small *private* farms run as *family* businesses, which is the exact opposite of Communist thinking on the matter. After 2 or 3 years the Communists managed to seize it, and the Communist peasant organisation which now supports a Communist Party pressing for the collectivisation of land is the same one which originally defended the interests of small farmers. Small farmers are hostile to the agrarian reform under which, since the early 1950s, farms have been growing larger while still remaining family businesses, and many farms too small to support a modern way of life have been disappearing, causing the very small farmers to feel themselves threatened; this is the source of the discontent of which the Communists make use despite the fact that it is the opposite of a demand for social ownership of land. The Communists, however, will seize any movement as long as it appears to them capable of mobilising the people.

It may be said that, wherever there is an organisation of any sort, there is a Communist attempt to take control of it. In the past, some movements, organisations and institutions put up great resistance to Communist infiltration. I am thinking in particular of the churches, and also of the Social Democrats, who for a long time warded off Communist infiltration. What has now become of the churches is a matter of record, and, looking at the present-day international policy of the Socialist International, one is forced to wonder whether it might not be the result of the infiltration of Communist elements into its ranks.

Which are the mass organisations through which the Communists attempt to make use of pacifist ideology, and where do they come from? Sometimes they are purpose-built by the Communists, but this is the least satisfactory method. Sometimes the Communists will seize an already existing organisation which has gained popularity through its own actions and put down roots in a section of public opinion. This is much better. The classic example of this technique is the French *Confédération Générale du Travail* (CGT, General Confederation of Labour). Founded in 1895, it had been in existence for 25 years before the Communist Party was set up in 1920, and the Communists took three attempts and 26 years to gain control of it. It was a political masterpiece: Machiavellian, true, but a masterpiece nonetheless.

There was a well-known and firmly established organisation with support among all occupational groups. Rather than set up a new organisation bearing their own stamp, which nobody would have joined, the Communists seized the old reformist organisation so as to harness it to Communist ideology.

The Communists did not altogether create the Peace Movement, in

France and abroad, out of nothing. A small movement of peace campaigners had been founded shortly before the Communists got their hands on it in late 1947. However, in France, the Peace Movement is entirely in the hands of the Communist Party.

In these mass organisations, sometimes in positions of leadership and often even in the most visible (but least influential) posts, such as that of chairman, there are always 'fellow-travellers', some quite innocent and some less so, who are known to the Communists as 'useful idiots'. These are the ones who are placed up front, where they find a gratifying sense of popularity and a ready supply of listeners and ovations (to which intellectuals are very partial). While the great majority of the rank and file of these organisations are not Communists, all the influential positions of leadership are held by Communists: between 85 per cent and 90 per cent in the CGT and a similar proportion in the Peace Movement. Even so, it is true that several events have caused ripples in the French Peace Movement. A number of fellow-travellers have found certain Soviet actions very hard to swallow – Afghanistan, for example, but it has all been sorted out fairly quickly: the Party has quickly regained control and consolidated its momentarily dented power.

Other organisations are only 50 per cent, 40 per cent or 30 per cent infiltrated, but the Communists make their presence felt despite being a minority, because the 'faction' which makes up this presence provides a hard core and a strong and unfailing resolve with solid backing from outside. Finally, there are many movements with non-Communist objectives and where the majority is anything but Communist, which have a small minority of Communists who have not seized power, but who are nevertheless in a position to act and to put the movement's policy off course. One sometimes looks like an anti-Soviet fanatic when one denounces some movement or other which is, objectively, serving Soviet policy, but which can in no sense be said to espouse the ideology or even the interests of the USSR. However, it is rarely a coincidence when a movement's actions conform with Soviet interests; often it is because there is a cell within the movement, more often than not invisible, but strong enough to direct overall policy.

A long-hidden Communist presence is now coming to light in a great many present-day French Catholic movements. There are a dozen Communist Party members on the Steering Committee of *Jeunesse Ouvrière Catholique* (JOC, Young Catholic Workers). That is quite extraordinary. These Communists definitely have an influence out of all proportion to their number; their influence is strengthened by the fact that this is a tightly structured group with clearly defined objectives and outside inspiration and support. It is a basic principle that a cell set up in a mass organisation must retain very close ties with the Party; otherwise, it might be 'cut off' by the mass organisation and end by supporting that organisation's interests while neglecting those of the Party which do not coincide with them.

This is not the place to examine in depth the methods used by the Communists, sometimes almost invisibly, to achieve their domination of a mass organisation, but nobody who has not studied those methods can claim to be a serious observer of national or international politics.

The Communists also make use of spontaneous movements, for such movements do of course exist. The movements I have in mind are those which have not been even indirectly inspired by Communists; movements which are sometimes created, not by parties or organised groups, but simply by private individuals acting on their own initiative, out of deep personal conviction or feeling. The Communists will attempt to make use of these movements, too, as soon as they become at all substantial.

At this point, a reply must be given to an objection which is well founded, but does not take sufficient account of the realities of Soviet propaganda and Communist methods of action.

At another conference, on the subject of neutralism, somebody took issue with what seemed to him to be a sort of obsessive fear afflicting those who see the hand of the Soviets everywhere. The gist of what he said was, 'Merely because Committees against the Vietnam War sprang up in a particular period in the United States — at one point there were hundreds of them — there is no reason to suspect the NKVD of being behind each one'. As I have said before, it is perfectly true that there are a great many organisations which do arise spontaneously, and which have nothing to do with the Communists at the outset, even if one or two of their objectives are the same as those of the Communists. Such parallelism is not in itself any proof of dependence. However, if there really is this parallelism, and if the association survives and grows, then the Communists will attempt to get their hands on it, to seize it. They will do this even where there is nothing to be gained, where the association does its job well, because they are ruled by their distrust of spontaneity, a sort of ideological quirk which makes them afraid that the association might escape or collapse unless it is given the structure of a mass organisation and covertly governed by the Party.

My next observation is crucial. Public opinion, both national and international, is profoundly influenced by Communist propaganda, and this influence is more often than not unsuspected by its victims. Many people are influenced without being aware of it, and therefore their actions, which they believe to be 'spontaneous', are nevertheless inspired from outside.

This point must be taken further. The Communist ideal and Communist thought are in very pronounced decline in intellectual circles and even elsewhere. This does not prevent the USSR and the world Communist movement from constituting a force of the first magnitude. It is a law of social physics that any force exerts an attraction. It follows that when the established order is destabilised in some part of the Western world (and unfortunately there is often every reason to challenge that established order) the destabilisation almost always serves the Soviet Union. This can give rise to crises of conscience. In Latin America, for example, there are political regimes which it is morally impossible to condone, yet it is more or less certain that if they are overthrown, even by democrats or liberals, nine times out of ten it will be to the advantage of Soviet policy. Thus we are often obliged to defend or protect systems which we disown or which are repugnant to us, because it would be still worse both domestically and internationally if those governments were to be overthrown.

Such is the power of Soviet propaganda in all its forms, then, that the Communist movement is able to make use of spontaneous movements of all sorts and even those which are hostile to it. Twenty years ago I allowed myself the flippancy of writing that Communism was the art of using discontent of whatever kind, and that if there existed an anti-Communist mass movement, the Communists would attempt to infiltrate it and to use it as a means of coming to power and creating the Communist revolution. Can they not from time to time be seen attempting to make use of anti-Stalinism? Do they not now call themselves anti-Stalinists, while continuing to act exactly as in the past?

Therefore, whenever one sees a movement working along the lines of Soviet policy, it is both one's duty and one's right, without worrying about being accused of having a warped mind, straight away to look, firstly for signs of Communist infiltration, and secondly for signs of the indirect ideological influence of the Communists on the movement.

I should like to make two final points. In contrast to the traditional pacifist movements, which, to use an excessively contemptuous phrase of that time, used to 'bleat for peace' and demand peace, period, as an end in itself and a supreme benefit, the Communists (whether operating directly or through the Peace Movement) are at pains to make the pacifist demand into something concrete, specific and precise on the one hand, and unilateral on the other. The demand does not remain in the abstract. It applies to a very concrete reality. Calls are made for action against the war in Indochina, against the atom bomb, against the Euromissiles. Participants thus feel that their action has a clearly defined point of application and that it is possible to achieve real and measurable results. On the other hand, the demand is always unilateral. It is directed against the actions of those who are not in the Soviet camp but in the other part of the world; directed against their actions or against the intentions attributed to them.

During the first three or four years of its existence, the post-World War II Peace Movement took the form of the 'Stockholm Appeal' and the struggle against the atom bomb. So what was this struggle, so brilliantly stage-managed, which made dupes of millions? It served to create a smoke-screen around what was going on in the USSR, so as to give the Soviets time to build their own atom bomb. The real aim of the Stockholm Appeal against the Bomb was the creation of a nuclear weapon in the USSR. I can still remember the disappointment and confusion of some supporters of peace, who had responded to the Stockholm Appeal with all the sincerity in the world, when they learnt of the first nuclear explosion in the USSR.

A similar phenomenon may be observed today. Those who campaign against Pershing missiles forget to campaign against the SS-20s. It sometimes happens – and the Communists tolerate it because it has its uses also – that some pacifist militant says that he is demonstrating against Pershing and SS-20 missiles at the same time; this argument was even used on one occasion by Mrs Deferre when speaking to journalists. Unfortunately a demonstration in Paris against Soviet missiles has no influence at all on the Soviet Government. It can therefore be allowed to happen. In recent times we have even had the comical sight of a peace march to the USSR organised by three or four hundred women from Northern Europe – Germany, Sweden, Norway and Finland. They crossed western Russia watchfully hemmed in by militants of the Soviet Peace Committee. However, there is a dissident Peace Committee whose members have been imprisoned; this one is not tolerated, while the official one was.

Permit me to end on a somewhat personal note.

I willingly acknowledge that not all the elements which comprise pacifism are of a high moral value. Some of them can even be quite mediocre. For this reason I am not an adherent of systematic idealisation in this respect. Nevertheless, I think I can say that some of the highest values in which I personally believe are also embodied in the pacifist movement. Communism has got its hands on it, and made a lie of the pacifist idea, which is one of those which require the most sincerity. It is truly painful for some of those who believe in peace to see that the most visible Peace Movements are dishonest to the core and profoundly distorted by Communist infiltration. In short, the Communists have acted in such a way that they have cast suspicion on the very word pacifism, so that genuine pacifists have come to the point where, when they hear the word spoken, they instantly react with distrust or hostility.

9 Threats to the Security of Europe

PIERRE GALLOIS

The different political threats which weigh upon the West have been set out and discussed elsewhere. My task is to address the question of military threats. These are a function of Moscow's intended international policy, of the degree of determination shown in putting this policy into effect and in seeing it through to completion, as well as of the nature and scope of Soviet armed forces.

1 MILITARY MEANS

The Soviet Union possesses the entire range of both modern conventional and nuclear weapons. It could destroy 7000 to 8000 targets in the western hemisphere and about that many in peripheral areas, that is non-Soviet Eurasia, the Middle East and a large proportion of the African continent. Obviously, this threat extends to the peninsulas, the archipelagos and all the oceans: the Arctic, Pacific, Indian and Atlantic. The Soviet submarine fleet is numerically the largest in the world, the Soviet surface fleet is the most modern, Soviet combat aircraft are powerful and Soviet strategic transport capabilities have already been proved, most notably during the period when Cuban volunteers were used to sustain military operations in Africa.

Russia has built up her military forces as circumstances demanded and has progressively mastered all the most effective arms techniques as they have been developed.

Initially, in the period after the Second World War, Russia retained and developed the vital conventional forces which had served first to defend Russian soil, then to drive the invader back as far as Berlin. As we know, the United States and Great Britain, on the other hand, lost no

171

time in demobilising. The Soviet Union, having thus secured the means of containing any enemy which might appear on the edges of the Eurasian continent, then progressively strove to match nuclear weapons developments in the United States.

At the start of the century, geopoliticians maintained that Russia held one of the few militarily inaccessible geographical zones. They called this zone the 'pivot of the World'. This refers approximately to the vast spaces running from the area north of Eurasia to the Urals. It is true that at that time these territories were not militarily accessible by land or sea. When the Allies' victory over the Third Reich conferred the role of superpower upon both the United States and Russia, it was clear that the Soviet Union, occupying this sort of position and having considerable armed forces, could become the world's major military power. However, this was without counting the strategic aircraft which had enabled the United States to defeat Japan. The first atomic bombs combined with American long-range bombers made this hitherto invincible 'pivot of the World' vulnerable to attack. Consequently, the United States government concentrated its efforts on developing a powerful strategic air force which would enable the United States to keep the Soviet Union, with its impressive conventional forces, at a respectful distance. If Soviet conventional forces were deployed in a regional or continental capacity, they could be brought to a standstill by the fear of an American strategic response at the very heart of the Soviet Union.

From Moscow's point of view, therefore, it was absolutely essential to be able to match a US advantage of this sort. In 1949, the first experimental Soviet atomic bomb was exploded and steps were taken to construct a long-range bomber. Later, as a result of developments in arms technology, ballistic missiles, launched from land-based silos and from diesel-propelled and later from nuclear-powered submarines, took the place of the air force, which from then on formed a relatively small part of Soviet strategic forces. It can be said that, by the late 1960s, the Russians had succeeded in achieving their aim: they had managed to neutralise American strategic nuclear forces. Since then, the inventory of Soviet strategic forces has continued to grow both in number and in effectiveness. Today, their destructive potential is nearly three times that of the United States (approximately 6700 megatons as opposed to 2600). However, the number of targets which could be reached is about the same for either side.

The third aim of the Soviet planners was to transform the coastal fleet of a state in which there had been little maritime tradition into a major ocean-going fleet. This transformation took place from the mid-1950s onwards, and was secured and carried through by the driving force of

Admiral Gorskhov, naval strategist and organiser, who virtually created the new Soviet fleet, since it came into his command in 1956 and remains his responsibility today. In terms of tonnage, the Soviet fleet as it stands today is equivalent to that of the United States, but it is more recent and appears to be less vulnerable to modern weapons.

A fourth component of Soviet defence, which has been gradually built up alongside the three outlined above, is military air transport. Transport planes have been developed from increasingly high-performance materials, such as the Ilyushin 76 or the Antonov 22; a new aircraft, the Antonov 40, is currently being produced and will be able to transport 120 tons over 5000 kilometres. This military force proper can be increased by the considerable capacities of Aeroflot, which is the largest airline company in the world. It so happens that Aeroflot uses aircraft which are similar to those of the military air force, and comes under the command of an air marshal. Lastly, the Russians, having dealt first with the defence of their continent (conventional forces), then with strategic air space (ballistic missiles), and sea and underwater areas, went on to tackle outer space. Their success is a familiar story.

Russian activity in outer space can be said to be more intense than that of the United States since, over the last ten years, the Russians have launched a new satellite every three or four days, a rate which is four to five times that of the United States.

2 POLITICAL WILL AND DETERMINATION

The above is a brief review of the Soviet Union's growing military power and a rapid breakdown of its military potential. But more important still are the policies which the Kremlin intends to pursue, and its determination to achieve the designs on which these policies are based. Russia is a country which is permanently expanding. In the fourteenth century the Great Duchy of Moscow was a minuscule state comparable in size to the *Ile de France*; today this core of Russian power has been extended, with varying fortunes, from West Berlin to the China Sea, and from the Arctic to Pakistan.

Between 1939 and 1949, in keeping with the strategy of the Tsars, the new Soviet leaders extended their grasp to some 120 million non-Russians, inhabitants of Eastern Europe, using armies of occupation to overrule the individual sovereignty of half a dozen states.

More recently, Moscow has turned towards Afghanistan, while, thanks to intervening sister parties and willing combatants, the Kremlin is extending its influence into all other parts of the world. It would seem that expansion of this sort is not only fundamental to the internal workings of the system, but that it also represents one of the facets of the Russian spirit.

3   ASYMMETRIES

In the current global situation, an undertaking of this kind is only possible because there are profound asymmetries between on the one hand the Soviet autocracy and on the other hand democracies which are powerful in terms of industry, the economy, and military capacity, but are politically weak, and the Third World countries which are dependent both economically and militarily. These asymmetries to some extent explain the success of Soviet undertakings and it is useful to remind ourselves of them here.

3.1   The Great Design

In the East, there is an autocracy committed to a far-reaching political and social design, which in future should be realised on a world scale. In the West, there is certainly concern about maintaining existing gains, yet their disappearance will clearly be accepted if it is necessary to fight in order to preserve them. In the East, there is no freedom, whereas the West compromises with moves towards the suppression of freedom.

3.2   Continuity in the Design: Power

In the East, there is a stable leadership, which has been in power for a long period and has had the time to formulate and apply their political and diplomatic conceptions; in the West, leaders make brief appearances on the international scene, with little time in which to learn how to handle affairs, still less to carry them through. One rather extreme example is this: whereas the Soviet Union has had only five leaders since 1917, France, during the same period, has had to endure more than sixty governments. Admittedly, the United States has been content with thirteen Presidents, but each new election has profoundly changed the state machinery, often to the detriment of effective government.

3.3 Continuity in the Action: Government Establishments

With reference still to the East, there has been more continuity in the Administration than in ruling circles. Gromyko has been in charge of his country's foreign policy since 1957. He no doubt regards as mere novices his Western counterparts who, in scores, have successively opposed him. Over a 26-year period − and he continues to do so today − Admiral Gorskhov has created and developed the Soviet war fleet. Admittedly, in doing so he has blocked the promotion of the entire admiralty. By contrast, in each democracy a dozen or so admirals have made it to the top, but they have had great difficulties in running their departments.

3.4 Freedom of Action in Relation to Public Opinion

In the East, public opinion has no right to be heard. The leaders and the high command have a free hand with a population which is kept ignorant of and indifferent to world affairs. In the West, there is vote-catching in which, more often than not, foreign policy is used for domestic political ends. In the East, there is the opportunity to conceive and implement a political project in utmost secrecy; in the West, there is the continual, untimely and often absurd intervention of the public in the running of the State. Whereas *Pravda* is the official organ of the truth, the *Washington Post* is prepared when necessary to compromise national interests to promote sales.

3.5 The Convergence of Efforts

In the East, the convergence of efforts and the gathering of forces serve a patient and prudent desire for power. Continual expansion is the Empire's very condition for existence. The Kremlin applies the Seventh Law of the Expansion of States, as defined by the German geographer, Ratzel (1844−1904): 'more space to conquer yet more space', or even 'on this small planet, there is room only for one great state'. In the West, there is only the drive for markets and the development of trade at any price and regardless of its object. Lenin was right: we would even sell the rope that will be used to hang us − and what is more, on credit.

These are some of the asymmetries and some of the striking differences between the two forms of society, which are irreconcilably opposed to one another throughout the world.

In the strategic area, there are differences which are just as obvious, although they are seemingly ignored in the West.

3.6 Initiative

In the East, there is initiative and of all kinds. But an enterprise is started only after the pros and cons have been carefully considered. In military terms, taking the initiative has the advantage of surprise. Given existing nuclear weapons, effective in small numbers and requiring only limited personnel to service them, the decisive act of war can precede mobilisation and even make it pointless. Consequently, providing these new weapons are made use of, it has become easy to take the enemy by surprise.

Since the Soviets were victims of surprise attack themselves in 1941 and witnesses to the gains made in this way by the Israelis in 1967 and by the Egyptians in 1973, they know that in war, surprise is the prerequisite for success. The doctrine that they parade and the arms that they deploy both bear witness to the importance that they attach to it. But the East alone is able to draw on the advantages of initiative and surprise.

Indeed, it is inconceivable in the West that the defensive coalition of free countries — and still more so that one, or even several of these countries — would ever initiate a strike against the Soviet Union, and this regardless of the behaviour of the Soviet Union. Western states, if they still have the means to do so, can only counter-attack. The fate of the West is to suffer the first strike, perhaps to retaliate, and definitely to negotiate. For the West has neither initiative nor surprise on its side. And in the age of the atom, this disparity is fundamental.

3.7 Geography

Even in geography, in terms of population and territory, there is asymmetry. In the East, there are vast areas of land, sparsely populated and, furthermore, the inhabitants — when there are any — are indifferent, even passive and would never think of protesting at the deployment of mobile batteries of ballistic missiles in their region.

However, in the West, there is limited land and a dense urban and even rural fabric, with people who expect to have a say in the running of their country's affairs and think they have the necessary know-how.

4 METHODS OF EXPANSION

Although these overlap according to the particular circumstances, it would seem that there are two fairly distinct and different methods of expansion: expansion into neighbouring states, and the exercise of political, military and social influence some distance from the frontiers of the Russian empire.

Let us consider first expansion through territorial contiguity. When Russia pushes her borders out to the west, east or south-east, this expansion into neighbouring states cannot be reversed. The Red Army is involved in this and as it is justifiably held to be invincible, because it guarantees the survival of the system, a serious defeat of the Army would shake the regime. The regime needs a 'cement' of some kind, i.e. some means of achieving cohesion, a need that increases as more and more non-Russian minorities are absorbed by the Kremlin. Russian military power therefore serves as the guarantor of the regime itself as well as of its conquests. It follows that it would be inadmissible for the Red Army to fail. When political leaders have miscalculated the degree of resistance by the inhabitants of an invaded territory, they pay the price of this error, as is currently happening in Afghanistan. Yet there can be no question of an about-turn, for the Red Army could not be defeated without shaking the structure of the Empire.

This kind of irreversibility of political and military action is not always understood by people in the West. They are quite wrong, for example, when they imagine that they could force the Soviets to 'play the game' of flexible response. If the Red Army was ordered to march westwards, it would not do so in order to be checked by the resistance with which it would probably meet. It would achieve its aims, whatever the cost. Any military engagement between East and West in which the Red Army is involved is an irreversible military engagement, in which all weapons necessary to secure victory will be used, including the most terrible. This calls into question the military concepts developed by NATO over the past twenty-five years.

Valéry Giscard d'Estaing once explained that he envisaged a European 'battle'. He mistook the times, for a battle of this sort would mean defeat and destruction for France. It is hard to imagine that Soviet units would be held in check by the fifteen half-divisions lined up by France, or that they would return to their barracks in the face of our feeble show of strength. This hypothesis still forms part of official doctrine. It is nonsense.

When, on the other hand, Soviet expansion occurs in non-neighbouring territory, the Red Army does not intervene, at least not in organised units.

The action is led by sister political parties and Cuban, East German or North Korean volunteers. Soviet forces themselves are only brought in, with their air force or sea fleets, by way of support; they do not fight. This permits them, if operations are not successful, to withdraw without losing face. This happened in Indonesia, in the Sudan, and in Egypt.

Thus Russian expansion has two different characteristics: 'irreversibility' when the empire itself is expanding, and possible 'reversibility' when expansion occurs in non-neighbouring territories.

Marshal Greshko announced the introduction of long-range action into Soviet strategy in 1974. This is what he said:

> The historical role of Soviet armed forces is not limited to the defence of the motherland and other socialist countries alone. In its foreign political activity, the Soviet State actively and intentionally opposes the export of counter-revolution, and policies of oppression; it supports the struggle for national liberation and is resolutely opposed to imperialist aggression in whichever distant region of the planet this may arise . . . the armed forces of the Soviet Union and of other socialist countries have thus acquired a new mission . . .

The result has been indirect intervention in South-East Asia, with the eviction of the Americans, the opening of two naval bases in the Indo-Chinese peninsula, Soviet presence in South Yemen, the transformation of the Aden base into a command post for Soviet forces in the Indian Ocean, and operations with which we are familiar in Angola and Ethiopia, which would introduce socialist-orientated regimes, such as in Mozambique and Madagascar. Thus, although the Russians have been absent from Africa until some 20 years ago, they have now, directly or indirectly, penetrated in strength.

To turn now to Western Europe, the threats to its security vary greatly.

As Claude Harmel reminded us, threats to the West are primarily of a social and political order. There are so many and they are so complex, that it would require a considerable length of time to set out and to analyse each one of them. This has already been done elsewhere.

Threats of a different order include those which in various ways aim to seize energy resources and raw materials which are vital to West European states, yet only available from elsewhere, outside their own national territory. And it is precisely there that the Soviets are extending their influence. The military staffs of Western states have often expressed the need to ensure channels of communication, which could be threatened by direct intervention. Doubtless this is so, yet it is hard to imagine the

USSR going in for piracy on the high seas. This would hardly represent its long-term interest. It is natural, however, that the Soviet Union seeks to instigate and uphold supportive political and social regimes in areas rich in natural resources. These regimes, under pressure from the Soviet Union, could use blackmail when selling their resources or direct them towards their powerful ally.

Another form of blackmail detrimental to customers in the West is that based on fear. The West is embarrassed by the Euromissile question. Why is this so? The background is, briefly, as follows.

In 1957, following the launch of the first Sputnik, Western Europe became frightened. Twenty years later, as the SS-20s were being installed, the same fear gripped Western Europe. In 1957, it looked to the United States for assistance. The then Eisenhower administration proposed the deployment of ballistic missiles. The Germans refused, on the grounds that their territory could not be the seat of an offensive against Russia, but the British, Italians and Turks accepted the American offer and a total of 72 Jupiter and Thor missiles were deployed in these three countries. During the Cuban crisis, Khrushchev had no difficulty in pointing out to President Kennedy just how uncomfortable it was to have ballistic missiles sited some 100 km from Soviet territory. Khrushchev withdrew his missiles and President Kennedy did likewise. This was explained to the West as a matter of modernisation. It was then proposed that these missiles should be replaced by nuclear submarines in the Mediterranean. Without too much thought, the entire Western intelligentsia agreed to this proposal. They were wrong to do so. When Thor and Jupiter were installed on Turkish territory, Russia was faced with two equally difficult choices: either to attack Turkey without preemptively destroying these missiles, risking them being fired against Russia, or to preemptively destroy them, which would incur the loss of American life, since the missiles were serviced by American specialist personnel. This would be a serious risk to take.

On the other hand, once the weapons were based at sea, the invasion by Russia of Turkish territory would mean that it would fall to the Americans to initiate a nuclear strike against Russian territory. This transfer of responsibility was disadvantageous to the West, but Western leaders, who failed to understand this transaction, applauded Kennedy's initiative.

Nevertheless, the missiles installed on European soil were withdrawn, and meanwhile the Soviets deployed theirs (known as SS-4s and SS-5s) — about 550 altogether. So between 1957 and 1980, Europe was under threat from these weapons, which moreover were inaccurate and therefore had very considerable megaton warheads to compensate for firing errors. Yet no one in Europe took offence at this and no government raised the least protest.

In 1972, Nixon and Brezhnev agreed on a so-called strategic arms limitation and signed the SALT I Accords on 26 May 1972, which among other articles allowed for the modernisation of their respective ballistic missiles. What did Brezhnev do? He replaced the SS-4s and SS-5s, built during 1955 and 1956, and deployed from 1961 to 1962 onwards, by more modern arms; he deployed the SS-20s, and then started modernising his arsenal, whilst remaining within the terms of the Accords. He might have said: 'The SS-4s and SS-5s were not accurate; in a conflict they would have destroyed at one and the same time towns and cities, and the civilian population, whereas the SS-20s, which are accurate to within 250–300 m rather than 2.5 km, would enable me to use far smaller warheads and to destroy military targets without affecting the civilian population. Therefore you stand to gain from this.' What is there to say in reply? Particularly as Brezhnev could deploy as many SS-20s as he wanted across a vast and sparsely populated territory.

By contrast, the installation of Cruise missiles in Holland, densely populated as it is, is bound to cause serious waves of protest from the civilian population.

Although they said nothing all the time that they were under threat from 550 SS-4s and SS-5s, both governments and their people were astonished by the installation of the SS-20s and their neutralisation by the deployment of Pershing II and Cruise missiles. Since they are less vulnerable than conventional contingents which form the basis of NATO defence, these new weapons are more difficult to locate and destroy. They are less of a 'sitting target' than existing conventional forces (fighter-bombers on airfields for example). Yet Western public opinion has interpreted the installation of Pershing II as amounting to a reduction in the security of Western Europe and an increase in the risks it faces, although this is not the case at all. This bears witness to the inability of Western statesmen to carry their countries' affairs through to a successful conclusion and to explain them to the public. What is to prevent the Soviets from making the most of such a shortcoming? The use of 'nuclear gesticulation', with the fears that this raises, is an additional means of destabilising the West.

Two other forms of threat must be mentioned, more or less plausible, but nonetheless worthy of consideration. The first is invasion by conventional means, with the Warsaw Pact taking advantage of the numerical superiority of all its conventional forces: men, tanks, aircraft, artillery, etc.

However, by doing this the Eastern bloc countries would lose the advantage of surprise, which is a decisive one. The Russians fell victim to it in 1941; they know how much the Egyptians gained by it in 1973, and the Israelis in 1967. Yet it is simply not possible to launch 25 000 - 30 000 assault tanks and the corresponding artillery without giving some indication of war preparations.

This form of battle would result in complete and utter carnage, since the fighting would cost the lives of some 50 million Germans, trapped and with no chance to flee. It is easy to imagine the damage caused by the onslaught of thousands of assault tanks across the highly urbanised West German plain, with some 50 million terrorised victims as mere pawns in the attack. This is a responsibility of a magnitude that the USSR, in my opinion, would hesitate to assume.

There is one more factor which must be taken into account: the urbanisation of the Rhine Valley, from Switzerland to the North Sea. This now forms a natural barrier, made up of a continuous high density settlement, some 600 km in length and 40—50 km wide, an environment in which tank formations would lose much of their effectiveness.

When General Sharon led his army, complete with tanks, across a plain and reached Beirut, he had to overcome street-fighting. He failed to do so. Since invasion by tank was the deciding factor in the Second World War, it is assumed that the same will be true tomorrow. Again it could be that we are mistaken by half a century.

There is still one final hypothesis which we should not overlook, for it is an intelligent one: the use of a selective attack, sufficient to paralyse NATO's military machinery. The first-generation SS-20 is not perhaps the right weapon; the second-generation SS-20 (expected to be accurate to within 150 m at a range of 2500 km) would allow the use of warheads in the subkiloton range, or kiloton warheads, without incurring major collateral damage. These missiles would make short work of blinding Western aviation by destroying radar systems, cutting pipelines out in the countryside, wiping out aircraft standing on airfields, destroying munition and artillery stores, and paralysing NATO's entire military machinery, without causing great loss of life. This action could even be selective enough to spare the territorial zone occupied by the American forces in Germany.

The increasing accuracy of long-range projectiles allows us to imagine a scenario which would be considered unreal today, although tomorrow it will be technically, if not politically, possible:

In the minutes following a surprise attack on NATO conventional forces deployed in the one Central-European Zone (a geographical zone which is crucial enough for the fate of NATO to depend on it), the Kremlin could communicate, in substance, the following message to the White House:

> It was difficult for us to endure any longer the build-up of men and weapons on our Western borders. All the more so because NATO's current weapons are more deadly and more accurate, and could reach Russian territory within minutes. Consequently, our warnings having fallen on deaf ears, we have decided to paralyse this military deployment by destroying at long range the elements which determine its possible operation. We have chosen to strike only military targets which are some way from civilian areas, in order to limit collateral damage. To achieve this, we have used accurate, low-yield missiles. Civilian and even military losses are slight, for the attack took place during a holiday period. We will not even proceed to invade or to occupy territories disarmed in this way. We simply demand the definitive withdrawal of American armed contingents from European soil and the installation, at the head of countries which come into our control in this way, of appropriate political and social regimes, open to exchanges of any nature with the USSR. What do you intend to do, given that we have carefully avoided the area in which American forces are deployed and that these have suffered no losses whatsoever?

In other words, rather than the two superpowers coming to blows, would it not be better to negotiate the disarmament – and thus the defeat – of your European allies? Within the framework of such a hypothesis, we might ask ourselves what the fate of NATO's Europe would be, that is the fate of countries who until now have only been secure because of the presence of American forces on their soil. In times of changing technology, the same security policy cannot be followed indefinitely. This is why, in the years to come, this scenario should not be disregarded, if only because it will be technically possible. Yet it is obvious that Western governments are unable either to conceptualise, or to act in accordance with, rapid technological developments.

One further failing must be added to the above. To date, countries with a liberal economy have been incapable of effectively organising to ensure their security, not merely in terms of defending their own territories, but of maintaining markets, freedom of trade and the unimpeded supply of raw materials and energy resources. This is largely beyond the scope of Europe alone. The economic centres in the Pacific for example, which more often than not are just as dependent on the outside world, are bound by the same constraints as West European countries and should join with them to resist the extension of Soviet influence and to limit the threats which the Soviet Union places on their security. The corresponding structures – political, economic, technical, cultural and military – have yet to be established.

10 How to Maintain Europe as One of the Safest Regions of the Globe

Wolf Graf von Baudissin

1 THE PROCESS OF *DETENTE*

The conflicts in the South are increasing in number, scope and intensity. The traditional foundations of our human existence, the existing social and economic structures as well as international relations are being widely destroyed by sweeping processes of development. Helplessness, uncertainty and destitution are gaining ground, bringing in their wake despair and impatience. There is an increase in the number of wars of all kinds and thus also in the number of dead and of refugees. Some regions suffer particularly from conflict, or are incapable of dealing with conflict. In these regions war has almost become the norm.

The North has succeeded in maintaining at least its non-war status for almost 40 years, despite all its differences in ideology and power political considerations, and there seems to be no plausible reason, indeed scarcely any opportunity, to undermine the prevailing strategic stability between East and West. The second-strike capability of both superpowers seems assured for the foreseeable future, although it is true that technology which may have a psychologically destabilising effect is being developed and in some cases is ready to be introduced. These technological developments also strengthen the momentum of the arms race. Yet the North appears to have learnt its lesson from the two world wars, namely that the increase in the destructive power of modern weapons has also meant increasing vulnerability for industrialised societies. Nuclear weapons drastically underline this fact and have made us more acutely aware of it.

An irritating revival of the Cold War is currently taking place, and its cause lies not least in the insecurity of the superpowers, who are experiencing considerable economic and social difficulties as well as political problems within each alliance, and who at the same time are losing influence over the South. In addition, there is much uncertainty on both sides about the intentions of their respective opponent. These consequences of the first phase of the process of *détente* could have been anticipated: increasing international stability has been paid for by internal instability. The contradictory political aims and expectations which each side linked with *détente* were also salient factors as were the particular threats experienced by each side and their essentially different strategies. The initial enthusiasm has ended in disappointment, the old distrust has been revived and 'worst-case thinking' once again has become apparently necessary.

The original aim of *détente*, according to Western understanding, was to develop a relationship which would allow the antagonistic political systems at least to accept each other as unchangeable realities, or better still as equivalent systems. Only then would it be possible to regulate all types of conflict through generally accepted structures and binding procedures. As cooperation is intensified, the number of conflicts will rise, although at the same time their political significance will decrease. The development of these types of relations involves a growing mutual interest in the stability of the opposing system, since this is a prerequisite for any willingness to compromise. Equally it becomes clear that cooperation is only rewarding with an efficient partner. Growing interdependence is thus no longer felt as an existential threat, but on the contrary as an element which promotes security.

The fact that Marxism—Leninism unceasingly propagates ideological class warfare irritates the West. There are indications however that these apparent offensives may in reality be the expression of a defensive posture. They serve more as the demarcation between the East and dangerously tempting Western influences than as the utopian aim of world revolution. Such an aim would scarcely be credible in view of the rapidly decreasing attractiveness of Marxist ideology and reality, the growing pluralism and the many bellicose conflicts within the Communist camp itself.

In any case, Moscow does not follow its ideological principles as far as the economic sphere is concerned. The Kremlin knows very well that without the strong economic, technological and financial support of the West, the Soviet Union can never become an equal competitor with the South. It is clearly in the interests of both East and West to intensify their contacts. This serves the economic development of all involved, leading eventually to a nexus of interests, or a 'North consciousness' which excludes the possibility of a war-like solution to any conflicts which may arise. The West should also realise that the transition of the Eastern bloc into an advanced industrialised society will in all probability also entail an ideological and social relaxation.

It is thus vitally important for all states, in both East and West, to recognise that the new Cold War is the consequence of unrealistic expectations and of incompetence; to accept the inevitable instability as the process of *détente* gets under way, and to look not solely at the antagonistic activities of the other side in order to explain the new confrontation. Only when governments recognise these factors, will they regain the flexibility, empathy and readiness to compromise which are necessary both for the maintenance of a serious dialogue and for initiatives on the regulation of conflicts without involving far-reaching concessions from either side. It is obvious that both German states should be particularly interested in a development of this kind.

2 STRATEGIC STABILITY

The continuation of the process of *détente* requires, from the point of view of security policy, a global military balance of forces, which I call strategic stability. Strategic stability acts both as a warning and a protection for all interested states against blackmail and the use of military force. Moreover, it is only because of strategic stability that states are able to run the risks involved in *détente*. Any attempt by either side to regulate or even to solve conflicts in Europe by direct or indirect use of military force represents an unacceptable risk.

Whilst strategic stability does exist, it could nonetheless be considerably improved if mutual cooperation meant that it became possible to:

(a) Gradually limit the extent and the political importance of military capabilities in such a way that each government's political freedom of action is guaranteed.
(b) Maintain structures and procedures of crisis management which are effective and binding.
(c) Adapt both the range and the potential use of the military forces to the 'minimum requirements' of security policy, which will in turn mean that the military forces will become less threatening, less vulnerable and less expensive.

The military strategy of mutual deterrence together with cooperative arms control make for stability, since both policies favour non-military solutions to conflicts; hence the destabilising effects of superiority in particular categories of weapons and political ambiguity can be avoided. Both concepts also discourage governments from making a drama out of inevitable inferiority in certain categories of weapons, which in any case is often merely temporary and without consequence. These policies advise against using these 'gaps' as a pretext for rearmament.*

Strategic defence doctrines currently being discussed under such varying titles as 'defensive concepts' and Air–Land–Battle 2000 are of dubious worth. The structure, armaments, logistics and training of our military forces are simply not adapted for what are fundamentally classic strategies. The adaptation of our forces would be a long-term project and could only be done at a high cost. More crucial, however, is the fact that this would involve war-fighting options which would make the outbreak of war more likely. Even under present operational and tactical conditions, the aggressor retains his initial advantage as well as the possibility of determining the geographic and temporal extent of the conflict and thus the possibility of fighting a limited war. It has become impossible for a nation which has been attacked to defend itself effectively; it is neither in a position to protect its population, nor to guarantee the continued functioning of its highly sensitive industrialised society. It is no longer even in the position, described by Clausewitz as one of the strengths of defence, of being able to let the aggressor exhaust himself before retaliating. The corollary of this is that extensive counter-offensives are once again being discussed as part of these defence plans.

The rejection of nuclear weapons and of deterrence, which, at first glance, appears intelligible, has led many people to concentrate on the consequences also of a conventional war in Europe, an area both densely populated and highly vulnerable. In view of these threats, the catastrophic effects of certain weapons, when used in war, cannot be the decisive criterion for strategies and forces, but rather the likelihood of their being able to prevent war.

For 15 years flexible response has been NATO's agreed and valid strategy. In case of an aggression the Western Allies are resolved to react to preserve the status quo, or to ensure that the aggressor accepts its re-establishment as soon as possible. The aggressor must be made afraid that a decisive success in the use of his conventional superiority will provoke

---

* *Editor's note*: Here the German is *Nachrüsten*, a term coined by Hans-Dietrich Genscher, the West-German Foreign Minister. It denotes rearmament by the West in an attempt to catch up with the Soviet Union, said to be engaged in *Vorrüsten*, arming itself first. Often used specifically in the context of the NATO dual-track decision, known in Germany as the *Nachrüstungsbeschluss*.

nuclear escalation, which, if continued, would very probably lead to a global nuclear war. Provided that this doctrine is maintained and is supported by the necessary military forces, there are no rational reasons – either in the short or the medium term – to fear the outbreak of war. Moreover, there are indications that the Soviet Union adheres to a similar strategic concept, albeit with stronger preemptive features, which can easily be explained by their geo-strategic doctrine and the way they perceive their own situation.

There is no doubt that mutual deterrence alone is not sufficient to guarantee strategic stability. The modernisation of military forces in industrialised countries can scarcely be avoided. Developments are neither parallel in nature nor synchronic but occur independently. Thus they cause temporary superiorities or inferiorities in certain parts of the armaments sector such as aircraft, warships, missiles or tanks. These imbalances are perceived as a threat, particularly when the aim of a given arms programme is not apparent and when new technologies create new defence and protection problems. In such cases arms control becomes a necessity, as only in this way can strategic stability be maintained by the process of adapting each side's military potential to that of the other.

Arms control is the subject of many negotiations: at the United Nations, the CSCE Follow-on meeting, the START, INF and MBFR talks. The results of these negotiations have certainly not been spectacular. All governments involved have experienced difficulties in acknowledging the others' often rather subjective security requirements, in relinquishing maximum security arrangements for themselves and in agreeing to a transparency of doctrines, of decision-making and armament processes, as well as of the military potential itself. For many governments, consistent arms control would involve a highly undesirable limitation of their sovereignty.

3   POSSIBILITIES FOR ARMS REDUCTION

A further problem is the fact that negotiations are normally slower than technological processes and that all negotiated limitations in one sector elicit changes in direction for arms research and development. Hence, a decisive factor for the future will be whether governments are prepared to shift the emphasis in arms control from the systems already operational to those which are still in the planning process. This would require international structures to coordinate the respective development programmes before production began, with the aim of evolving a preventive arms control. Here too, the decisive criteria would be the maintenance of stability and undermining the dynamics of the arms race.

There are, understandably, many impatient voices calling for General and Complete Disarmament – at first glance, a captivating idea. Yet it is debatable whether successful disarmament of all countries would make the world any more peaceful. Such a situation would require, in any case, effective means of control in order to prevent rearmament even on a minor scale which would give one side an overwhelming superiority over its weaponless neighbours. However, complete and global disarmament could not eliminate most of the existing social and international conflicts. Complete disarmament would require a new world order which would guarantee, particularly to minority groups and small nations, a peaceful and fair solution to conflicts, and thus guarantee, in the first place, their continued survival. It should also prevent more powerful neighbouring states from violating treaties and attacking smaller nations. Thus, once again, it is clear that the problem we are dealing with is primarily a political one rather than a military-technical one.

Similarly, the often proposed abolition of nuclear weapons and the introduction of nuclear-weapons-free zones in politically tense areas seems to be rather problematic. The dangers of a security policy advocating purely a denuclearisation of our military potential have already been mentioned. Furthermore, it would be exceedingly difficult to verify a halt in the production of nuclear weapons, particularly if they were to be made available for use with launchers of conventional weapons. A drastic, verifiable reduction in short-range systems would seem to be more useful, since this would eliminate early and rapid escalation to battlefield nuclear weapons, whilst at the same time retaining the threat of disaster and thus preventing war. The proposals for nuclear-weapons-free zones also contain certain weaknesses. It is important to distinguish between those zones which have not previously had nuclear weapons (a situation which has been codified in international law), and other zones where denuclearisation would have to take place. This would require 'transarmament' and possibly also changes in strategy, thus giving new weight to the balance of conventional forces. This could awaken renewed fear amongst the populations concerned. It would depend greatly on the overall political climate whether such an agreement would be seen as a sign of the goodwill of those governments involved, and thus build up confidence which would lead to a relaxation of tension. To speak of being free of nuclear weapons seems illusory, at any rate from the military point of view, considering the high manoeuvrability of the launchers and the high accuracy of even long-range weapons. Moreover, it would be virtually impossible to verify the implementation of a denuclearisation agreement, and both sides would have to face the possibility of it being broken.

4   INF AS AN EXAMPLE OF ARMS CONTROL

The NATO dual-track decision of December 1979 has been exposed to much criticism from West Europeans. As a proponent of consistent arms control, I have always warned both sides against unilateral arms programmes which are not absolutely necessary. I have particularly warned against decisions which may seem threatening to the other side and so endanger both strategic and political stability.

I am therefore highly critical of certain aspects of the NATO decision. However, it cannot be denied that the Kremlin began this modernisation process, despite the fact that its own Eurostrategic systems had long become obsolete. There was no longer any need to keep Western Europe 'hostage', since thousands of Soviet warheads based in silos, submarines and aircraft now directly threaten US territory. These already represented a credible deterrent against an attack on Soviet targets. Furthermore, the Soviet Union violated significant arms control practices:

(a) There was no publication of definitive deployment ceilings and, despite having announced parity on several occasions, the Soviet Union has continued to build up her arms.

(b) The Kremlin initiated negotiations too late and made only abstract offers of a moratorium, despite the fact that the clear Soviet advantage in this area meant that even a production freeze would not have put the Soviet Union in a disadvantageous position.

Constant threats from the Soviet Union also reduced NATO's willingness to negotiate. First the dual-track decision itself, and then NATO's refusal to revoke it, were declared by the Soviet Union to be insurmountable obstacles to reaching any agreement. Today the deployment of the first Pershing, which in itself will not have the slightest impact on strategic stability, has been similarly elevated to a matter of prestige, as has, for many NATO governments, the importance of keeping to the Brussels deployment schedule. They want to demonstrate their solidarity and their resolve in the face of all Soviet attempts to intimidate them.

Despite differing opinions on both the history and the content of the Brussels decision, the West has to realise that:

(a) Only loyalty towards this carefully prepared decision, which was thoroughly discussed and arrived at only after concessions on the part of all the NATO-Allies, affords other governments the opportunity of influencing the aims, timing and progress of superpower negotiations.

(b) Apparently only the solidarity of the Allies can persuade the Soviet

Union to accept a compromise and give up the illusion that NATO can be blackmailed by Soviet-influenced public opinion in the West. Equally, the Kremlin will be forced to realise that it will not be able to avoid committing itself to a reduction in its own systems.

(c) A mutually acceptable agreement should not be difficult to reach, since it is extremely unlikely that the Eurostrategic systems would ever be used. Their numbers are significant politically and in terms of arms control, rather than in strategic terms. An interim agreement, followed by the combining of START and INF talks would enable a resolution of issues currently still problematic and would then facilitate progress at other discussions of arms control — in Geneva, Vienna and Stockholm.

(d) NATO's dual-track offer gives precise information about an arms programme which was consciously limited. Three years before their possible introduction NATO gave notification of the types and exact numbers of the planned systems, as well as their deployment areas. And, most importantly, NATO linked the implementation of this decision to the result of the negotiations.

The aspects noted above make the dual-track decision a very promising model for future arms control negotiations. It is therefore regrettable that Moscow has reacted only with obscure counter-offers.

Whilst it is perfectly understandable that many people feel outraged by, and reject, the further accumulation of arms in central Europe, it seems unfounded to dramatise these modernisation steps at one level of armaments into an immediate cause of danger of war. For neither in the East nor the West is there any doubt that the use of these weapons would trigger off a global nuclear war, which would completely destroy the North. These systems do not give first-strike capability to either side and their mobility prevents them from being sitting targets for a first-strike themselves. The use of these weapons would be far more likely to provoke a direct attack on the aggressive superpower's own strategic targets.

5   CONCLUSION

(a) Peace is endangered all over our rapidly and fundamentally changing world. Yet in Europe war is proving to be a particularly inappropriate instrument for solving internal and external conflicts. The most dangerous approach towards these conflicts is one of hostility and impatience, incorporating the desire for quick and clear-cut solutions and the 'all or nothing' postulate inherent in ideologies. This approach is incapable of dealing with conflict, it is nonpeaceful and is moreover a relic of the 19th century.

(b) War can be prevented only by the maintenance of strategic stability. Peaceful relations and political stability can develop only through close cooperation, by creating interdependence in as many fields as possible. Since any *rapprochement* of opposing systems will by no means eliminate conflict, however, structures will be required to regulate conflicts nonviolently.

(c) Increasingly, both direct and indirect threats may be anticipated from and within the South, and these will frequently overshadow East–West relations. This should not generate resentment against the South but rather should encourage the North to develop in the interests of all, a common concept for global crisis management and aid vis-à-vis the South.

11 A Proposal to End the Danger of War in Europe

MORTON A. KAPLAN

The recent anti-nuclear demonstrations in Western Europe and the United States have aroused much controversy. Their proponents argue that they are the beginning of a popular tidal wave that will eliminate, or at least reduce, the danger of nuclear war in Europe. Opponents argue that, even if the drive is not being orchestrated from Moscow, it will have asymmetric effects that will weaken the defensibility of the West and increase the chances of war, including nuclear war.

Although the size of the demonstrations is clearly disproportionate to the actual risk of war in Europe, the concern that is being expressed is warranted by the nature of the catastrophe that would occur if war, and in particular nuclear war, broke out in Europe. Yet history provides little support for those who believe that reducing numbers of weapons or refusing to engage in an arms race lessens the probability of war. Most analysts now agree that political lack of support for rearmament in the democracies in the 1930s played a significant role in reinforcing Hitler's plans for conquest. Even if we dismiss, as I would, the argument some make that the Soviet Union is planning additional conquests in Europe, the repeated crises within Eastern Europe and the dismal state of the Soviet economy might lead the Soviet high command — if the West is weak or seems irresolute — to seek a solution to its problem through threat, bluff, or extortion. And, even if this is not very likely, the demonstrations would make no sense if the risk of war is negligible. Surely no one in his right mind expects NATO to attack the East.

There can be no doubt that the present heavy concentrations of military force in Europe, which are driven by the huge size of the military forces that the Soviet Union unilaterally built up, are morally obscene.

Justifications for this build-up often refer to Russian history. The Russian concern with military space for defence is understandable in these terms. Both Napoleon and Hitler invested the Moscow area, and only defensive territorial space saved Russia.

Today, however, it is Western Europe that lacks space for defence. From the border between the Germanies to Paris is less than 300 miles or roughly the width of the state of Pennsylvania. Contending armies, even without the use of nuclear weapons, would employ unprecedented explosive power in areas of concentrated population. It is little wonder, therefore, that some in Western Europe worry about the new Pershing II nuclear launchers that have been proposed for Europe. They are provocative because they can hit Moscow, dangerous because they can be hit by preemptive attack, and are seen as signifying — even though this is factually incorrect — an American willingness to engage in nuclear war that would be limited to European terrain. Western European demonstrators have particular reason to be concerned given the unprecedented and unnecessary concentration of Soviet nuclear power directed against them, not merely in tactical nuclear weaponry, but in the MIRVed SS-20s as well.

1   NO REASONABLE OBJECTIVE CAN VALIDATE THE RISK OF WAR

It can be taken as a given that no European nation will today begin a war for the reason that led to the wars of the last century and this. Not trade, colonies, space, or other similar motives will lead the authorities of either East or West deliberately to initiate a war in Europe. War in Europe, if it comes, will come from miscalculation or from some uncontrollable incident. Although an equilibrium in strength between NATO and the WTO (Warsaw Treaty Organisation) is a guarantee against a war by miscalculation, it not only is no guarantee against war arising from an uncontrollable incident but provides a large part of the explosive power that would be set off by the flame arising out of an incident.

There is a plan presented here that will guard against both war by miscalculation and war arising from an uncontrollable incident. It will be consistent with the national security of all the nations of Eastern and Western Europe. In addition, by reducing drastically the huge expenditures for military forces, it will release the economic and creative energies of the populations of both areas.

This plan may not be received with enthusiasm by the leaders of either bloc. Leaders of large entities tend to be extremely conservative and often lack imagination. They tend to be responsive to vested interests that have a stake in the current situation. And it is possible that the non-legitimate nature of Soviet rule may inhibit acceptance for fear of loss of personal political position and power. I am not, therefore, arguing that the plan will be accepted, at least initially, but only that it is acceptable in terms of the national, international and human interests of the parties to whom it is addressed.

The threat of war stems from the huge build-up of forces in Europe, not from nuclear weapons as such. In the absence of a massive confrontation in Europe, even entirely conventional, nuclear war in Europe would not be a threat.

It is inconceivable that the leaders of East or West would resort to the use of nuclear weapons over a European issue unless a conventional European war were in progress or about to be initiated. If only modest forces were present in Europe — so small that they would be incapable of producing the conquest of other nations — then it is difficult to believe that nuclear weapons would be resorted to. It is only in a disordered fantasy that one imagines leaders in Moscow or Washington pressing the red button in the absence of a threat to the survival of the nation.

However, if survival is threatened, the resort to nuclears is not unlikely. Because the losing side is not unlikely to resort to nuclears, the attacking force is motivated to preempt whether or not it has agreed not to use nuclear weapons first. Even if all nuclear weapons are removed from Europe and strategic forces savagely reduced, the losing party is still likely to resort to strategic nuclear weapons, whether sea- or land-based.

Therefore, if one wishes significantly to reduce or to eliminate the threat of nuclear war in Europe, the first step is to reduce or eliminate the threat of war in Europe; and this threat lies in the conventional confrontation.

The possibilities just sketched are sufficient reason for proposing a conventional disarmament plan such as the one in this proposal. However, the next generation of nuclear weapons constitutes an additional reason for considering nuclear disarmament proposals — valuable though they may be as auxiliary considerations after conventional disarmament — as largely irrelevant to the avoidance of nuclear war.

I am indebted to General Gallois for a better understanding of the sub-kiloton nuclear missiles that are on the horizon. These weapons are so small they can be easily shielded and hidden. A freeze to prevent their manufacture cannot be verified effectively for control purposes. They can be fired from dual-purpose launchers so that no distinction can be made between conventional and nuclear launchers. And they can be shot accurately from Western Europe to Eastern Europe and the Soviet Union and vice versa with little likelihood of extensive collateral damage.

Thus, they may produce a preemptive hair trigger in a crisis if they are deployed or presumed to be deployed. The preempting side may believe that it can avoid disaster, change the European balance, and run only a slight risk of strategic nuclear retaliation if there has been only minimal civilian damage. This estimate may be correct and that would be bad enough for the losing side. But it may well be wrong and then the nuclear holocaust would be upon us. However, in the absence of targets requiring nuclear attack to be disabled and also of the extensive forces needed to consolidate gains — and both would be absent with the present proposal — the hair trigger is gone, for both the threat and the targets that invoke it are gone. (This is an additional reason for the removal of tactically oriented nuclear weapons to the seas in the back-up proposal; but the best solution is that of massive conventional disarmament.)

2   CONVENTIONAL ASPECTS

Except for 10 000 American and 10 000 Soviet troops in the respective Germanies as guarantees against forcible attempts to reunite Germany, all US ground forces would be removed from Europe and all Soviet ground forces from areas west of the Urals. The Soviet armies must be behind the Urals because otherwise they would constitute a threat to other European nations. Such major reductions by the United States and Soviet Union obviously would be dependent upon the minimisation of the other conventional armies in Europe either as a threat to each other or to the Soviet Union, although it is difficult to imagine that the Poles, Rumanians, or Bulgarians would attack the Russians, even if the Russian armies are behind the Urals. Moreover, one might perhaps admit 50 000 to 100 000 Russian soldiers on the frontier as part of this proposal. In any event, therefore, the other European armies would require substantial limitation. Although this would have to be negotiated with them, one possibility is that all national European armies other than the Soviet be limited to 50 000 men on active duty and 200 000 men in reserves. Furthermore, except for the Soviet Union, all forces under ministries of the interior and all national police forces, except for small customs and air and seaport forces, should be eliminated because they might serve as disguised armies. Police forces should be local only.

All tanks should be removed from Europe within the specified area. In addition, the Soviet and United States tank forces should be limited to 1000 tanks apiece. All other tanks should be destroyed. No armoured equipment should be permitted in excess of 5 tons. All guns larger than 2 inches should be removed from the specified areas.

All combat aircraft should be removed from the specified area. The Soviet Union and the United States should be restricted to 1000 fighter aircraft apiece and 100 medium-range and 100 long-range military aircraft apiece.

The ground forces of the United States should be restricted to 1 000 000 men in the continental United States and of the Soviet Union to 1 000 000 men, who would be east of the Urals. The reserves should be restricted to 500 000 men.

Following such European agreements, sustained efforts should be made to reach similar agreements in Asia and particularly on the Soviet–China border. If this can be done, the American, Soviet, and Chinese forces should be reduced to 250 000 men and the reserves reduced accordingly.

Adequate on-site inspection and also remote sensor inspection arrangements must be agreed to.

All European nations and the United States should sign agreements to the non-first-use of force and to non-interference in internal political changes within other nations, even those involving system changes.

There should be an agreement to arbitrate all disputes that might lead to war.

This should be a first stage in an effort to remove the threat of major war from the world. In particular, proposals should be explored for the Middle East and Asia, areas that, although not as likely as Europe to lead to nuclear war, cannot entirely be excluded as danger zones.

The parties to the agreement should pledge themselves not to sell the weapons that are eliminated but to destroy them and also permit inspection of re-supply facilities. In addition, they should pledge themselves to bring within strong control the sales of armaments abroad. It is assumed that the arrangements they have agreed to would make this advisable, particularly because the great comparative advantage that the United States and Soviet Union have over other nations would be greatly reduced.

Some European analysts believe that the force levels proposed here for Europe, exclusive of Russia, are so small that Russia quickly could invade Western Europe anyway. However, although the size and composition of the reduced European forces certainly require extensive discussion, the subsequent potential threat from the Soviet Union should not be exaggerated. If Russia does not mobilise, it will denude its Asian front. If it mobilises, there likely is time for European and American mobilisation. The Soviet Union, moreover, would have to move through an independent Poland and this would provide both a time and space buffer. In addition, the major Soviet threat is not of an actual attack but of political blackmail and of the threat of attack. This would be far more difficult at a distance.

And it is hard to think of the precipitating factors.

Furthermore, the proposal could include provisions for civilian reserves trained in and equipped with small arms and anti-tank weapons, which could be so widely dispersed that the preemptive strike mentioned earlier would not be feasible. Other weapons more effective in defence than offence and for use by civilian militias might also be permitted. It is true that these details are important and require extensive discussion, as do the actual sizes of the reduced European forces, but the general thrust of the proposal seems superior to present arrangements.

3   NUCLEAR ASPECTS

All land-based nuclear weapons should be removed from Western and Eastern Europe, including Great Britain and the Soviet Union west of the Urals.

The sea-based weapons of France and England should not be eliminated by this proposal; but neither should Russian sea-based weapons. In any event, the land-based weapons are the ones that may provoke a preemptive strike in Europe.

A world in which this proposal is accepted is a world in which it will be enormously easier to negotiate massive nuclear reductions and to inhibit proliferation. In a world in which there are few conventional arms, it is inconceivable that nations would lob nuclear weapons at each other. If this does not make the issues of nuclear balance meaningless, it certainly makes them much less critical than in the current world. Because the minor nuclear powers can never compete with the major ones anyway, the reduction or elimination of their systems as a condition for the reduction or elimination of the systems of the major powers may succeed in reducing or eliminating the serious threat of nuclear proliferation. The small powers may well accede to this pressure because they will not wish to live in a world in which the major powers can punish them severely if they use nuclear weapons. This will be particularly true if they receive guarantees of assistance if invaded and promises of sanctions against invaders.

4   SOVIET RESPONSE

Although the Soviet Union initially may turn this plan down for fear of its consequences in Eastern Europe, or even inside the Soviet Union, its eventual implementation would enhance the national security of the

Soviet Union and remove an albatross from the neck of its economy. Even though the Russian public does not directly determine national policy, the plan, if beamed in by broadcast, or even eventually by a kind of osmosis, likely will become enormously popular with a people that has long suffered from immense economic hardships, a decreasing life span, and great harshness in living conditions. The West, therefore, should manifest great persistence in pursuing this plan and, if necessary, might even attempt to implement it by stages – if they are not destabilising – as an alternative to the cosmetic SALT and MBFR (Mutual Balanced Force Reduction) negotiations. (The current START proposals may widen the window of vulnerability and may produce less flexibility than proposals similar to the back-up proposal that is specified below.) These in fact are mostly propaganda ploys: offensive on the part of the Soviet Union, which is attempting to disrupt Western unity; and defensive on the part of a NATO that is trying to prevent a deterioration in its position. Although the confidence-building measures proposed by the Rumanians, and elaborated on recently by President Reagan, such as notices concerning manoeuvres, are certainly valuable, they are only marginal with respect to the threat of war. Europe certainly deserves something much better.

There is a good reason why Russia would stumble over its own feet in rejecting this proposal, as it likely will do initially. Russia is still committed to the Litvinov proposals of the 1930s for complete and absolute disarmament. Although this proposal does not go that far, it takes a giant step in that direction. Furthermore, there is no reason why the West should not offer to work toward that goal with a proposal similar to this one as a major step in that direction.

5   EUROPEAN TRANSITIONS AND EASTERN EUROPE

In my opinion the threat of war in a Europe from which both the United States and the Soviet Union have removed their forces and in which the Soviet relationship with Eastern Europe has been attenuated would be minimal. However, because of the highly urbanised character of Europe, the dangers involved in modern weapons technology, and the aspirations of the peoples of the area, it would nonetheless be immoral not to attempt to reduce even that minimal risk. Therefore, even a joint US–USSR withdrawal should be accompanied by a series of intra-European arms control and confidence-building agreements.

Furthermore, although differences in the natures of the Eastern and Western economies would make difficult any intimate linking between the

Common Market and the Eastern European economies, a military withdrawal should be accompanied by a series of intra-European economic measures. Our object throughout should be to leave behind a safer, and more independent, Europe.

At least two European regimes likely would collapse during this process with dire consequences for the leaders of these regimes: East Germany and Czechoslovakia. Therefore, it would be important for some tacit, if not formal, agreements between the United States, the Soviet Union, Poland, and the democracies of Western Europe to be reached to insure continued consultation and process insulation in order to minimise the potential destabilising consequences of collapses of those regimes. That might place limits on the free popular choices of the people of the two countries that it would be difficult to justify theoretically. But it would be far less moral to leave Soviet hardliners with an argument for war in order not to fail completely in their obligations to their clients.

6 BACK-UP PROPOSAL

Suppose that this proposal is rejected and that no significant arms-control proposals appear likely of joint adoption by the United States and the Soviet Union. What are the things that the United States and its allies could do unilaterally that would increase deterrence, decrease the provocatory character of present arrangements, place European nations in control of their own destiny, and not reduce the comparative war capability of NATO?

7 NUCLEAR POSITIONING

Some of the suggestions made here have been made previously by me; I refer briefly to their history only to indicate my persistent interest in such measures. As early as 1971, I suggested to the Pentagon that the Pershing and Sergeant weapons be eliminated from the NATO arsenal and that the nuclear-armed QRA (Quick Reaction Aircraft) be withdrawn to Great Britain or the United States. That proposal is repeated now with a further specification for the unilateral removal of all nuclear launchers with ranges exceeding 250 kilometres. Weapons of this kind that are easily located and that can hit the Soviet Union are obvious targets for a Soviet first strike. In the original proposal I argued that the presence of these weapons might have destabilising effects during periods of tension. On the other hand, removing the QRA's to Britain and the United States not only removes them from the sites of likely targeting but permits their potential recall as an element in deterrence.

Any required nuclear targeting in the event of a war in Europe, with the exception of massed tanks, can be accomplished through the employment of Poseidon and/or Trident missiles. It may be that the United States may wish to reconsider the actual number of nuclear missile submarines to be employed within this strategy and that some of its allies may wish to assist in the financing of them.

The great threat that the arrangements specified here do not account for is that of massed tank attacks. Shorter-range Lances can be used for this purpose. If it were not for the propaganda tag that has been tacked on to the neutron bomb (or the enhanced radiation weapon), it would be the weapon of choice. It is not true that it was developed to kill people while leaving buildings intact. The object was rather to develop a weapon the lethal effects of which could be more narrowly contained than is the case with standard nuclear weapons. If the alliance should decide to resort to this weapon system, it should recommend as part of its declaratory policy that the Soviet Union remove its standard nuclear shells and replace them with neutron shells. Although there is no possibility that NATO forces will attack eastward, reasons of appropriate symmetry recommend this. In time, smart conventional weapons may be able to do this job.

It is true that the previous proposals run counter to the sentiment of many Americans for a nuclear non-first-use proclamation by NATO. Such suggestions have been made in an effort to reduce the risk of nuclear war. However, such a proclamation would be counter-productive. It is extremely unlikely that the Soviet Union would begin an invasion of Western Europe if it could not mass its tanks. The only current significant threats to massed tanks are nuclear mines and shells. Although a nuclear non-first-use proclamation would not in fact necessarily stop us from resorting to nuclear weapons if a successful Soviet campaign is launched against the West, the belief that we might not resort to such weapons is likely to reduce substantially deterrence of a Soviet attack and to increase, rather than to reduce, the risk of war — and hence of nuclear war — in Europe. The proclamation in 1982 by Russia of a non-first-use doctrine, however, was cost free; for the West will not attack the East and the WTO has superior conventional forces. Some proponents of the nuclear non-first-use proposal argue that it will not reduce deterrence because the Russians are unlikely to believe it. This is too tricky.

A careful reading of the debates between Admiral Yamashita and his staff and the Japanese naval general staff on the Pearl Harbor campaign indicates the extremely dubious character of the venture. If it had not been for Admiral Yamashita's great prestige, the attack would not have been approved. Even so, the attack would not have been launched if the fleet had not been stationed in bases, if it had not regularised its activities, and if other defensive measures had been taken. This is merely one example in military history that illustrates (a) that risky operations *do* get undertaken and (b) that both their success and their initiation could have been avoided by appropriate measures. Wishful thinking does not make good policy. And unnecessary marginal reductions of deterrence can invoke very heavy costs. However, if smart weapons actually develop sufficiently they can and should substitute for nuclear weapons in Europe.

It would be better to make an announcement that can be believed because it is inherently credible. NATO should announce that it will not initiate the first use of force or the threat of force in the entire NATO/WTO area; that if the Russians use modest local force in the NATO area, NATO will respond in kind without escalation; that if the Russians attempt to change NATO boundaries in Europe by the use of force, NATO will do whatever is required to defeat this. In the attempt to defeat this, nuclear weapons will be employed only if necessary. NATO should also announce that it knows that Russian operational manuals specify, and that their wargaming employs, nuclear weapons in the event of a central, that is, European, war and announce that a significant employment of nuclear weapons in Western Europe will invoke the use of nuclear weapons against the territory of the Soviet Union.

8   DISSUASION

Because of WTO conventional superiority, it is important to reduce WTO cooperation with the Soviet Union in an attack on the West. Because of the number of targets in Eastern Europe, there are prospects for dissuading Eastern European nations from cooperating with a Soviet attack.

In a prolonged central war, missiles from submarines would be aimed at the Soviet Union and at choke points in Eastern Europe, including marshalling yards, large military dumps, and naval and air bases. Similar facilities within the Soviet Union would also be subject to such attack.

In a variant of the dissuasion strategy I first proposed to the Pentagon in 1971 and then publicly in 1973, the list of targets in Eastern Europe subject to these attacks would remain quite limited to prevent extensive collateral damage provided that these countries refrain from actively assisting the Russian attack and that their forces do not hold border areas essential to NATO counterattack. Under these circumstances, we would also guarantee them from other consequences of belligerency. The East Germans would be particularly vulnerable inasmuch as their territory would be the only effective staging ground for a WTO attack on the West (with the exception of a direct Russian attack on the northern flank). It is extremely unlikely that the Russians would mount such an attack on the central NATO front without the cooperation of the East Germans; and this is a lesson that should be taken closely to heart by the East Germans, lest they be subjected to severe damage. Inasmuch as the East Germans, unlike the other Warsaw Treaty Organisation states, seem unlikely to cooperate with a dissuasion strategy, it perhaps may be the case that NATO would agree to limit counterattacks in East Germany if there were massive civilian resistance and sabotage. This is an instance in which the dropping of anti-tank and anti-aircraft weapons might play an important role.

After this tactic was publicly proposed in 1973, NATO officers in Washington got feedback from Eastern European nations' officials many of whom began to ask what they would have to do to stay out of the line of reprisals. This type of reaction is one that the Russians would have to take very seriously. They could not remove these governments during times of calm, for that would be excessively costly because of active and passive resistance and the need to maintain a minimum of consensus. During a crisis, it would be too late to do this effectively because it would be a sign of disunity and, thus, would weaken the WTO threat to their west and their assurance in threatening or conducting war.

9 THE COUPLING PROBLEM

The dispute between the Soviet Union and the United States over the installation of Pershing IIs in response to the Soviet SS-20s is primarily political rather than military or strategic. The Soviet Union is fully capable of saturating Western Europe with nuclear weapons other than the SS-20s. And the targeting that will be assigned to the Pershing IIs could be taken over by the American submarine fleet.

The Soviet objective in implanting massive numbers of SS-20s is to convince the Europeans that they are decoupled from American strategic deterrence. The objective of the United States in putting Pershing IIs into Europe is to convince them of the contrary. The Soviet Union behaved in a threatening way before the recent German elections in the hope that Germans would be frightened into voting for the Social Democrats, who in turn would back off from the decision on the Pershing IIs.

When the former tactic failed, at least in part, because of the Christian Democratic victory, the Soviet Union turned its threats against the United States by proposing that the use of the Pershing IIs would lead to a nuclear counterattack against the United States. This represented an effort to influence the debate in the Congress over a nuclear freeze. If the freeze won, the Russians hoped that its advocates would resist new deployments while negotiations were in progress.

The political asymmetries between the NATO and WTO blocs have concerned me since the late 1950s, when I made the first proposal for a joint NATO nuclear force, a force that would have operated under NATO command without veto under certain standardised conditions. By the time this proposal emerged from the bureaucratic process as a multilateral fleet that operated on the surface and with six vetos, I disowned it.

In 1971 in a project that was done for the army, I advocated pulling the Sergeants and Pershings out of Europe, rebasing the quick reaction aircraft in England and the United States, and doing NATO strategic nuclear targeting from the seas. My argument was that nuclear weapons in Europe, particularly if they could hit the Soviet Union or were highly vulnerable, would be such a symbolic target that they would be divisive of the alliance during a crisis. And the Russians would particularise their threats to heighten this divisiveness. To maintain the strategic coupling, I proposed a quick transfer capability for nuclear submarines. There would have been previous training of officers of a particular nation if it was attacked or under immediate threat of attack. This was nearly accepted by Operations and Plans, but ultimately it proved too difficult to get the army to give up its intermediate-range nuclear weapons in a world in which the air force and navy had intercontinental missiles.

Recently I revised that proposal. In a discussion of the plan in Europe, the major criticism was that in a crisis the United States might not turn the submarines over.

There is a solution to the problem and I propose it here. Any NATO ally that so wishes may place on an agreed number of American nuclear submarines a parallel command officer and fire-control officer plus a certain number of other personnel. There will be a treaty between the United States and each ally that so desires that specifies that, under an attack of agreed dimensions, according to the NATO situation report, that ally may take command of the particular submarines and use them according to national orders. Each member of the crew of each appropriate submarine must attend a briefing on the arrangement and sign a statement specifying that the treaties of the United States are the law of the land and that he will obey the command of the treaty-designated command officer.

This proposal, in addition to being enforceable, has an additional advantage over my earlier proposal. Command of specified submarines would be taken over not merely by the nation under immediate threat but by any other NATO ally that considers the attack against that nation to be threatening to its interests. As a consequence of this, the Soviet Union would not be able to direct its retaliatory threats against a particular NATO country because it could not know which NATO country might fire. Moreover, because any substantial conventional attack on NATO would threaten the Soviet Union with intercontinental warfare, the extremely high deterrence that the United States had in the middle 1950s when it had nuclear superiority would be restored. The alliance would be coupled and the Soviet threats would lose their destabilising capability. We would have neutralised the SS-20s much more effectively than can the Pershing IIs.

10 CIVILIAN ASPECTS

Although the value of anti-tank and anti-aircraft hand-held weapons against mass attacks has been much exaggerated, those weapons can be of considerable use under appropriate circumstances. There should be stockpiles of such weapons in Western Europe. There will be two ways in which such stockpiles can be used. In the first place, there should be large, trained civilian militias that can use them if a NATO nation is invaded. In the second place, they can be dropped into Eastern European countries if Soviet forces attack one of those nations or the West.

There may be better versions both of the principal plan and of the fall-back plan. The present proposals are intended primarily to clarify the character of the options that face us. If statesmen in the United States and the Soviet Union adopt a comparable plan, that would remove the threat of holocaust from Europe and, thus, likely from the entire world. Wars, and even nuclear uses, elsewhere are not as likely to escalate as catastrophically as might be the case in Europe (although such escalation, even in Europe, also is much less likely than many believe). Even the unilateral fall-back position in this proposal, which fails to remove the gruesome threat that hangs over Europe and the world, mitigates that threat to a significant extent by increasing deterrence, by decreasing provocation, by putting European nations in charge of their own destiny, and by maintaining the comparative defensibility of the West at least as well as, and probably better than, existing arrangements.

12 Comments on Kaplan's Proposal

(i) JEAN KLEIN

In 1973 I was privileged to participate in a colloquium of the *Inter-University Seminar on Armed Forces and Society*, in Chicago and I remember participating in a panel chaired by Professor Morton Kaplan. The debate concerned the relations between the two superpowers and the security interests of the medium powers. I took the opportunity to express a European viewpoint, and already at this time it was clear that there were significant differences between Europeans and Americans over these issues. I am afraid that transatlantic differences have become even more pronounced since then, and that my comments will be no better received now than they were 10 years ago.

I would like to start by saying how stimulating I found Kaplan's proposals. He has no hesitation in leaving the beaten track and proposing a drastic remedy for solving problems relating to international security and the regulation of arms. However, as he is under no illusion as to the way his recommendations will be received by those in power, he wisely suggests alternatives.

Kaplan's proposals suggest two different approaches to problems of security. The first comes under the heading of general and complete disarmament and the underlying assumption is that the arms build-up, particularly in Europe, poses a threat to peace; by ridding ourselves of the instruments of war, it would be possible to guarantee lasting peace. This thesis is not new; Victor Hugo, whose gospel was progress, believed that arms were the cause of conflict and that the only way of preventing the outbreak of violence was to scrap them. This view is no longer held by people working in international relations and conflict studies.

Kaplan's 'alternative' approach draws its inspiration from a different philosophy. He has broken away from the utopian idea of a general dis-

206

armament that would seem unrealistic in the medium term and recognises the need to bring about a balance of forces that guarantees peace in Europe and to avert the risks of war through misunderstanding, accident and miscalculation. To this end, he makes proposals which are less far-reaching, but whose advantage is that they can be put into practice without any major change in the structure of international relations.

I would like to make some brief comments on these two strands of Kaplan's proposals.

Firstly, I would like to refer to his ideas about the drastic reduction of conventional and nuclear forces deployed in Europe. We really need to ask ourselves if a reduction of this kind would effectively avert the danger of war. Kaplan seems to hold that the concentration of conventional forces in Europe is primarily responsible for the climate of insecurity and to consider that any departure from the existing balance, which would incur further arms build-up on both sides in response to initiatives taken by the other, could escalate into generalised nuclear war. Kaplan argues that this must be avoided at all costs and that moves must be made towards a significant reduction of armed forces in the European theatre.

Personally, I am not convinced that dissymmetries in conventional weapons in Europe can be exploited for aggressive purposes by the Soviet Union and General Gallois has explained that in his view a deliberately triggered war is an unlikely hypothesis. If, however, the Soviet Union were to take the initiative in an armed conflict, its counterforce nuclear capability would pose a greater threat than its conventional forces, since it would enable the Soviet Union to inflict a defeat on its enemy without a battle. We should also be more concerned about the possibility of a pre-emptive nuclear strike and pay less attention to hypotheses about the likelihood of conventional war, since it is hard to imagine that the Soviets woud opt for the type of action that could lead to nuclearisation of the conflict in circumstances least favourable to them. Whatever our views on this, Kaplan goes on from his initial premise to logically deduce that substantial reductions must be made in conventional forces deployed in the geostrategic space stretching from 'the Atlantic to the Urals'.

Kaplan's model for disarmament is more satisfactory than the one tried out in Vienna, as part of the MBFR negotiations. Indeed, the agreed measures would apply to a zone which takes in the entire European continent, whereas the 19 states which are taking part in the Vienna talks on mutual and balanced force reduction only envisage disarmament in an area of central Europe. However, all the experts agree that this zone where reductions would take place is too limited to have any positive effect in terms of increasing European security.

On the other hand, we need to consider the relevance of Kaplan's proposals for the reduction of arms and armed forces. Other speakers have already drawn attention to the disadvantages of total withdrawal of American forces, with the exception of 10 000 men stationed in West Germany in order to guarantee the maintenance of the status quo and the division of Germany. I would add here that the modalities of the reduction of Soviet forces do not appear to conform to the principle of 'equal security' and balance. The main body of Soviet forces (1 million on active service, 500 000 reservists) would be transferred beyond the Urals, but a cordon of troops (50 000 to 100 000 men, with 1000 tanks and 1000 fighter planes) could be deployed along the western borders of the USSR. Other European states could retain only 50 000 men in the armed forces (plus 200 000 reservists), equipped with light weapons.

Furthermore, Draconian measures would be imposed on European countries to prevent them from rearming under the pretext of increasing their police forces, yet the same restrictions would not be imposed upon the Soviet Union. A certain ambiguity remains concerning the deployment of the bulk of Soviet forces, as it has been suggested that they would be stationed somewhere between Moscow and the Urals.

It is clear that if these measures for disarmament were adopted it would be to the disadvantage of European states. The Soviet Union would have sufficient armed forces to intimidate them and could possibly declare war against them. The instability which we hoped to correct would be codified by treaty and the security of Western European states would be in greater jeopardy than before. It follows that the Soviet Union would stand to gain everything from accepting this proposal, whereas the West would be foolish to agree to it.

On the subject of nuclear weapons, Kaplan proposes the removal of all land-based systems deployed in Europe; the Moscow meridian would be the eastern limit of the nuclear-weapon-free zone. Moreover, intermediate-range ground-to-ground missiles such as the SS-20 would be transferred to the east of the Urals, from where they could reach targets in Western Europe and pose a serious threat to the West. Soviet ground-to-ground intercontinental missiles would not be affected by these measures.

Kaplan's zero option is therefore less radical than President Reagan's, because Reagan is not satisfied simply by a redeployment of the SS-20s beyond the Urals, but is demanding that they should be dismantled or taken out of service under effective control. What is more, Europeans who have welcomed the long-standing nature of US involvement in European defence would seem to be justifiably concerned about the weakening of the guarantee now on offer within the framework of the alliance, and would see American withdrawal as the expression of an isolationist policy. It is true that Kaplan has emphasised that nuclear cover could be assured by nuclear-powered ballistic missile submarines (SSBN), yet we are right to question the effectiveness of a flexible-response strategy based on this weapon system, which excludes the land-based systems considered by the allies to be the key instruments of the 'coupling'.

We cannot fail to be surprised at the bold nature of some of Kaplan's formulations when he considers the possible measures which could be taken in response to a blunt refusal from the Soviet Union to his maximalist proposal. Hence, in order to dissuade the Soviets from initiating war in Europe, the defection of armies within the Eastern bloc would be encouraged and renegades would be provided with arms which would then be used against the USSR.* In order to prompt them to do this, responses would be designed to minimalise collateral damage in friendly states. Quite apart from the fact that such measures would militate against our objective, that is stabilising the relations of mutual deterrence, it is hard to imagine how such measures could be taken without incurring greater risk.

Elsewhere, Kaplan proposes a recast version of the MLF, which offers European countries the opportunity to participate in a nuclear force of Poseidon submarines. At one stage, the MLF did win some support, but also met with increasing reservations in France and Great Britain. Eventually, it failed on two counts: shared decision-making and the nonproliferation of nuclear arms. The United States is no more inclined today to share with its allies decisions about the firing of nuclear weapons than it was before and it is important not to underestimate the reactions that German participation in this type of collective deterrent system would inevitably entail. The Soviets would not fail to invoke the obligations of the Non-proliferation Treaty and one of the preconditions laid down by Moscow for signing the Treaty was that the MLF project would be abandoned.

As Kaplan sets great store by measures whose aim is to contain the spread of nuclear weapons, there is no doubt that he would not wish to compromise results achieved in this area by insisting on establishing a defence system which allows for a more equitable distribution of responsibilities between allies, but whose efficacy is doubtful.

On the other hand, Kaplan is right to emphasise the risks of war through accident or misunderstanding and to suggest measures against what Daniel Frei calls 'unintentional nuclear war' (in a book recently pub-

* *Editor's note*: In Kaplan's revised proposal, this suggestion has been dropped.

lished under the auspices of UNIDIR). It is possible to conceive of defence formulae that would allow us to circumvent the recourse to nuclear weapons on the battlefield. Furthermore, we do not need to rely solely on land-based nuclear weapons systems, which are known to be vulnerable and which are even more likely to invite preemption, rather than strengthen deterrence capability. It would also be useful to adopt measures intended to prevent premature recourse to nuclear arms during a crisis. On all of these points Kaplan makes suggestions which should be taken on board. I have more reservations than Kaplan about neutron weapons, which do not appear to have the advantages that they are said to possess against armoured divisions.

As far as negotiation is concerned, priority should be given to measures aimed at promoting a stable deterrence relationship. The two superpowers are already bound by agreements intended to prevent nuclear war, and the United States has made new proposals within START. Confidence-building measures are being discussed at the CSCE Follow-up Conference in Madrid and there is an attempt to convene a 35-nation conference on disarmament which would give all European countries the opportunity of putting forward their own ideas and stating their interests. In September 1983, a consensus emerged at Madrid on this issue, and the Conference on confidence and security building measures and disarmament in Europe started in Stockholm, on 17 January 1984. I am surprised that Kaplan has not mentioned this initiative, for arms control should not remain the sole prerogative of the two nuclear protagonists, but should be a matter for all interested states, big and small.

Finally, if we set ourselves an objective as ambitious as disarmament, certain principles must be borne in mind. Firstly, disarmament is not an end in itself but needs to be seen as part of a general peace policy. Secondly, it must be brought about progressively, and the security of the parties must be guaranteed at all stages of the process. Finally, an undertaking of this kind can only be equitable if it is multilateral. If disarmament was no more than the result of bargaining between big powers, whereby they impose their views on others, other states would have good grounds for suspicion; they will gain nothing from the game of disarmament if it is to remain a 'sport of kings' ('jeu de princes').

(ii)   WOLF GRAF VON BAUDISSIN

Kaplan's proposals represent a thoroughly interesting contribution to the arms control debate, for which one can only be grateful, since it is always of great benefit to be challenged to reconsider one's own position.

What follows are comments on some specific issues:

(a) The paper emphasises the danger of war from miscalculation or due to an uncontrollable incident. Whilst it convincingly states that miscalculation is virtually impossible as long as both NATO and the Warsaw Pact have a balanced and adequate strength, the author does not clarify what type of incident he is thinking of. It is difficult to imagine any East—West crisis that would totally suspend political rationality, leaving no room for political decisions. The political decision-making process would have to be introduced at the very latest to decide on a nuclear first-use policy.

(b) The issue of Nuclear free Zones should be analysed primarily in a political and arms control context, the technical and tactical consequences being of secondary importance. In the light of the MBFR experiences, the prospects seem rather dim.

(c) An important part of the Helsinki Final Document is the declaration of non-intervention. The North Atlantic Treaty already contains a renunciation of all first use of force. A further commitment to a 'non-first use of any weapon' policy within the MBFR framework could prove to be a confidence-building measure, although it is doubtful whether such a declaration would really hold in a crisis situation.

Neither the Soviet Union nor the USA has yet agreed to this commitment at a global level. However, such an agreement together with the setting up of intervention-free zones would be valuable instruments of global security policy. These would be of particular importance for the South. On the other hand it is true that many such declarations and agreements do already exist; additional affirmations will not necessarily enhance their credibility. States will either have to come to some degree of mutual trust or will continue in their suspicion of each other, and this regardless of any new declarations.

(d) An urgent need for security policy would be to reach an agreement on the limitation of international weapons transfers. There is no need to elucidate the way in which international weapons transfers cause suppliers to be dependent on the politics of the buyers, involving them in their local and regional conflicts. The 'London Suppliers' Club' with its self-imposed limitations on the spread of civil nuclear technology could be a useful model to follow and could be combined with some measure of UN control.

Certain proposals seem to me to be not only of dubious value, but even dangerous:

(e) I reject all nuclear proliferation, including horizontal proliferation as represented by the delegation of the decision to release nuclear weapons to the submarine commanders. Flexible response must not develop into 'flexible responsibility'. It is the American President who should take the decision to release each individual nuclear weapon in the US arsenal or for NATO. To act otherwise would be to conventionalise and depoliticise nuclear weapons, making escalation politically uncontrollable.

(f) Nuclear aid for Eastern partisans or for an anti-tank guerilla force in Western Europe would neither bring any advantages for security policy, nor increase the credibility of deterrence. It would lead to a disregard for human rights and would primarily endanger the civilian population.

Index